COUNTIES ARMAGH, MONAGHAN & CAVAN

A

TOPOGRAPHICAL DICTIONARY

OF THE PARISHES, VILLAGES AND TOWNS
OF THESE COUNTIES IN THE 1830s

ILLUSTRATED WITH
CONTEMPORARY MAPS AND ENGRAVINGS

BY SAMUEL LEWIS

PREFACE

BY BRIAN M. WALKER

BELFAST

PUBLISHED BY FRIAR'S BUSH PRESS

2005

THIS SELECTED EDITION
PUBLISHED 2005
BY FRIAR'S BUSH PRESS
160 BALLYLESSON ROAD
BELFAST, BT8 8JU
NORTHERN IRELAND

FIRST PUBLISHED 1837
BY S. LEWIS & CO.
87 ALDERSGATE STREET, LONDON

ISBN 0-946872-65-1

TEXT COPIED BY IRISH TIMES (IRELAND.COM)

PRINTED BY DATAPLUS PRINT & DESIGN
13 HILL STREET, DUNMURRY, BT17 OAD

PREFACE

––––––––––

This volume brings together three important contemporary sources of information about life and society in Counties Armagh, Monaghan and Cavan in the 1830's. The text is taken from the monumental two-volumed topographical dictionary of Ireland, published by Samuel Lewis in 1837. His work covered all of Ireland in alphabetical order in a grand total of 1405 double columned pages. Maps of the main towns have been photographed from the first edition Ordnance Survey maps, which were published in the mid 1830's, and are integrated into the text. A considerable number of engravings, mostly from the 1830's, has also been included. In the case of all three components of this book-the topographical text, the maps and the engravings, the period of the 1830's witnessed new heights in the availability and worth of such sources. Brought together here in this particular form, the material presents a special view of these parishes, villages and towns in the period before the great changes of Victorian Ireland. It gives a compelling record of agriculture, industry, population, buildings and antiquities over one hundred and sixty years ago.

Samuel Lewis, publisher

Our knowledge about the life of Samuel Lewis is fairly limited. We do know, however, that during the 1830's and 1840's he ran a publishing business in London, first at 87 Aldersgate Street and secondly at 13 Finsbury Place South. He died in 1865. More is known about the outcome of his publishing efforts, in particular the very successful series of topographical dictionaries for which he was responsible. His 4 volumed topographical dictionary for England appeared in 1831 (7th edition 1849) to be followed a year later by a similar two volumed work for Wales (4th edition 1849). In 1837 he produced a two volumed dictionary for Ireland (2nd edition 1842), accompanied by an atlas of the counties of Ireland. Finally, he published a three volumed topographical dictionary for Scotland in 1846.[1]

Production of the Irish dictionary involved a vast entreprenurial enterprise.[2] Starting in early 1833, agents were dispatched to all parts of Ireland to gather information for the work and also to obtain advance subscribers. The dictionary was priced at two guineas per volume while the atlas was also available for two guineas. As was explained in the preface to the first volume, compared to England and Wales, there was less available for Ireland in the form of county histories and other such work, so it was important to gain extensive personal information. His principal sources of information were local landowners and clergy. When the dictionary appeared finally in 1837, the list of subscribers (including many of his informants) ran to a total of nearly 10,000 names, including large numbers in these counties.

The publication of the Irish dictionary led to considerable controversy, caused not by the content of the volumes but by objections from some of those listed as subscribers to being included on the list. A number of legal cases ensued over questions of liability for payment for the two books. There seems to have been relatively little debate over the accuracy of the contents. The 1842 revised edition made some corrections but also updated the figures in accordance with the 1841 census and replaced educational material with extra material on the railways. The entries reprinted here are from the first edition and so relate to the 1830's.

This dictionary by Lewis gives a unique coverage of life in Ireland, parish by parish and town by town. No-one before had produced such an extensive survey. At the same time as the appearance of these volumes by Lewis an enterprise was underway to record Irish society and economy as part of the Ordnance Survey (O.S.) with the writing of memoirs to accompany the production of the first O.S. maps for Ireland. This project collapsed finally in 1840, however, after only the northern counties had been investigated, and just one volume was published for the parish of Templemore in County Londonderry. Only in the last decade of the twentieth century have the memoirs been published.[3] These volumes by Lewis are very valuable for us today not just because he gathered important personal information at local level but also because he availed of much of the statistical and factual information which was now becoming available for Ireland, often through parliamentary papers and reports. In particular, he used the 1831 census report, new educational data and O.S. acreage figures.

At the same time, we must be aware of some of the perspectives and weaknesses of the material. A man of his time, Lewis approached his work from the standpoint of a society run by the gentry. The parishes are those of the Church of Ireland which was the established church. We must appreciate that some of his accounts of Irish pre history and archaeology would be questioned by historians and archaeologists today. His information on these matters reflects the state of knowledge about them at the time, which changed considerably in the course of the nineteenth century, thanks to the work of people such as John O'Donovan. For example his references to 'druidical altars', and some of his accounts of the origins of the early people of Ireland would not now be accepted. Those interested in the composition of placenames should check Lewis's interpretation with modern works on the subject.[4] It should also be noted that Lewis gives distances in Irish miles (10 Irish miles equal a little over 12 miles British). Spellings of names have been left as found in the original text.

Maps and map makers
Run by officers of the Royal Engineers, and starting in the 1820's, a complete mapping survey of the whole country was carried out under the auspices of the Ordnance Survey of Ireland, based at Phoenix Park in Dublin.[5] This led to the appearance in 1833 of the first six inches to the mile maps for County Londonderry, to be followed by similar maps for all the Irish counties over the next nine years. The first maps for County Armagh were published in 1836 while those for Counties Monaghan and Cavan appeared in 1837. This surveying project was a vast undertaking which involved considerable expenditure and manpower. The result was a very extensive cartographic record for Ireland, which had no equivalent in the world at the time.

In this volume plans of the main towns in the three counties have been copied from the original 6 inch O.S. maps. For sake of greater clarity the town maps have been magnified by 40 per cent. Map publication dates have been recorded, but it should be noted that the actual surveying could have been done in the previous one or two years. We have also included a map of each of the three counties from Lewis's atlas. One of the advantages of this map is that it gives the location of the parishes, and, while it does not show the parish boundaries, it can be helpful to give people some idea of which parish their area is located in. The maps in the atlas were based on drawings reduced from the Ordnance Survey and other surveys.

Artists and engravers

The period from the early 1820's to the early 1840's witnessed an upsurge in the appearance of topographical views of Ireland, partly due to technological advances, such as the advent of line engraving on steel in the early 1820's. There are few views of these three counties for the 1830's, so material has been drawn from as early as the 1780's and as late as the mid 1850's. The publication of the weekly *Dublin Penny Journal*, 1832–5, with its many wood engravings, was an important new departure in the level of illustrated material available at a low cost. The journal carried topographical articles and illustrations on many parts of Ireland. Besides the *Dublin Penny Journal*, there now appeared a large number of illustrated books, covering special areas or all of the country. Well known artists, such as George Petrie (who worked for the Ordnance Survey for a time in the 1830's), were employed to provide drawings to be engraved for these works.

Of special interest in this activity is the work of a number of northern artists. Views by the Belfast born Andrew Nicholl (1804–86) appeared frequently, both in the *Dublin Penny Journal* and in various published tours and guides. James Howard Burgess (c.1817–90) of Belfast was a skilled topographical artist who provided 25 views for S.C. Hall's *Ireland: its scenery, character, &c.* (London, 1846).[6] The *Irish Penny Journal*, which ran only for the year 1840, contained work by Burgess and other artists. The year 1819 saw the publication of James Stuart's *Historical memoirs of Armagh* which included 5 engravings by John Bell.[7]

In recent times engravings such as these have often been used to illustrate texts, but usually there has been little attempt to name the artist and engraver involved or to accurately date the picture. In this volume, however, an effort has been made to identify both the artist and engraver responsible for a particular piece of work. This has not been possible in every case and where the full information has not been given this is because it is not available. The title of the book, and the date and place of publication, have been given with each print so that we can establish a date for the particular view.

Brian M. Walker   **Belfast, 2005**

References

[1]   See Frederick Boase, (ed.) *Modern English biography*, vol. 2 (London, 1965), p. 417.

[2]   See Tim Cadogan's introduction to *Lewis's Cork* (Cork, 1998).

[3]   Angelique Day and Patrick McWilliams, *Ordnance survey memoirs of Ireland*, vols 1–40 (Belfast, 1990–8).

[4]   See Patrick McKay, *A dictionary of Ulster place-names* (Belfast, 1999). See also relevant volumes published by the Northern Ireland Placenames Project.

[5]   See J.H. Andrews, *A paper landscape: the ordnance survey in nineteenth century Ireland* (Oxford, 1993; second edition, Dublin, 2002).

[6]   See John Hewitt, *Art in Ulster* (Belfast, 1977). Bio. notes by Theo Snoody.

[7]   James Stuart, *Historical memoirs of the city of Armagh…* (Newry, 1819).

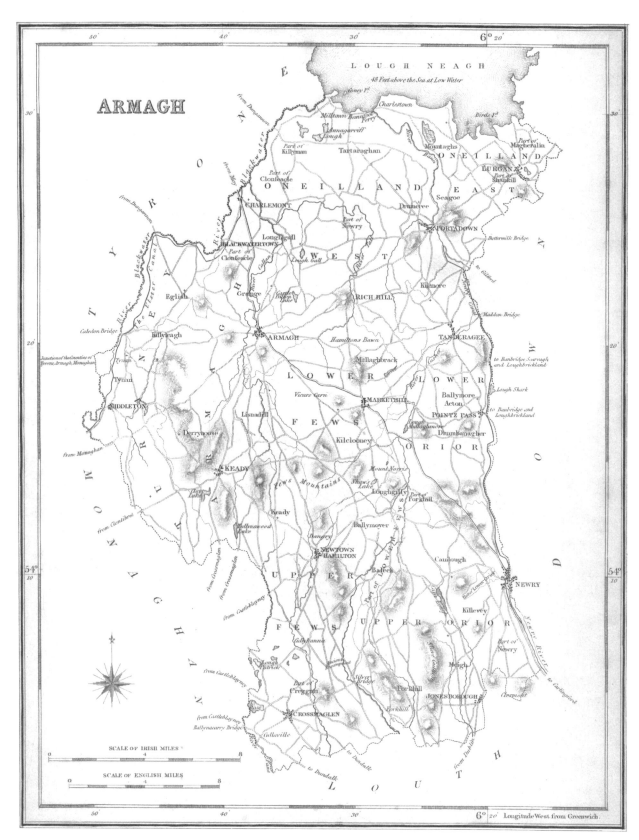

Armagh. Drawn by R. Creighton and engraved by I. Dower. From Lewis's Atlas, *(London, 1837).*

COUNTY ARMAGH

A

TOPOGRAPHICAL DICTIONARY

ARMAGH (County of), an inland county, in the province of ULSTER, bounded on the north by Lough Neagh, on the east by the county of Down, on the south-east by that of Louth, on the south-west by Monaghan, and on the west and north-west by Tyrone: it is situated between 54° 3′ and 54° 31′ (N. Lat.), and between 6° 14′ and 6° 45′ (W. Lon.); and comprises, according to the Ordnance survey, 328,076 statute acres, of which 267,317 acres are tillable, 17,941 are covered with water, and the remainder is mountain and bog. The population, in 1821, was 197,427; and, in 1831, 220,134.

This tract is supposed to have been part of that named by Ptolemy as the territories of the Vinderii and Voluntii: it afterwards formed part of the district called Orgial, which also comprised the counties of Louth and Monaghan. The formation of this part of Ireland into a separate dominion is said to have taken place so early as the year 332, after the battle of Achaighleth-derg, in Fermoy, in which, as recorded by Tigernach, abbot of Clonmacnois, who died in 1068, Fergus Feagha, son of Froechair the Brave, the last of the Ultonian kings who resided in Eamania, was killed by the three Collas, who then expelled the Ultonians from that part of the province to the south of Lough Neagh, and formed it into an independent state, to which they gave the name of Orgial, afterwards corrupted into Oriel or Uriel, names by which it was distinguished to the beginning of the seventeenth century.

The county was made shire ground, under its present name, in 1586, by the lord-deputy, Sir John Perrott, who, not relying with confidence on the vigilance and care of Henry O'Nial and Sir Henry Bagnell, to whom the government of Ulster had been entrusted, projected the division of the greater part of that province into seven counties, of which Armagh was one, and took its name from the chief town in it. For each of these counties he appointed sheriffs, commissioners of the peace, coroners, and other officers. Previously to this arrangement, the chief part of the property of the county had centred in the families of the

O'Nials, the MacCahans, and the O'Hanlons. At the commencement of the seventeenth century, it was principally vested in those of MacHenry, Acheson, O'Nial, Brownlow, and O'Hanlon, exclusively of the great territories settled on Moharty, which the Mac Cahans had forfeited in rebellion, and a large tract of country called Oirther, afterwards Orior, a district in the southern part, which also escheated to the crown by rebellion of a branch of the O'Hanlons. According to a project for planting, by Jas. I, the whole of the arable and pasture land, amounting to 77,580 acres, was to be allotted in 61 proportions of three classes of 2000, 1500, and 1000 acres each, among the English and Scottish undertakers, the servitors, and the Irish natives. A portion was also assigned to the primate, another for glebes for the incumbents (of whom there was to be one for each proportion), another for the four corporate towns of Armagh, Mountnorris, Charlemont, and Tanderagee, and a fourth for a free grammar school. The native Irish were to be distributed among a few of the several proportions, with the exception of the swordsmen, who were to migrate into waste lands in Connaught and Munster. The project, which was but partially effected, was not acted upon until 1609, when a royal commission was issued to inquire into the king's title to the escheated and forfeited lands in Ulster, with a view to the plantation there. Inquisitions were consequently held, the return of which for Armagh, made in August of the same year, states that the county was then divided into the five baronies of Armaghe, Toaghriny, Orier, Fuighes, and Onylane or O'Nealane, and enumerates with great particularity the names and tenures of the proprietors. In 1618, a second commission was issued to Captain Pynnar and others, to ascertain how far the settlers located there in the intervening period had fulfilled the terms of their agreement. It is somewhat remarkable that, although the inquisition names five baronies, three only are noticed in Pynnar's survey; those of Armaghe and Toaghriny being omitted, probably because they contained no forfeited property. The number of the proportions specified in the survey are but 22, eleven of which, situated in O'Neylan, were in the hands of English undertakers; five in the Fuighes, in those of Scottish undertakers; and seven in Orier were allotted to servitors and natives. The number of tenants and men capable of bearing arms in the two first proportions amounted to 319 of the former, and 679 of the latter; the number in Orier is not given.

The county is partly in the diocese of Dromore, but chiefly in that of Armagh. For civil purposes it is now divided into the baronies of Armagh, Turaney, O'Neilland East, O'Neilland West, Upper Fews, Lower Fews, Upper Orior, and Lower Orior. It contains the city and borough of Armagh; part of the borough, seaport, and market-town of Newry; the market and post-towns of Lurgan, Portadown, Tanderagee, Market-hill, and Newtown-Hamilton; the disfranchised borough of Charlemont; the post-towns of Richhill, Keady, Blackwatertown, Loughgall, Tynan, Forkhill, and FlurryBridge; and the market-towns of Middleton and Crossmeglan, which, with Killylen, have each a penny post. Prior to the Union it sent six members to the Irish parliament, two for the county at large, and two for each of the boroughs; but at present its representation consists of three members in the Imperial parliament, two for the county at large, and one for the borough of Armagh. The election takes place at Armagh; and the constituency, as registered in Oct. 1836, consisted of 384 £50, 324 £20, and 2384 £10 freeholders; 5 £50 and 19 £20 rent-chargers; and 122 £20 and 573 £10 leaseholders; making a total of 3811. It is in the north-east circuit: the assizes are held at Armagh, where the county court-house and gaol are situated; and quarter sessions at Armagh, Lurgan, Markethill, and Ballybott, of which the three last have each a courthouse and bridewell. The number of persons charged with criminal offences and committed to the county gaol, in 1835, was 385, and of civil bill commitments, 111. The local government is vested in a lieutenant, vice-lieutenant, 13 deputy-lieutenants, and 63 other magistrates; besides whom there are the usual county officers, including three coroners. There are 17 constabulary police stations, having in the whole a force of a stipendiary magistrate, sub-inspector, paymaster, 5 chief and 19 subordinate constables, and 99 men, with 5 horses maintained equally by Grand Jury presentments and by Government. The amount of Grand Jury presentments, for 1835, was £27,259.2.3$\frac{1}{2}$, of which £4704.0.3 was for the public roads of the county at large £9974.1.7$\frac{1}{2}$ for the public roads, being the baronial charge; £1475.11.4 in repayment of loans advanced by Government; £2279.10.7 for the police, and £8525.18.6 for public establishments, officers' salaries, buildings, &c. The public charitable institutions are a district lunatic asylum, and the county infirmary and fever hospital at Armagh; and dispensaries at Crossmeglin, Forkhill, Market-hill, Jonesborough, Keady, Blackwatertown, Seagoe, Loughgall, Richhill, Lurgan, Newtown-Hamilton, Poyntz-Pass, Tynan, Portadown, Tanderagee and Ballybott, supported by equal Grand Jury presentments and private subscriptions. There

are also dispensaries at Tanderagee, Portadown, and Tullyhappy, built and supported by the Earl and Countess of Mandeville; and a fever hospital at Middleton, built and supported by the Trustees of Bishop Sterne's munificent bequest. In the military arrangements this county is within the northern district, of which Armagh is the headquarters, where there are an ordnance-depot and an infantry barrack constructed to accommodate 12 officers, 174 men, and 5 horses: at Charlemont there is a fort, with an artillery barrack for 5 officers, 151 men, and 79 horses, to which is attached an hospital for 22 patients.

The northern verge of the county, near Lough Neagh, the north-western adjoining Tyrone, and the neighbourhoods of Armagh, Market-hill, and Tanderagee, are level; the remainder is hilly, rising in the southern parts into mountains of considerable elevation. The highest is Slieve Gullion, rising, according to the Ordnance survey, 1893 feet above the level of the sea; it is about seven miles from the southern border, and is considered to be the loftiest point of land in Ulster, except Slieve Donard, in the neighbouring county of Down. Slieve Gullion sinks on the east into the Fathom Hills, which skirt the Newry water. One of the finest and most extensive prospects in Ulster is obtained from its summit, which commands the bay of Dundalk; and the bold and picturesque features of mountain scenery are confined to this immediate vicinity, including the Doobrin mountains and the neighbourhood of Forkhill. Westward to the Fews the country exhibits a chain of abrupt hills, the greater part of which can never be reduced to a state of profitable cultivation. Further west are the Fews mountains, a subordinate range, lying in a direction from south-east to north-west. The fertility of the more level districts towards the eastern, northern, and north-western confines is very remarkable, especially in the views from Richhill, the numerous demesnes being sufficiently wooded to ornament the whole country, and the surface generally varied by pleasing undulations. From the shores of Lough Neagh, however, extend considerable tracts of low, marshy, and boggy land. The other lakes are few and small: that of Camlough, romantically situated on the northern verge of Slieve Gullion, is the largest. Lough Clay, in the western part of the county, which gives rise to one of the branches of the Callen river, is the next in size; but neither of them would be noticed for extent or beauty if situated in some of the neighbouring counties. A chain of small lakes occupying the south-western boundary of the county is valuable from the supply of water afforded by them to the mills in their neighbourhood. Coney Island, near the southern shore of Lough Neagh, and between the mouths of the Blackwater and Bann rivers, is the only island in the county; it is uninhabited. The climate is more genial than most of the other counties in Ulster, as is evinced by the greater forwardness of the harvests: this advantage has been attributed to the nature of the soil and subsoil, the gentle undulation of the surface, the absence of moor or marshy land, and the protection by mountains from the cooling breezes of the sea.

The soil is generally very fertile, especially in the northern part, the surface of which is a rich brown loam, tolerably deep, on a substratum of clay or gravel. There is an abundance of limestone in the vicinity of Armagh, and in Kilmore and other places; and there are quarries near Lough Neagh, but the stone lies so deep, and they are subject to such a flow of water, as to be of little practical use. Towards Charlemont there is much bog, which yields red ashes, and is easily reclaimable; the substratum of this is a rich limestone. The eastern part of the county consists of a light friable soil. In the south the country is rocky and barren: huge rocks of granite are found on the surface promiscuously mixed with blocks of limestone, as if thrown together by some convulsion of nature. All the limestone districts make good tillage and meadow ground: the natural meadow found on the banks of the rivers, and formed of a very deep brown loam, yields great crops without manure. The hilly district is generally of a deep retentive soil on a gravelly but not calcareous substratum: a decayed freestone gravel, highly tinged with ferruginous ore, is partially found here: the subsoil is sometimes clay, slate. In these districts heath is peculiarly vigorous, except where the judicious application of lime has compelled it to give place to a more productive vegetation. Except near Newtown-Hamilton, there is but little bog among these hills. The valleys which lie between them have a rich and loamy soil, which yields much grain, and does not abound in aquatic plants, although the poa fluitans grows in them in great luxuriance. The general inequality of surface which pervades the county affords great facilities for drainage.

In consequence of the dense population the farms are generally very small, and much land is tilled with the spade. Wheat is a very general crop in the baronies of Armagh, the O'Neillands, and Turaney; the main crops in the other baronies are oats, flax, and potatoes. In the smaller farms potatoes constitute the first and second crops, sometimes even a third; and afterwards flax occupies a portion of the potatoe plot, and barley the remainder, if the soil be dry and fine, but if otherwise, crops of oats are taken in succession. The treatment of the wheat crop consists of one harrowing and one ploughing, to level the potatoe furrows; if two crops of potatoes have preceded, a small quantity of ashes is scattered over the surface. The seed most in use is the red Lammas wheat, and the quantity sown is about three bushels to the acre. Potatoe oats are commonly sown on the best lands; black oats, and sometimes white oats, on land manured with lime, in the mountainous districts; this latter species, when sown on mountain land not previously manured and drained, will degenerate into a black grain in two or three seasons. Flax is invariably sown on potatoe ground, the plot being tilled with the spade, but not rolled Dutch seed is sown on heavy soils, American on light soils. The seed is not saved, and therefore the plant is pulled just before it changes colour, from an opinion that when thus prepared it makes finer yarn. More seed was sown in 1835

than was ever before known, in consequence of the increased demand from the spinners in England and Ireland. The pasturage is abundant and nutritious; and though there are no extensive dairies, cows are kept by all the small farmers of the rich northern districts, whence much butter is sent to the Belfast market: a considerable quantity of butter, generally made up in small firkins, is also sent to Armagh and Newry for exportation.

The state of agriculture in modern times has very much improved; gentlemen and large farmers have introduced all the improved agricultural implements, with the practice of drainage, irrigation, and rotation crops. Mangel-wurzel, turnips, clover, and all other green crops are now generally cultivated even upon the smallest farms, particularly around Market-hill, Tanderagee, Banagher, and other places, where the greatest encouragement is given by Lords Gosford, Mandeville, and Charlemont, and by Col. Close and other resident gentlemen, who have established farming societies and expend large sums annually in premiums. The Durham, Hereford, North Devon, Leicester, Ayrshire, and other breeds of cattle have been introduced, and by judicious crosses a very superior stock has been raised: some farmers on good soils have also brought over the Alderney breed, which thrives remarkably well; but in some of the mountain districts the old long-horned breed of the country is still preferred, and a cross between it and the old Leicester appeals to suit both soil and climate, as they grow to a large size, give great quantities of milk, and fatten rapidly. The breed of sheep and horses has also been greatly improved; the former kind of stock is chiefly in the possession of gentlemen and large farmers. The horses used in farming are mostly a light active kind; but the best hunters and saddle horses are brought hither by dealers from other counties. Numerous herds of young cattle are reared on the Fews mountains, which are the only part of the county where grass farms are extensive. Goats are numerous, and are allowed to graze at liberty in the mountainous districts. Hogs are fattened in great numbers; the gentry prefer the Chinese breed, but the Berkshire is preferred by the country people, as being equally prolific and more profitable. Lime and dung are the general manures; the former is usually mixed with clay for the culture of potatoes, and is also applied to grass lands as a surface dressing preparatory to tillage, sometimes even three years before the sod is broken, as being deemed more effective than manuring the broken ground; the average quantity of lime laid on an acre is from 30 to 40 barrels. Thorn hedges well kept are the common fences in the richer districts, and with scattered timber trees and numerous orchards give them a rich woody appearance. In the mountainous district, too, the same fences are rising in every direction. Many parts of the county, particularly in the barony of Armagh, are decorated with both old and new timber: and in comparison with neighbouring districts it has a well-wooded appearance; but there are no extensive woodlands, although there is, near Armagh, a large public nursery of forest trees.

The geological features of the county are various and interesting. The mountain of Slieve Gullion, in its south-eastern extremity, is an offset of the granite district of Down, and is remarkable for the varieties of which it is composed. It is in the form of a truncated cone, and presents on some sides mural precipices several hundred feet in height, from which it acquires an appearance of greater elevation than it really attains the summit is flat, and on it is a lake of considerable extent. The granite of this mountain, particularly that procured near the summit, is frequently used for millstones, being extremely hard and fine-grained, and composed of quartz, feldspar, mica, and hornblende. This, indeed, is here the common composition of this primitive rock, the feldspar being grey and the mica black. Sometimes the hornblende is absent, in which case the rock is found to be a pure granite; and at others it graduates into a beautiful sienite composed of flesh-coloured feldspar and hornblende- Flesh-coloured veins of quartz are also found to variegate the granite, in a beautiful manner, in several places. On the south, towards Jonesborough, the sienite succeeds to the granite, and afterwards passes into porphyry, which is succeeded by silicious slate. The Newry mountains and the Fathom hills are composed of granite. Around Camlough mica slate is found in vast beds. Westward the granite district of Slieve Gullion extends to the hill above Larkin-mill, on the western declivity of which the granite basis is covered by almost vertical strata, composed first of an aggregation of quartz and mica with steatite, which in the distance of about a quarter of a mile is occasionally interstratified with greenish grey clay-slate, of which the strata still further west are wholly composed. Several slate quarries have here been opened and partially worked, but none with spirit or skill: the principal are at Dorcy, Newtown-Hamilton, Cregan-Duff, and in the vicinity of Crossmeglan. Further distant this becomes grauwacke slate, by being interstratified with grauwacke. In the neighbourhood of Market-hill the strata comprise also hornblende slate and greenstone porphyry. Sandstone is also connected with this district; there is a quarry of remarkably fine freestone at Grange; and on the surface of the southern confines is seen the intermixture of grit and limestone rocks above noticed. Trap rocks, forming a hard stone varying in hue between dark green and blue, here called whin, are found in various places in huge blocks and boulders, or long narrow stones. The substratum of the eastern portion of the county varies between a silicious schistus and an argillaceous deposit, forming a grauwacke district, which extends across to the western confines of the county. The west and middle of the county is limestone, which is generally white, except in the vicinity of the city of Armagh, where it assumes a red tinge, exhibiting that colour more distinctly as it approaches the town, improving also in quality, and increasing in the varieties of its shades. The minerals, as connected with metallurgy, are so few as scarcely to deserve notice, lead only excepted, a mine of which was worked in the vicinity of Keady, on a property held by the Earl of Farnham, under Dublin College; but after much expenditure the operations were discontinued in consequence of the loss incurred, which, however, has been attributed to the want of skilful or honest superintendence. Lead ore has also been found near Market-hill, in several places near Newtown-Hamilton, on the demesne of Ballymoyer, near Hockley, in Slieve Cross, near Forkhill, and in the parish of Middleton. Some indications of iron, imperfect lead, regulus of manganese, and antimony, have been found in a few spots. The other mineral substances found here are potters' clay and a variety of ochres. Various kinds of timber, particularly oak, pine, and yew, have been raised out of the bogs; petrified wood is found on the shores of Lough Neagh; and fern, spleenwort, and mosses have been discovered in the heart of slaty stones.

The woollen trade flourished extensively in this county until interrupted by the legislative measures enacted by William III, and cloth of every description was manufactured. The linen manufacture is now pursued in all its branches, the finest goods being produced in the northern parts. The extent of the manufacture cannot easily be ascertained, because much comes in from the outskirts of the neighbouring counties, though the excess thus arising is most probably counterbalanced by the goods sent out of Armagh to the markets in the adjoining counties. At the commencement of the present century, the value of its produce annually was estimated at £300,000, and at present exceeds £500,000. Large capitals are employed by bleachers, who purchase linen and bleach it on their own account; the principal district is on the river Callan, at Keady. Considerable sums are also employed in the purchase of yarn, which is given out to the weaver to manufacture. Woollen goods are made solely for home consumption, and in only small quantities. Manufactories for the necessaries of life in greatest demand, such as candles, leather, soap, beer, &c. are numerous; and there are mills for dressing flax and spinning linen yarn, and numerous large flour-mills.

The two principal rivers are the Blackwater and the Bann, which chiefly flow along the north-eastern and north-western boundaries of the county, the former discharging itself into the western side of Lough Neagh, and the latter into the southern part of the same lake, at Bann-foot ferry. The Newry water, after flowing through a narrow valley between the counties of Down and Armagh, empties itself into the bay of Carlingford, below Newry. The Callan joins the Blackwater below Charlemont: the Cusheir falls into the Bann at its junction with the Newry canal; and the Camlough, flowing from the lake of the same name, discharges itself into the Newry water. This last named river, during its short course of five miles, supplies numerous bleach-works, and corn, flour, and flax mills: its falls are so rapid that the tail race of the higher mill forms the head water of the next lower. The Newtown-Hamilton river is joined by the Tara, and flows into Dundalk bay, into which also the Flurry or Fleury, and the Fane, empty themselves. The total number of main and branch streams is eighteen, and the combined lengths of all are 165 miles. The mouths of those which flow into Lough Neagh have a fine kind of salmon trout, frequently 30lb in weight: the common trout is abundant and large, as are also pike, eels, bream, and roach. An inland navigation along the border of the counties of Armagh and Down, from Newry to Lough Neagh, by the aid of the Bann and the Newry water, was the first line of canal executed in Ireland. Commencing at the tideway at Fathom, it proceeds to Newry, and admits vessels drawing nine or ten feet of water, having at each end a sea lock. From Newry to the point where the Bann is navigable, a distance of fifteen miles, is a canal for barges of from 40 to 60 tons, chiefly fed from Lough Brickland and Lough Shark, in the county of Down. The river Bann, from its junction with the canal to Lough Neagh, a distance of eleven miles and a half, completes the navigation, opening a communication with Belfast by the Lagan navigation, and with the Tyrone collieries by the Coal Island or Blackwater navigation. The chief trade on this canal arises from the import of bleaching materials, flax-seed, iron, timber, coal, and foreign produce from Newry; and from the export of agricultural produce, yarn, linen, firebricks, pottery, &c. The canal from Lough Erne to Lough Neagh, now in progress, enters this county near Tynan, and passes by Caledon, Blaekwatertown, and Charlemont to its junction with the river Blackwater above Verner's bridge, and finally with Lough Neagh. A line of railway from Dublin to Armagh, and thence to Belfast, and another from Armagh to Coleraine, have been projected. The roads are generally well laid out, and many of them of late have been much improved.

Among the relics of antiquity are the remains of the fortress of Eamania, near Armagh, once the royal seat of the kings of Ulster. The Danes' Cast is an extensive line of fortification in the south-eastern part of the county, and stretching into the county of Down. The tumulus said to mark the burial-place of "Nial of the hundred battles" is still visible on the banks of the Callan. The Vicar's Cairn, or Cairn-na-Managhan, is situated near the city of Armagh. Cairn Bann is in Orior barony, near Newry. A tumulus in Killevy parish contains an artificial cavern. Two ancient brazen weapons were found in a bog near Carrick, where a battle is said to have been fought in 941. Spears, battle-axes, skeyns, swords, the golden torques, and collars, rings, amulets, and medals of gold, also various ornaments of silver, jet, amber, &c., have been found in different places, and are mostly preserved. Near Hamilton's Bawn, in 1816, was found the entire skeleton of an elk, of which the head and horns were placed in the hall of the Infirmary at Armagh, and in the same year also the body of a trooper was discovered in a bog near Charlemont, of which the dress and armour appeared to be of the reign of Elizabeth. The religious houses, besides those of the city of Armagh, of which any memorial has been handed down to us were Clonfeacle, Killevey or Kilsleve, Kilmore, Stradhailloyse, and Tahellen. The most remarkable military remains are Tyrone's ditches, near Poyntz Pass, Navan fort, the castles of Criff-Keirn and Argonell, the castle in the pass of Moyrath, and Castle Roe.

The peasantry are in possession of superior comforts in their habitations as well as in food and clothing, which cannot be attributed solely to the linen manufacture, as their neighbours of the same trade in the adjoining counties of Cavan and Monaghan are far behind them in this respect. The county possesses sufficient fuel for domestic consumption; but coal is imported from England by the Newry canal, and from the county of Tyrone by the Blackwater. In no other county do the working classes consume so much animal food. The general diffusion of the population is neither the result of a predetermined plan, nor of mere accident it arises from the nature of the linen manufacture, which does not require those employed in it to be collected into overgrown cities, or congregated in crowded factories. Engaged alternately at their loom and in their farm, they derive both health and recreation from the alternation. Green lawns, clear streams, pure springs, and the open atmosphere, are necessary for bleaching: hence it is that so many eminent bleachers reside in the country, and hence also the towns are small, and every hill and valley abounds with rural and comfortable habitations.

In the mountainous districts are several springs slightly impregnated with sulphur and iron. The borders of the bogs sometimes also exhibit ferruginous oozings, one of which in the Fews mountains is said to be useful in scrofulous complaints. The same effect was also formerly attributed to the waters of Lough Neagh, in the north-western limits of this county. Boate states, in addition to this, that the temperature of the sand at the bottom of the bay in which this sanative quality is perceived, alternates frequently between cold and warmth. A petrifying quality, such as that said to exist in some parts of Lough Neagh, has been discovered at Rosebrook, near Armagh, the mansion-house of which was built, in a great measure, of petrifactions raised from a small lake there. Petrified branches of hawthorn have been found near the city of Armagh; and fossil remains of several animals have also been discovered in the limestone rocks in the same vicinity. Petrifactions of the muscle, oyster, leech, together with dendrites, belemnites, and madreporites, are also found; and in the mountain streams are pure quartz crystals, of which a valuable specimen, found near Keady, is in the possession of Dr. Colvan, of Armagh.

ACTON, a parish, in the barony of LOWER ORIOR, county of ARMAGH, and province of ULSTER, 3 miles (S.S.E.) from Tanderagee, on the old road from Newry to that place; containing 3843 inhabitants, of which number, 257 are in the village. The village was originally founded by Sir Toby Pointz, who, for his military services, obtained a grant of 500 acres of land, part of the forfeited estates of the O'Hanlons, and erected a bawn 100 feet square, a house of brick and lime for his own residence, and 24 cottages for so many English settlers, and called the place Acton, after his own native village in England. It consists of one main street, and at present contains about 50 houses indifferently built. Under the authority of an order of council, in 1789,

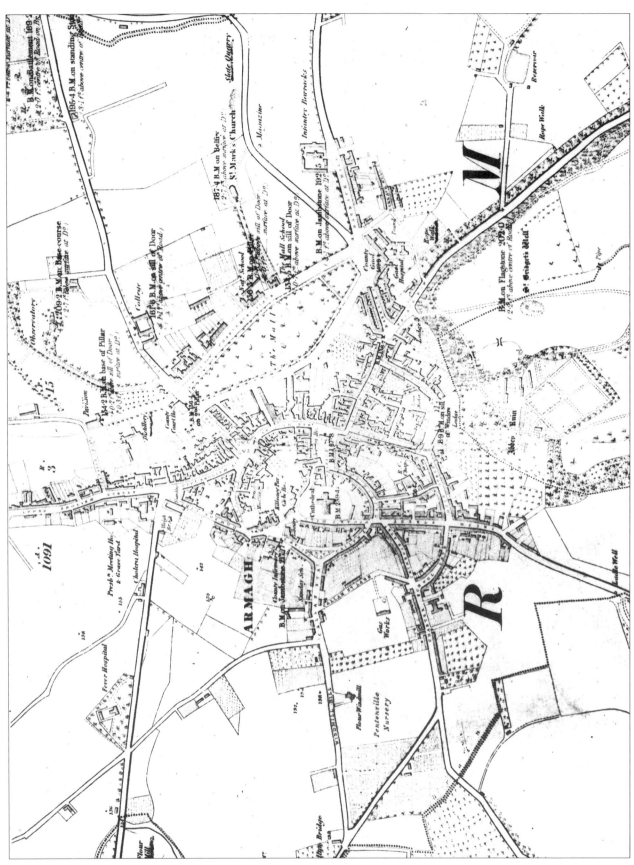

Armagh. Part of 6 inch O.S. map of Co.Armagh, sheet 12, published 1836 (reproduced at 140%).

nineteen townlands were severed from the parish of Ballymore, and erected into the parish of Acton, which comprises 4395 statute acres, and is intersected by the Newry canal. The improved system of agriculture has been extensively introduced, the lands are well drained and fenced, and the bogs have been all drained and brought into cultivation by the proprietor, Col. Close. The weaving of linen cloth, diapers, checks, and calicoes is extensively carried on by the small farmers and cottiers in the parish. The principal gentlemen's seats are Acton House, the residence of R. Conway Dobbs, Esq.; and Drominargoole, of D. Lucas, Esq. The living is a perpetual curacy, in the diocese of Armagh, and in the patronage of the Prebendary of Ballymore in the cathedral church of St. Patrick, Armagh: the income arises from a fixed stipend of £50 per annum, payable by the rector or prebendary of Ballymore, and an augmentation of £25 per annum from Primate Boulter's fund. The church, erected at Pointz Pass in 1789, is a neat edifice, in the early English style. The glebe-house, situated about half a mile from the church, is a handsome residence; and the glebe comprises 21 acres of good land. In the R.C. divisions this parish is in the union or district of Ballymore: the chapel is a small building, situated at Pointz Pass. There are two places of worship for Presbyterians in connection with the Seceding Synod, situated respectively at Tanniokee and Carrickbrack, or Tyrone's Ditches, the latter of the first class. There are four schools, of which two are aided by annual donations from Col. Close and the Rev. Mr. Darby, and in which are about 220 boys and 160 girls; also a private pay school of about 30 boys and 30 girls. The remains of a church built by Sir Toby Pointz, in 1684, under the chancel of which he lies interred, are situated in the midst of a wood, and have a very interesting appearance; a tablet is still preserved, with an inscription to his memory.

ARMAGH, a city, market and post-town. and a parish, partly in the barony of O'NEILLAND WEST, but chiefly in that of ARMAGH, county of ARMAGH (of which it is the capital), and province of ULSTER, 31 miles (S.W. by W.) from Belfast and 65¾ (N.N.W.) from Dublin; containing 10,518 inhabitants, of which number, 9470 are within the limits of the borough.

The past importance of this ancient city is noticed by several early historians, who describe it as the chief city in Ireland. St. Fiech, who flourished in the sixth century, calls it the seat of empire; Giraldus Cambrensis, the metropolis; and, even so lately as 1580, Cluverius styles it the head of the kingdom, adding that Dublin was then next in rank to it. The original name was Druim-sailech, "the hill of sallows," which was afterwards changed to Ard-sailech, "the height of sallows," and, still later, to Ard-macha, either from Eamhuin-macha, the regal residence of the kings of Ulster, which stood in its vicinity, or, as is more probable, from its characteristic situation, Ard-macha, signifying "the high place or field."

Armagh is the head of the primacy of all Ireland, and is indebted for its origin, and ecclesiastical pre-eminence, to St. Patrick, by whom it was built, in 445. He also founded,

near his own mansion, the monastery of St. Peter and St. Paul, for Canons Regular of the order of St. Augustine, which was rebuilt by Imar O'Hoedegan, and was the most distinguished of the religious establishments which existed here, having materially contributed to the early importance of the place. This institution received numerous grants of endowment from the native kings, the last of whom, Roderick O'Connor, made a grant to its professors, in 1169; in-somuch that its landed possessions became very extensive, as appears from an inquisition taken on its suppression. Attached to it was a school or college, which long continued one of the most celebrated seminaries in Europe, and from which many learned men, not only of the Irish nation, but from all parts of Christendom, were despatched to diffuse knowledge throughout Europe. It is said that 7000 students were congregated in it, in the pursuit of learning, at one period; and the annals of Ulster relate that, at a synod held by Gelasius at Claonadh, in 1162, it was decreed that no person should lecture publicly on theology, except such as had studied at Armagh. The city was destroyed by accidental conflagrations in the year 670, 687, and 770, and also sustained considerable injury in the last-mentioned year by lightning. In subsequent periods it suffered severely and repeatedly from the Danes, a band of whom having landed at Newry, in 830, penetrated into the interior, and having stormed Armagh established their headquarters in it for one month, and on being driven out, plundered and reduced it to ashes. In 836, Tergesius or Thorgis, a Danish chieftain, equally celebrated for his courage and ferocity, after having laid waste Connaught and a great part of Meath and Leinster, turned his arms against Ulster, which he devastated as far as Lough Neagh, and then advancing against Armagh, took it with little difficulty. His first act, after securing possession of the place, was the expulsion of the Bishop Farannan, with all the students of the college, and the whole body of the religions, of whom the bishop and clergy sought refuge in Cashel. The numerous atrocities perpetrated by the invaders at length excited a combined effort against them. Nial the Third collected a large army, and after having defeated the Danes in a pitched battle in Tyrconnel, advanced upon Armagh, where, after a second successful engagement, and while preparing to force his victorious way into the city, the main position of the enemy in these parts, he was drowned in the river Callan, in an attempt to save the life of one of his followers. Malachy, his successor, obtained possession of the city, in which a public assembly of the princes and chieftains of Ireland was held, in 849, to devise the means of driving their ferocious enemies out of the island. In their first efforts the Danes suffered several defeats; but, having concentrated their forces, and being supported by a reinforcement of their countrymen, they again marched against Armagh, and took and plundered it about the year 852.

The subsequent annals of Armagh, to the commencement of the 11th century, are little more than a reiteration of invasions and conquests by the Danes, and of successful but brief insurrections of the natives, in all of which this devoted city became in turn the prize of each contending army, and suffered all the horrors of savage warfare. In 1004, the celebrated Brian Boru entered Armagh, where he presented at the great altar of the church a collar of gold weighing 20 ounces; and after his death at the battle of Clontarf, in 1014, his remains were deposited here, according to his dying request, with those of his son Murchard, who fell in the same battle. From this period to the English invasion the history of Armagh exhibits a series of calamitous incidents either by hostile inroads or accidental fires. Its annals, however, evince no further relation to the events of that momentous period than the fact of a synod of the Irish clergy having been held in it by Gelasius, in 1170, in which that assembly came to the conclusion that the foreign invasion and internal distractions of the country were a visitation of divine retribution, as a punishment for the inhuman practice of purchasing Englishmen from pirates and selling them as slaves; and it was therefore decreed that every English captive should be liberated. The city suffered severely from the calamities consequent on the invasion of Edward Bruce, in 1315, during which the entire see was lamentably wasted, and the archbishop was reduced to a state of extreme destitution, by the reiterated incursions of the Scottish army.

During the local wars in Ulster, at the close of the 15th and the beginning of the 16th centuries, this city was reduced to a state of great wretchedness; and in the insurrection of Shane O'Nial or O'Neal, Lord Sussex, then lord-lieutenant, marched into Ulster to oppose him; and having attacked him successfully at Dundalk, forced him to retire upon Armagh, which the lord-lieutenant entered in Oct. 1557, and wasted with fire and sword, sparing only the cathedral. In 1566, O'Nial, to revenge himself on Archbishop Loftus, who had transmitted information of his hostile intentions to Government, even before the Irish chieftains and the lord-deputy had preferred their complaint against him, resolved on a special expedition against this city, and on this occasion committed dreadful havoc, not even sparing the cathedral. In the year 1575, Sydney, the lord-deputy, marched into Ulster against Turlogh O'Nial, and fixed his head-quarters at Armagh, whither that chieftain, after some ineffectual negotiations through the agency of his wife, proceeded, and having surrendered himself, was permitted to return home without molestation. In the short but sanguinary war carried on between the English Government and Hugh O'Nial, Earl of Tyrone, towards the close of the reign of Elizabeth, the earl obtained possession of this place by stratagem; but unfavourable events in other parts soon obliged him to evacuate the place. In the course of the same war, Armagh was again invested, in 1598, by this chieftain, who hoped to reduce it a second time by famine, but was baffled by the treachery of his illegitimate son, Con O'Nial, who, having deserted to the English, discovered a private road by which Sir Henry Bagnall, the British commander, was enabled to send in such a supply of men and provisions as completely

frustrated the earl's efforts. Soon after, the English were utterly defeated, and their commander killed, in a desperate attempt to force O'Nial's intrenchments, the immediate consequence of which was their evacuation of Armagh, which, however, was retaken in 1601, by Lord Mountjoy, who made it one of his principal positions in his Ulster expedition, and occupied it with a garrison of 900 men. In the early part of the 17th century, a colony of Scottish Presbyterians settled here, from which it is supposed Scotch-street, near the eastern entrance of the town, took its name.

At the commencement of the war in 1641, Armagh fell into the hands of Sir Phelim O'Nial, who, on being soon after forced to evacuate it, set fire to the cathedral, and put to death many of the inhabitants. On the breaking out of the war between James II and William, Prince of Orange, the Earl of Tyrconnel, then lord-lieutenant under the former sovereign, took the charter from the corporation, and placed a strong body of troops in the town; but they were surprised and disarmed by the people of the surrounding country, who had risen in favour of the new dynasty: the garrison was permitted to retreat without further injury to Louth, and Lord Blayney, having taken possession of the town, immediately proclaimed King William. This nobleman, however, was soon afterwards compelled to evacuate it, and retreat with his forces to Londonderry, at that period the last refuge of the Protestants. James, in his progress through the north to and from the siege of Derry, rested for a few days at Armagh, which he describes as having been pillaged by the enemy, and very inconvenient both for himself and his suite. In 1690, Duke Schomberg took possession of it, and formed a depot of provisions here. No important event occurred after the Revolution until the year 1769, when this city furnished a well-appointed troop of cavalry to oppose Thurot at Carrickfergus. In 1778, on the apprehension of an invasion from France and of civil disturbances, several of the inhabitants again formed themselves into a volunteer company, and offered the command to the Earl of Charlemont, by whom, after some deliberation, it was accepted. In 1781, an artillery company was formed; and in the following year, a troop of volunteer cavalry, of which the Earl of Charlemont was also captain. In 1796, this nobleman, in pursuance of the wishes of Government, formed an infantry company and a cavalry troop of yeomanry in the town, whose numbers were afterwards augmented to 200: they were serviceable in performing garrison duty during the temporary absence of the regular troops in the disturbances of 1798, but in 1812 were disbanded by order of the lord-lieutenant.

The city, which is large, handsome, and well built, is delightfully situated on the declivity of a lofty eminence, round the western base of which the river Callan winds in its progress to the Blackwater. It is chiefly indebted for its present high state of improvement to the attention bestowed on it by several primates since the Reformation, especially by Primate Boulter, and, still more so, by Primate Robinson, all of whom have made it their place of residence.

The approaches on every side embrace interesting objects. On the east are the rural village and post-town of Rich-hill, and the demesne of Castle-Dillon, in which the late proprietor erected an obelisk on a lofty hill in memory of the volunteers of Ireland. The western approach exhibits the demesnes of Caledon, Glasslough, Woodpark, Elm Park, and Knappagh; those from Dungannon and Loughgall pass through a rich and well-wooded country; that from the south, descending through the fertile, well-cultivated, and busy vale of the Callan, the banks of which are adorned with several seats and extensive plantations, interspersed with numerous bleach-greens and mills, is extremely pleasing; and that from the south-east, though less attractive, is marked by the classical feature of Hamilton's Bawn, immortalised by the sarcastic pen of Swift. Many of the streets converge towards the cathedral, the most central point and the most conspicuous object in the city, and are connected by cross streets winding around the declivity; they have flagged pathways, are Macadamised, and are lighted with oil gas from works erected in Callan-street, by a joint stock company, in the year 1827, but will shortly be lighted with coal gas, the gasometer for which is now in progress of erection; and since 1833 have been also cleansed and watched under the provisions of the general act of the 9th of Geo. IV, cap. 82, by which a cess is applotted and levied on the inhabitants. A copious supply of fresh water has been procured under the authority of two general acts passed in 1789 and 1794. Metal pipes have been carried through all the main streets, by which a plentiful supply of good water is brought from a small lake or basin nearly midway between Armagh and Hamilton's Bawn, in consideration of a small rate on each house; and fountains have also been erected in different parts of the town occupied by the poorer class of the inhabitants. The city is plentifully supplied with turf, and coal of good quality is brought from the Drumglass and Coalisland collieries, 11 miles distant. A public walk, called the Mall, has been formed by subscription, out of ground granted on lease to the corporation, originally in 1797, by the primate, being a part of the town commons, which were vested in the latter for useful purposes by an act of the 13th and 14th of Geo. III: the enclosed area, on the eastern side of which are many superior houses, comprehends nearly eight acres, kept in excellent condition. In addition to this, the primate's demesne is open to respectable persons; and his laudable example has been followed by two opulent citizens, who have thrown open their grounds in the vicinity for the recreation of the inhabitants. The Tontine Buildings, erected as a private speculation by a few individuals, contain a large assembly-room having a suite of apartments connected with it, a public news-room, and a savings' bank. Dramatic performances occasionally take place in this edifice, from the want of a special building for their exhibition.

The public library was founded by Primate Robinson, who bequeathed for the free use of the public his valuable collection of books, and endowed it with lands at Knockhamill and houses in Armagh yielding a clear rental of £339. He also erected the building, which is a handsome edifice in the Grecian style, situated to the north-west of the cathedral, and completed in 1771, as appears by the date in front, above which is the appropriate inscription "ΤΟ ΤΗΣ ΨΥΧΗΣ ΙΑΤΡΕΙΟΝ." The room in which the books are deposited is light, airy and commodious, and has a gallery: there are also apartments for a resident librarian. In 1820, an additional staircase was erected, as an entrance at the west end, which has in a great measure destroyed the uniformity and impaired the beauty of the building. The collection consists of about 20,000 volumes, and comprises many valuable works on theology, the classics, and antiquities, to which have been added several modern publications. In the record-room of the diocesan registry are writings and books bequeathed by Primate Robinson to the governors and librarian, in trust, for the sole use of the primate for the time being. The primate, and the dean and chapter, by an act of the 13th and 14th of Geo. III, are trustees of the library, with liberal powers. The observatory, beautifully situated on a gentle eminence a little to the north-east of the city, was also erected by Primate Robinson, about the year 1788, on a plot of 15 acres of land: the building is of hewn limestone, and has on its front the inscription, "The Heavens declare the glory of God;" it comprises two lofty domes for the observatory, and a good house for the residence of the astronomer. The munificent founder also provided for the maintenance of the astronomer, and gave the impropriate tithes of Carlingford for the support of an assistant astronomer and the maintenance of the observatory, vesting the management in the primate for the time being and twelve governors, of whom the chapter are eight, and the remaining four are elected by them as vacancies occur. Primate Robinson dying before the internal arrangements were completed, the establishment remained in an unfinished state till 1825, when the Right Hon. and Most Rev. Lord J. G. De La Poer Beresford, D.D., the present primate, furnished the necessary instruments, &c., at a cost of nearly £3000. This city is usually the station of a regiment of infantry: the barracks occupy an elevated and healthy situation, and are capable of accommodating 800 men. In the immediate vicinity is the archiepiscopal palace, erected in 1770 by Primate Robinson, who also, in 1781, built a beautiful chapel of Grecian architecture nearly adjacent, and embellished the grounds, which comprise about 800 acres, with plantations tastefully arranged.

Though an increasing place, Armagh has now no manufactures, and but little trade, except in grain, of which a great quantity is sent to Portadown and Newry for exportation: much of the flour made in the neighbourhood is conveyed to the county of Tyrone. After the introduction of the linen manufacture into the North of Ireland, Armagh became the grand mart for the sale of cloth produced in the surrounding district. From a return of six market days in the spring of 1835, the average number of brown webs sold in

Armagh. Drawn by T. Creswick and engraved by S. Fisher. From S.C. Hall, Ireland: its scenery, character &c. *vol. iii (London, 1846).*

the open market was 4292, and in private warehouses 3412, making a total of 7704 webs weekly, the value of which, at £1.11 each, amounts to £620,942.8.0 per annum. But this does not afford a just criterion of the present state of the trade, in which a great change has taken place within the last 20 years; the quantity now bleached annually in this neighbourhood is nearly double that of any former period, but only a portion of it is brought into the market of Armagh. The linen-hall is a large and commodious building, erected by Leonard Dobbin, Esq., M.P. for the borough: it is open for the sale of webs from ten to eleven o'clock every Tuesday. A yarn market is held, in which the weekly sales amount to £3450, or £179,400 per annum. There are two extensive distilleries, in which upwards of 25,000 tons of grain are annually consumed; an ale brewery, consuming 3800 barrels of malt annually; several extensive tanneries; and numerous flour and corn mills, some of which are worked by steam. The amount of excise duties collected within the district for the year 1835 was £69,076.5.8$\frac{1}{2}$. The Blackwater, within four miles of the city,

affords a navigable communication with Lough Neagh, from which, by the Lagan canal, the line of navigation is extended to Belfast; and to the east is the navigable river Bann, which is connected with the Newry canal. A canal is also in progress of formation from the Blackwater, to continue inland navigation from Lough Neagh to Lough Erne, which will pass within one mile of the city. The markets are abundantly supplied; they are held on Tuesday, for linen cloth and yarn, pigs, horned cattle, provisions of all kinds, vast quantities of flax, and flax-seed during the season; and on Saturday, for grain and provisions. Fairs are held on the Tuesday after Michaelmas, and a week before Christmas, and a large cattle market has been established on the first Saturday in every month. By a local act obtained in 1774, a parcel of waste land adjoining the city, and containing about 9$\frac{1}{2}$ plantation acres, was vested in the archbishop and his successors, to be parcelled into divisions for holding the fairs and markets, but only the fairs are now held on it.

The market-house, an elegant and commodious

building of hewn stone, erected by Archbishop Stuart, at an expense of £3000, occupies a central situation at the lower extremity of Market-street; the old shambles, built previously by Primate Robinson, have been taken down, and a more extensive and convenient range, with markets for grain, stores, weigh-house, &c., attached, was erected in 1829 by the committee of tolls: the supply of butchers' meat of very good quality is abundant, and the veal of Armagh is held in high estimation: there is also a plentiful supply of sea and fresh-water fish. Several of the inhabitants, in 1821, raised a subscription, by shares (on debentures or receipts) of £25 each, amounting to £1700, and purchased the lessee's interest in the tolls, of which a renewal for 21 years was obtained in 1829: eight resident shareholders, elected annually, and called the "Armagh Toll Committee," have now the entire regulation and management of the tolls and customs of the borough, consisting of market-house, street, and shambles' customs, in which they have made considerable reductions, and the proceeds of which, after deducting the expenses of management and five per cent, interest for the proprietors of the debentures, are applied partly as a sinking fund for liquidating the principal sum of £1700, and partly towards the improvement of the city and the places for holding the fairs and markets. The Bank of Ireland and the Provincial Bank have each a branch establishment here; and there are also branches of the Northern and Belfast banking companies. The post is daily: the post-office revenue, according to the last return to Parliament, amounted to £1418.4.0½.

The inhabitants were incorporated under the title of the "Sovereign, Free Burgesses, and Commonalty of the Borough of Ardmagh," in 1613, by charter of Jas. I, which was taken from them by Chas. II, who granted one conferring more extensive privileges; but Wm. III restored the original charter, under which the corporation consists of a sovereign, twelve free burgesses, and an unlimited number of freemen, of whom there are at present only two a town-clerk and registrar, and two serjeants-at-mace are also appointed. The sovereign is, by the charter, eligible by the free burgesses from among themselves, annually on the festival of the Nativity of St. John the Baptist (June 24th); the power of filling a vacancy in the number of free burgesses is vested in the sovereign and remaining free burgesses; the freemen are admitted by the sovereign and free burgesses; and the appointment of the inferior officers is vested in the corporation at large. By charter of King James, the borough was empowered to send two representatives to the Irish parliament, but the right of election was confined to the sovereign and twelve burgesses, who continued to return two members till the union, when the number was reduced to one. The nature of the franchise continued the same until the 2nd of Wm. IV, when the free burgesses not resident within seven miles of the borough were disfranchised, and the privilege of election was extended to the £10 householders; and as the limits of the district called "the corporation" comprehend 1147 statute

acres unconnected with the franchise, a new electoral boundary was formed close round the town, comprising only 277 acres: the number of voters registered, according to the latest classified general return made to Parliament, amounted to 454, of whom 443 were £10 householders and 11 burgesses; the number of electors qualified to vote at the last election was 541, of whom 360 polled; the sovereign is the returning officer.

The seneschal of the manor of Armagh, who is appointed by the primate, holds his court here, and exercises jurisdiction, both by attachment of goods and by civil bill process, in all causes of action arising within the manor and not exceeding £10: the greater part of the city is comprised within this manor, the remainder being in that of Mountnorris adjoining. The assizes and general quarter sessions are held twice a year; a court for the relief of insolvent debtors is held three times in the year; and the county magistrates resident in the city and its neighbourhood hold a petty session every Saturday. The corporation grand jury consisted of a foreman and other jurors, usually not exceeding 23 in number, chosen from among the most respectable inhabitants by the sovereign, generally within a month after entering upon his office, and continued to act until the ensuing 29th of September; but its dissolution took place at the close of the year 1832, when a new grand jury having been formed amidst much political excitement, they determined, under an impression that the inhabitants would resist any assessment which they might make, to abrogate their functions, and the system appears to be abandoned. The inconvenience which resulted from the dissolution of the corporation grand jury induced the inhabitants to adopt measures for carrying into effect the provisions of the act of the 9th of Geo. IV, cap. 82, previously noticed. The sessions-house, built in 1809, is situated at the northern extremity of the Mall: it has an elegant portico in front, and affords every accommodation necessary for holding the courts, &c. At the opposite end of the Mall stands the county gaol, a neat and substantial building, with two enclosed yards in which the prisoners may take exercise, and an infirmary containing two wards for males and two for females: there is also a tread-wheel. It is constructed on the old plan, and does not afford convenience for the classification of prisoners, but is well ventilated, clean, and healthy. The females are instructed by the matron in spelling and reading. In 1835, the average daily number of prisoners was 85; and the total net expense amounted to £1564.14.6. Armagh is a chief or baronial constabulary police station, of which the force consists of one chief officer, four constables, and twelve men.

THE SEE OF ARMAGH, according to the common opinion of native historians, was founded by St. Patrick, who in that city built the cathedral and some other religious edifices, in 445. Three years after, he held a synod there, the canons of which are still in existence; and in 454 he resigned the charge of the see (to which, on his recommendation, St. Binen was appointed), and spent the remainder of a life protracted to the patriarchal period of 120 years, in visiting and confirming the various churches which he had founded, and in forming others. Prior to the year 799, the bishop of Armagh and his suffragan bishops were obliged to attend the royal army during the military expeditions of the king of Ireland; but on a remonstrance made by Conmach, then archbishop, the custom was discontinued. A tumult which broke out in the city, during the celebration of the feast of Pentecost, in 889, between the septs of Cinel-Eoghain, of Tyrone, and Ulidia, of Down, affords an instance of the great power exercised by the archbishops at this period. Moelbrigid, having succeeded in quelling the disturbance, mulcted each of the offending parties in a fine of 200 oxen, exacted hostages for their future good conduct, and caused six of the ringleaders on each side to be executed on a gallows. The commencement of the twelfth century was marked by a contest as to the right of the primacy, which had been monopolised during fifteen episcopal successions by a single princely tribe, as an hereditary right. "Eight married men," says St. Bernard, "literate indeed, but not ordained, had been predecessors to Celsus, on whose demise the election of Malachy O'Morgair to the primatial dignity, by the united voice of the clergy and people, put an end to the contest, though not without some struggles." Malachy resigned the primacy in 1137, and in lieu of it accepted the bishoprick of Down, which see he afterwards divided into two, reserving one to himself. His object seems to have resulted from a wish to procure leisure for a journey to Rome, with a view to prevail upon the pope to grant palls to the archbishops of Armagh and Cashel; but in this he was, on his first journey, disappointed, by being informed that so important a measure could only be conceded in pursuance of the suffrage of an Irish council. On making a second journey for the same purpose, he fell sick on the road, and died at the abbey of Clarevall, in the arms of his friend, St. Bernard. Nevertheless, this object was soon after accomplished, even to a greater extent than he had proposed. In 1152, Cardinal Paparo arrived in Ireland as legate from Pope Eugene III, with four palls for the four archbishops, to whom the other Irish bishops were subjected as suffragans. The following sees, several of which are now unknown even by name, were then placed under the provincial jurisdiction of the archbishop of Armagh; viz., Connor, Dumdaleghlas (now Down), Lugud, Cluniniard or Clonard, Connanas, Ardachad, (now Ardagh), Rathboth (now Raphoe), Rathlurig orRathlure, Damliag, and Darrick (now Derry).

The origin of a dispute between the Archbishops of Armagh and Dublin, regarding their respective claims to the primatial authority of Ireland, may be traced to this period, in consequence of a papal bull of 1182, which ordained that no archbishop or bishop should hold any assembly or hear ecclesiastical causes in the diocese of Dublin, unless authorised by the pope or his legate: but it was not until the following century that this dispute acquired a character of importance. The rank of the former of the prelates among the bishops of Christendom was determined at the council of Lyons, where, in the order of subscription to the acts, the name "Albertus Armachanus" preceded those of all the bishops of France, Italy, and Spain. In 1247, Archbishop Reginald or Rayner separated the county of Louth from the diocese of Clogher, and annexed it to Armagh. Indeed, before this act, the inadequacy of the revenue to maintain the dignity of the see occasioned Hen. III to issue a mandate to the lord justice of Ireland, to cause liberty of seisin to be given to the Archbishop of Armagh of all the lands belonging to the see of Clogher: but this writ was not carried into effect. In 1263, Pope Urban addressed a bull to Archbishop O'Scanlain, confirming him in the dignity of primate of all Ireland; but the authenticity of the document has been disputed. This bull did not put an end to the contest about precedency with the Archbishop of Dublin, which was renewed between Lech, Archbishop of Dublin, and Walter Jorse or Joyce, then primate, whose brother and successor, Rowland, persevering in the claim, was resisted by Bicknor, Archbishop of Dublin, and violently driven out of Leinster, in 1313. Again, in 1337, Primate David O'Hiraghty was obstructed in his attendance On parliament by Bicknor and his clergy, who would not permit him to have his crosier borne erect before him in the diocese of Dublin, although the king had expressly forbidden Bicknor to offer him any opposition. In 1349 Bicknor once more contested the point with Fitz-Ralph, Archbishop of Armagh; and, notwithstanding the king's confirmation of the right of thelatter to erect his crosier in any part of Ireland, the lord justice and the prior of Kilmainham, being bribed, as is supposed, by Bicknor, combined with that prelate in opposing the claims of the primate, who thereupon excommunicated the resisting parties.

Shortly after both Bicknor and the prior died; and the latter, on his death-bed, solicited Fitz-Ralph's forgiveness through a special messenger. After his decease, his body was refused Christian burial, until absolved by the primate in consequence of his contrition. In 1350, the king, through partiality to John de St. Paul, then Archbishop of Dublin, revoked his letter to Fitz-Ralph, and prohibited him from exercising his episcopal functions in the province of Dublin; and, in 1353, Pope Innocent VI: decided that Armagh and Dublin should be both primatial sees; the occupant of the former to be styled Primate of all Ireland, and of the latter, Primate of Ireland. In 1365, the Archbishops Milo Sweetman and Thomas Minot renewed the controversy, which, after that period, was suffered to lie dormant till Richard Talbot, Archbishop of Dublin, prevented Primate Swain from attending his duty in five successive parliaments held in 1429, 1435, and the three following years. Primates Mey and Prene experienced similar opposition; but after the decease of Talbot, in 1449, their successors enjoyed their rights undisturbed till 1533, when John Alen, Archbishop of Dublin, revived the contest with Primate Cromer, but seemingly without success. Edw. VI divested Archbishop Dowdall of the primacy, in 1551, in order to confer it on

George Browne, Archbishop of Dublin, as a reward for his advocacy of the Reformation; but on the same principle the right was restored to Dowdall on the accession of Mary. In 1623, Launcelot Bulkeley revived the contest with Primate Hampton, and continued it against his successor, the distinguished Ussher, in whose favour it was decided by the Earl of Strafford, then lord-deputy, in 1634.

At the commencement of the Reformation, Primate Cromer was inflexible in his determination to oppose its introduction into the Irish church; and on his death, in 1542, his example was followed by his successor, Dowdall, who, after the accession of Edw. VI, maintained a controversy on the disputed points with Staples, Bishop of Meath, in which both parties claimed the victory. The English government, finding him determined in his opposition to the new arrangements, issued a mandate rendering his see subordinate to that of Dublin, which caused Dowdall to quit the country and take refuge on the continent. The king, deeming this act a virtual resignation of the see, appointed Hugh Goodacre his successor; but Dowdall was restored by Queen Mary, and held the see till his death in 1558, the year in which his protectress also died. Notwithstanding the ecclesiastical superiority of the see of Armagh over that of Dublin, the income of the latter was so much greater, that Adam Loftus, who had been appointed Archbishop of Armagh on the death of Dowdall, was removed a few years after to Dublin, as being more lucrative: he was only 28 years of age on his first elevation, being the youngest primate of all Ireland upon record, except Celsus. In 1614–15, a regrant of the episcopal property of Armagh, together with a large additional tract of land, accruing from the forfeited estates of the Earls of Tyrone and Tyrconnel, was made to Primate Hampton. His immediate successor was the celebrated James Ussher, during whose primacy Chas. I endowed anew the college of vicars choral in the cathedral, by patent granted in 1635, by which he bestowed on them various tracts of land, the property of the dissolved Culdean priory. Ussher was succeeded by Dr. Bramhall, a man also of great learning and mental powers, who was appointed by Chas. II immediately after the Restoration. Dr. Lindsay, who was enthroned in 1713, endowed the vicars choral and singing boys with £200 per annum out of lands in the county of Down, and also procured for them a new charter, in 1720. Dr. Boulter, who was translated from the see of Bristol to that of Armagh, on the death of Lindsay in 1724, is known only as a political character; a collection of his letters is extant. He was succeeded by Dr. Hoadly, translated from Dublin, who published some sermons and other works; and the latter by Dr. Stone, also an active participator in the political events of the time. His successor was Dr. Robinson, Bishop of Kildare, and after his translation created Baron Rokeby, of Armagh, whose history may be best learned in the contemplation of the city over which he presided, raised by his continued munificence from extreme decay to a state of opulence and respectability, and embellished with various

useful public institutions, worthy of its position among the principal cities of Ireland; and from the pastoral care evinced by him in an eminent degree in the erection of numerous parochial and district churches for new parishes and incumbencies, to which he annexed glebes and glebe-houses, and in promoting the spiritual concerns of his diocese.

Of the R.C. archbishops, since the Reformation, but little connected with the localities of the see is known. Robert Wauchope, a Scotchman, who had been appointed by the pope during the lifetime of Dowdall, may rightly be considered the first; for Dowdall, though a zealous adherent to the doctrines of the Church of Rome, had been appointed solely by the authority of Hen. VIII Peter Lombard, who was appointed in 1594, is known in the literary and political circles by his commentary on Ireland, for which a prosecution was instituted against him by Lord Strafford, but was terminated by Lombard's death at Rome, in 1625, or the year following. Hugh McCaghwell, his successor, was a man of singular piety and learning, an acute metaphysician, and profoundly skilled in every branch of scholastic philosophy: a monument was erected to his memory by the Earl of Tyrone. Oliver Plunket, appointed in 1669, obtained distinction by his defence of the primatial rights against Talbot, Archbishop of Dublin; but his prosecution and death for high treason, on a charge of favouring a plot for betraying Ireland to France, have rendered his name still more known. Hugh McMahon, of the Monaghan family of that name, was appointed in 1708: his great work is the defence of the primatial rights, entitled "Jus Primitiale Armacanum," in which he is said to have exhausted the subject.

The Archbishoprick, or Ecclesiastical Province of Armagh comprehends the ten dioceses of Armagh, Clogher, Meath, Down, Connor, Derry, Raphoe, Kilmore, Dromore, and Ardagh, which are estimated to contain a superficies of 4,319,250 acres, and comprises within its limits the whole of the civil province of Ulster; the counties of Longford, Louth, Meath, and Westmeath, and parts of the King's and Queen's counties, in the province of Leinster; and parts of the counties of Leitrim, Roscommon, and Sligo, in the province of Connaught. The archbishop, who is primate and metropolitan of all Ireland, presides over the province, and exercises all episcopal jurisdiction within his own diocese; and the see of Down being united to that of Connor, and that of Ardagh to the archiepiscopal see of Tuam, seven bishops preside over the respective dioceses, and are suffragan to the Lord-Primate. Under the Church Temporalities' Act of the 3rd of Wm. IV, the archiepiscopal jurisdiction of the province of Tuam will become extinct on the death of the present archbishop, and the dioceses now included in it will be suffragan to Armagh.

The diocese of Armagh comprehends the greater part of that county, and parts of those of Meath, Louth, Tyrone, and Londonderry: it comprises by computation a superficial area of 468,550 acres, of which 1300 are in Meath, 108,900 in

Louth, 162,500 in Tyrone, and 25,000 in Londonderry. It was anciently divided into two parts, the English and the Irish, now known as the Upper and Lower parts: the English or Upper part embraces that portion which extends into the counties of Louth and Meath, and is subdivided into the rural deaneries of Drogheda, Atherdee or Ardee, and Dundalk; and the Irish or Lower part comprehends the remaining portion of the diocese in the counties of Armagh, Tyrone, and Londonderry, and is subdivided into the rural deaneries of Creggan, Aghaloe, Dungannon, and Tullahog. In all ancient synods and visitations the clergy of the English and Irish parts were congregated separately, which practice is still observed, the clergy of the Upper part assembling for visitation at Drogheda, and those of the Lower at Armagh. The see of Clogher, on the first avoidance by death or translation, will, under the Church Temporalities' Act, become united to that of Armagh, and its temporalities will be vested in the Ecclesiastical Commissioners for Ireland. There are 100,563 statute acres belonging to the see of Armagh, of which 87,809 are profitable land, the remainder being bog or mountain; and the gross amount of its yearly revenue on an average is about £17,670, arising from chief rents, fee farms, and copyhold leases. On the death of the present primate the sum of £4500 is, under the above act, to be paid out of the revenue annually to the Ecclesiastical Commissioners. The chapter consists of a dean, precentor, chancellor, treasurer, archdeacon, and the four prebendaries of Mullaghbrack, Ballymore, Loughgall, and Tynan, with eight vicars choral, and an organist and choir. The dean and precentor are the only dignitaries for whom houses are provided; five houses are assigned for the vicars choral and organist. Each dignity and prebend has cure of souls annexed, as regards the benefice forming its corps. The economy estate of the cathedral yields an annual rental of £180.1.5, which is expended in the payment of salaries to the officers of the cathedral, and in defraying other charges incident to the building. The diocese comprises 88 benefices, of which, 14 are unions consisting of 45 parishes, and 74 consist of single parishes or portions thereof. Of these, 4 are in the gift of the Crown, 51 in that of the Lord-Primate, 12 are in lay and corporation patronage, and 21 in clerical or alternate patronage. The total number of parishes or districts is 122, of which 91 are rectories or vicarages, 23 perpetual cures, 1 impropriate, and 7 parishes or districts without cure of souls; there are 22 lay impropriations. The number of churches is 88, besides 11 other buildings in which divine service is performed, and of glebe-houses, 74.

In the R.C. Church the archbishoprick of Armagh, as originally founded, is the head or primacy of all Ireland; and the same bishopricks are suffragan to it as in the Protestant Church. The R.C. diocese comprises 51 parochial benefices or unions, containing 120 places of worship, served by 51 parish priests and 65 coadjutors or curates. The parochial benefice of St. Peter, Drogheda, is held by the archbishop; and the union of Armagh, Eglish, and Grange is annexed to the deanery. There are 68 Presbyterian meeting-houses, and

44 belonging to other Protestant dissenters, making in the whole 331 places of worship in the diocese.

The parish of Armagh comprises, according to the Ordnance survey, 4606¾ statute acres, of which 1051¼ are in the barony of O'Neilland West, and 3555½ in that of Armagh. The rural district is only of small extent: the system of agriculture has very much improved of late; the land is excellent, and yields abundant crops. Limestone prevails, and is mostly used in building and in repairing the roads; in some places it is beautifully variegated, and is wrought into chimney-pieces. The principal seats are the Primate's palace; Ballynahone, that of Miss Lodge; Beech Hill, of T. Simpson, Esq.; Tullamore, of J. Oliver, Esq.; and those of J. Simpson, Esq., and J. Mackey, Esq., at Ballyards. The living consists of a rectory and vicarage, in the diocese of Armagh consolidated by letters patent of the 11th and 12th of Jas. I, and united, in the reign of Chas. I, to the parishes of Eglish, Lisnadell, and Ballymoyer, in the patronage of the Lord-Primate. These parishes, having been so long consolidated, are not specifically set forth in the incumbents' titles, so that Armagh has practically ceased to be, and is no longer designated a union in the instruments of collation. The deanery is in the gift of the Crown, and is usually held with the rectory, but they are not statutably united, and the former has neither tithes nor cure of souls: it is endowed with five tenements and a small plot of land within the city, the deanery-house and farm of 90 acres, and five townlands in the parish of Lisnadill, comprising in all 1142 statute acres, valued at £274.13.7½. per annum. The deanery-house, situated about a quarter of a mile from the cathedral, was built in 1774. The rectorial glebe-lands comprise about 380 acres, valued in 1831 at £368.6.9 per annum. The tithes of Armagh and Grange amount to £500: and the gross value of the deanery and union of Armagh, tithe and glebe inclusive, amounts to £2462.1.2½. There are six perpetual cures within the union, namely, Grange, Eglish, Killylea, Lisnadill, Armaghbreague, and Ballymoyer, the endowments of which amount to £440 per annum, paid by the rector out of the tithes. The Ecclesiastical Commissioners have recommended that the union, on the next avoidance of the benefice, be partially dissolved, and the district of Ballymoyer erected into a new parish; and that the deanery and consolidated rectory and vicarage, now belonging to different patrons, be united and consolidated, the respective patrons presenting and collating alternately, agreeably to the Irish act of the 10th and 11th of Chas. I, cap. 2, (or that the advowson of the deanery be vested solely in the patron of the rectory and vicarage, which are of much greater value than the deanery, the patron of which to be compensated by being allowed the right of presentation to the new parish of Ballymoyer.

The cathedral church, originally founded by St. Patrick in 445, was burnt by the Danes of Ulster, under Turgesius, who, in 836, destroyed the city. At what time the present building was erected is not accurately known; the crypt appears to be of the 11th or 12th century, but there are several

The archbishop's palace, Armagh. Drawn by John Bell and engraved by I. Martin, Dublin. From James Stuart's Historical memoirs of the city of Armagh *(Newry, 1819).*

portions of a much earlier date, which were probably part of a former, or perhaps of the original, structure. It appears from an existing record that the roof, which for 130 years had been only partially repaired, was, in 1125, covered with tiles; and in 1262 the church was repaired by Archbishop O'Scanlain, who is supposed to have built the nave and the elegant western entrance. The cathedral was partially burnt in 1404 and 1566, after which it was repaired by Primate Hampton, who in 1612 rebuilt the tower; it was again burnt in 1642 by Sir Phelim O'Nial, but was restored by Archbishop Margetson, at his own expense, in 1675, and was further repaired in 1729 by the Dean and Chapter, aided by Archbishop Boulter. Primate Robinson, in 1766, roofed the nave with slate, and fitted it up for divine service; the same prelate commenced the erection of a tower, but when it was raised to the height of 60 feet, one of the piers, with the arch springing from it, yielded to the pressure from above, and it was consequently taken down even with the roof of the building. The tower was again raised to its present height and surmounted by a spire, which, from a fear of overpowering the foundation, was necessarily curtailed in its proportion. Primate Beresford, on his translation to the see, employed Mr. Cottingham, architect of London, and the restorer of the abbey of St. Alban's, to survey the cathedral with a view to its perfect restoration, and the report being favourable, the undertaking, towards

which His Grace subscribed £8000, was commenced under that gentleman's superintendence in 1834.

The piers of the tower have been removed and replaced by others resting upon a more solid foundation, in the execution of which the whole weight of the tower was sustained without the slightest crack or settlement, till the new work was brought into contact with the old, by a skilful and ingenious contrivance of which a model has been preserved. The prevailing character of the architecture is the early English style, with portions of the later Norman, and many of the details are rich and elegant, though long obscured and concealed by injudicious management in repairing the building, and, when the present work now in progress is completed, will add much to the beauty of this venerable and interesting structure. The series of elegantly clustered columns separating the aisles from the nave, which had declined from the perpendicular and will be restored to their original position, was concealed by a rude encasement, with a view to strengthen them; and many of the corbels, enriched with emblematical sculpture, were covered with thick coats of plaister. Among other ancient details that had been long hidden is a sculpture of St. Patrick with his crosier, in a compartment surmounted with shamrocks, which is perhaps the earliest existing record of that national emblem; and another of St. Peter, with the keys, surmounted by a cock, discovered in the wall under the rafters of the choir. There are several splendid monuments, of which the principal are those of Dean Drelincourt, by Rysbrach; of Primate Robinson, with a bust, by Bacon; of Lord Charlemont, who died in 1671, and of his father, Baron Caulfield. The ancient monuments of Brian Boru or Boroimhe, his son Murchard, and his nephew Conard, who were slain in the battle of Clontarf and interred in this cathedral, have long since perished. The church, which was made parochial by act of the 15th and 16th of Geo. III, cap. 17th, occupies a commanding site; it is $183\frac{1}{2}$ feet in length, and 119 in breadth along the transepts.

To the east of the cathedral and Mall, on an eminence in front of the city, is a new church, dedicated to St. Mark: it is a handsome edifice in the later English style; the interior is elegantly finished; the aisles are separated from the nave by a row of arches resting on clustered columns, from the capitals of which spring numerous ribs supporting a handsome groined roof. This church, which is indebted for much of its decorations to 'the munificence of the present primate, was built at an expense of £3600, and contains about 1500 sittings, of which 800 are free. There are also six other churches within the union. In the R.C. divisions this parish is the head of a union or district, which comprises also the parishes of Eglish and Grange, and forms one of the benefices of the primate: the union contains three chapels, situated at Armagh, Annacramp, and Tullysaren. The first was built about the year 1750, on ground held under different titles, the proprietors having successively devised a permanent interest therein to the congregation at a nominal rent; the building has of late been much enlarged and improved, but is still too small for the R.C. population; it is triple-roofed, as if intended for three distinct buildings, yet has a good effect. The places of worship for dissenters are, one built in 1722 with part of the ruins of the church and monastery of St. Peter and St. Paul, and having a substantial manse in front, for a congregation of Presbyterians in connection with the Synod of Ulster, who settled here about the year 1670, and endowed with a first class grant of royal bounty; one for Seceders, built about the year 1785, and endowed with a second class grant; one for the Evangelical or Independent congregational union; one for Wesleyan Methodists, built in 1786, with a comfortable house for the minister attached, and situated near the spot where Mr. Wesley, in 1767, frequently preached; and one near it for Primitive Wesleyan Methodists.

The free grammar-school, to the south of the observatory, is endowed with seven townlands in the parish of Loughgilly, comprising 1514 acres, and producing a clear rental of £1377, granted in trust to the primate and his successors in 1627, for the support of a grammar school at Mountnorris: part of the income is applied to the maintenance of several exhibitions at Trinity College, Dublin. The buildings occupy the four sides of a quadrangle, the front of which is formed by a covered passage communicating on each side with the apartments of the head-master and pupils; on the fourth side is the school-room, 56 feet long by 28 broad, behind which is a large area enclosed by a wall and serving as a play-ground. They were completed in 1774, at an expense of £5000, defrayed by Primate Robinson, and are capable of conveniently accommodating 100 resident pupils. A school for the instruction of the choir boys has been established by the present primate, the master of which receives a stipend of £75 per annum, and is allowed to take private pupils. The charter school was founded in 1738, and endowed with £90 per ann. by Mrs. Drelincourt, widow of Dean Drelincourt, for the maintenance and education of 20 boys and 20 girls, who were also to be instructed in the linen manufacture, housewifery, and husbandry. In that year the corporation granted certain commons or waste lands, called the "Irish-Street commons," comprising upwards of 8 statute acres, on which the school premises, including separate residences for the master and mistress, were erected, and to which Primate Boulter annexed 13 statute acres adjoining. The endowment was further augmented with the lands of Legumin, in the county of Tyrone, comprising about 107 acres, and held under a renewable lease granted in trust by Primate Robinson to the dean and chapter: the present annual income is £249.8.2. The primate and rector are trustees, and the officiating curate is superintendent of the school, in which only ten girls are now instructed in the general branches of useful education; the surplus funds have been allowed to accumulate for the erection of premises on a more eligible site, and it is in contemplation to convert the establishment into a day school for boys and girls. In 1819, Primate Stuart built and endowed a large and handsome edifice, in which 105 boys and 84 girls are at present taught on the Lancasterian plan, and about 160 of them are clothed, fifteen by the dean, and the remainder principally by Wm. Stuart, Esq., son of the founder. The income is about £100 per annum; £31.10.0. is given annually by the present primate and Mr. Stuart. The building is situated on the east side of the Mall, and consists of a centre and two wings, the former occupied as residences by the master and mistress, and the latter as school-rooms. There is a national school for boys and girls, aided by a grant of £50 per ann. from the National Board of Education and by private subscriptions, for which a handsome building is now in course of erection by subscription, to the east of the Mall, with a portico in front. In Callan-street is a large building erected for a Sunday school by the present primate, who has presented it to the committee of an infants' school established in 1835, and supported by voluntary contributions. At Killurney is a National school for boys and girls, built and supported by the Hon. Mrs. Caulfeild; and there are other schools in the rural part of the parish. The total number of children on the hooks of these schools is 653, of whom 285 are boys and 368 are girls; and in the different private schools are 270 boys and 200 girls.

The county hospital or infirmary is situated on the north-western declivity of the hill which is crowned by the cathedral, at the top of Abbey-street, Callan street, and

Dawson-street, which branching off in different directions leave an open triangular space in front. It is a line old building of unhewn limestone, completed in 1774, a tan expense of £2150, and consisting of a centre and two wings; one-half is occupied as the surgeon's residence, the other is open for the reception of patients; there are two wards for males and one for females. The domestic offices are commodious and well arranged, and there are separate gardens for the infirmary and for the surgeon. The entire number of patients relieved in 1834 was 3044, of whom 563 were admitted into the hospital, and 71 children were vaccinated: the expenditure in that year amounted to £1145.8.8, of which £500 was granted by the grand jury, and the remainder was defrayed by private subscription. Prior to the establishment of the present county infirmary by act of parliament, the inhabitants had erected and maintained by private contributions an hospital called the "Charitable Infirmary," situated in Scotch-street, which they liberally assigned over to the lord primate and governors of the new establishment, and it was used as the county hospital until the erection of the present edifice. The fever hospital, situated about a furlong from the city, on the Caledon road, was erected in 1825, at an entire cost, including the purchase and laying out of the grounds, &c., of about £3500, defrayed by the present primate, by whose munificence it is solely supported. It is a chaste and handsome building of hewn limestone, 50 feet in length and 30 in width, with a projection rearward containing on the ground floor a physician's room, a warm bath and washing-room, and on the other floors, male and female nurses' rooms and slop-rooms, in the latter of which are shower baths. On the ground floor of the front building are the entrance hall, the matron's sitting and sleeping-rooms, and a kitchen and pantry: the first and second floors are respectively appropriated to the use of male and female patients, each floor containing two wards, a fever and a recovery ward, the former having ten beds and the latter five, making in all thirty beds. The subordinate buildings and offices are well calculated to promote the object of the institution: there is a good garden, with walks in the grounds open to convalescents; and with regard to cleanliness, economy, and suitable accommodation for its suffering inmates, this hospital is entitled to rank among the first in the province. The Armagh district asylum for lunatic poor of the counties of Armagh, Monaghan, Fermanagh, and Cavan, was erected pursuant to act of parliament by a grant from the consolidated fund, at an expense, including purchase of site, furniture, &c., of £20,900, to be repaid by instalments by the respective counties comprising the district, each of which sends patients in proportion to the amount of its population, but is only charged for the number admitted. It has accommodation for 122 patients, who are admitted on an affidavit of poverty, a medical certificate of insanity, and a certificate from the minister and churchwardens of their respective parishes. The establishment is under the superintendence of a board of directors, a resident manager and matron, and a physician. Thirteen acres of ground are attached to the asylum, and are devoted to gardening and husbandry. The male patients weave all the linen cloth used in the establishment, and the clothing for the females; gymnastic exercises and a tennis-court have been lately established. From the 14th of July, 1825, when the asylum was first opened, to the 1st of Jan., 1835, 710 patients were admitted, of whom 400 were males and 310 females: of this number, 305 recovered and were discharged; 121 were discharged relieved; 70 unrelieved and restored to their relations; 89 died, and 1 6 were transferred to the asylum at Londonderry; leaving in this asylum 109. The average annual expense for the above period amounted to about £1900, and the average cost of each patient, including clothing and all ether charges, was about £17 per annum.

Among the voluntary institutions for the improvement of the city the most remarkable is the association for the suppression of mendicity, under the superintendence of a committee, who meet weekly. For this purpose the city is divided into six districts, and eight resident visiters are appointed to each, one of whom collects the subscriptions of the contributors on Wednesday, and distributes them among the paupers on the ensuing Monday. The paupers are divided into three classes, viz., those wholly incapacitated from industrious exertion; orphans and destitute children; and paupers with large families, who are able in some measure, though not wholly, to provide for their subsistence. The visiters personally inspect the habitations of those whom hey relieve, and report to the general committee. The paupers are employed in sweeping the streets and lanes, by which means the public thoroughfares are kept in a state of great cleanliness; and itinerant mendicants are prevented from begging in the streets by two authorised beadles. "The Robinson Loan Fund" consists of an accumulated bequest of £200 by Primate Robinson, in 1794, held in trust by the corporation, and lent free of interest, under an order of the Court of Chancery made in Feb. 1834, in sums of from £10 to £30, to tradesmen and artificers resident or about to settle in the city, and repayable by instalments at or within 12 months; and there is another fund for supplying distressed tradesmen with small loans to he repaid monthly. A bequest was made by the late Arthur Jacob Macan, who died in India in 1819, to the sovereign and burgesses and other inhabitants of Armagh, for the erection and endowment of an asylum for the blind, on the plan of that at Liverpool, but open indiscriminately to all religious persuasions, and, if the funds should allow of it, for the admission also of deaf and dumb children, with preference to the county of Armagh. The benefits derivable under the will are prospective, and are principally contingent on the death of certain legatees.

Basilica Vetus Concionaria, "the old preaching church," was probably used in later times as the parish church: a small fragment still remains contiguous to the cathedral, where the rectors of Armagh were formerly inducted. The

Original design by Thomas Duff of new cathedral, c. 1840. From John Gallogly, The History of St. Patrick's Cathedral Armagh, *(Dublin, 1880).*

priory of the Culdees, who were secular priests serving in the choir of the cathedral, where their president officiated as precentor, was situated in Castle street, and had been totally forsaken for some time prior to 1625, at which period the rents were received by the archbishop's seneschal, and the whole of its endowment in lands, &c., was granted to the vicars choral. Temple Bridget, built by St. Patrick, stood near the spot now occupied by the R.C. chapel. He also founded Temple-na-Fearta, or "the church of the miracles," without the city, for his sister Lupita, who was interred there, and whose body was discovered at the commencement of the 17th century in an upright posture, deeply buried under the rubbish, with a cross before and behind it. The site of the monastery of St. Columba was that now occupied by the Provincial Bank, at the north-east corner of Abbey-street; the two Methodist chapels stand on part of its gardens. There are many other vestiges of antiquity in the city and its vicinity. The most ancient and remarkable is Eamhuin Macha or Eamania, the chief residence of the Kings of Ulster, situated two miles to the west, near which several celts, brazen spear heads, and other military weapons have been found. Crieve Roe, adjoining it, is said to have been the seat of the only order of knighthood among the ancient Irish; its members were called "Knights of the Red Branch," and hence the name of the place. In the same neighbourhood is the Navan Fort, where also numerous ornaments, military weapons, horse accoutrements, &c., are frequently found; and on the estate of Mr. John Mackey, in the townland of Kennedy, are the remains of two forts, where petrified wood

and other fossils have been found. In the primate's demesne are extensive and picturesque ruins of an abbey; near the asylum are the walls of Bishop's Court, once the residence of the primates; and on the banks of the Callan are the remains of the tumulus of "Nial of the hundred battles." On a lofty eminence four miles to the south-east is Cairnamnhanaghan, now called the "Vicar's Cairn," commanding an extensive and pleasing prospect over several adjacent counties. It is a vast conical heap of stones in the parish of Mullaghbrack, covering a circular area 44 yards in diameter, and thrown together without any regularity, except the encircling stones, which were placed close to each other, in order to contain the smaller stones of which the cairn is composed. Its size has been much diminished by the peasantry, who have carried away the large stones for building; but the proprietor, the Earl of Charlemont, has prohibited this destruction. Coins of Anlaff the Dane, Athelstan, Alfred, and Edgar have been found in and around the city. Armagh gives the title of Earl to his Royal Highness Prince Ernest Augustus, Duke of Cumberland.

ARMAGH-BREAGUE, a district parish, partly in the barony of ARMAGH, and partly in the barony of LOWER FEWS, county of ARMAGH, and province of ULSTER, 7 miles (S.) from Armagh, on the road from Keady to Newtown-Hamilton; containing 3632 inhabitants, it was formed into a parish under the provisions of an act of the 7th and 8th of Geo. III, cap. 43, by taking three townlands from the parish of Lisnadill, and three from that of Keady, the former principally heath and mountain, and the latter tithe-free; and comprises 9113 statute acres, of which 5000 are arable, and the remainder waste and bog. The mountains abound with clay-slate; and there are also indications of lead and copper ores, but no attempt has yet been made to work either. About two miles from the village is Mountain Lodge, the residence of Hugh Garmany, Esq. At Linen Vale there is an extensive bleach-green, where 20,000 pieces of linen are annually finished for the English markets. The inhabitants are chiefly employed in the weaving of linen and in agricultural pursuits. The living is a perpetual curacy, in the diocese of Armagh, and in the alternate patronage of the Rectors of Armagh and Keady, the former of whom contributes £60 and the latter £40 per annum as a stipend for the curate there is neither glebe-house nor glebe. The church, situated on the summit of one of the Fews mountains, is a small neat edifice, in the early English style; it was built in 1831, at an expense of £600, a gift from the late Board of First Fruits. In the R.C. divisions this parish is one of three that form the union or district of Lisnadill or Ballymacnab, and contains a small chapel at Granemore. In the parochial school are 80 boys and 40 girls; the master has a house and three roods of land rent-free. The school-room, a large and commodious building, was erected by subscription in 1826. There are also a Sunday school for gratuitous instruction, and a hedge school. Lough Aughuagurgan, the source of the river Callan, is in this district; and on the summit of one of the mountains stands the South Meridian Arch belonging to the observatory of Armagh.

BALEEK, or BELLEEK, a parish, partly in the baronies of UPPER and LOWER FEWS, and partly in that of LOWER ORIOR, county of ARMAGH, and province of ULSTER, 6 miles (S.E.) from Market-Hill; containing 3396 inhabitants, of which number, 129 are in the village. In the reign of Elizabeth an English garrison was stationed at this place; but it was besieged and taken by O'Donnell, of Tyrconnell, who put every individual to the sword. The village is situated on the road from Newry to Newtown-Hamilton, and contains about 20 houses. The parish was constituted in 1826, by the separation of twelve townlands, comprising 5509 statute acres, from the parish of Loughgilly, of which eight pay tithes to the perpetual curate, and four to the rector of Loughgilly. The living is a perpetual curacy, in the diocese of Armagh, and in the patronage of the Rector of Loughgilly: the tithes amount to £331.3.0, of which £179.3.0 is payable to the curate, and the remainder to the patron. The church, built in 1827, is a plain small edifice in the ancient style, with a lofty square tower. There is no glebe-house: the glebe comprises 20 acres in the townland of Lisnalee. In the R.C. divisions the parish is one of three forming the union or district of Loughgilly, and contains a chapel. There is a place of worship for Presbyterians. Two schools afford instruction to about 160 boys and 110 girls; and there are also two hedge schools, in which are about 50 children, and three Sunday schools.

BALLYMORE, or TANDERAGEE, a parish, in the barony of LOWER ORIOR, county of ARMAGH, and province of ULSTER: containing, with the town of Tanderagee, the village of Clare, and the greater part of the village of Poyntz-Pass (all which are separately described) 7963 inhabitants. This parish is situated on the road from Newry to Portadown, and comprises, according to the Ordnance survey, 14,158$\frac{3}{4}$ statute acres, of which 13,958 are applotted under the tithe act and valued at £10,052 per annum: about 100 acres are under plantation, 300 are bog, and 60 waste and water; the remainder is all arable land, remarkably good and in a high state of cultivation, producing abundant crops. There are veins of potters' clay and fullers' earth, both of excellent quality and lying near the surface close to the town; but neither have been worked. Several quarries in the parish yield excellent building stone; that at Tullyhue is now being worked for building the splendid castle of Tanderagee, and produces stone of very superior quality. This castle, which is now being rebuilt by its proprietor Viscount Mandeville, is situated near the town, and forms a conspicuous and highly interesting feature in the view. The other seats are Dromenargoole house, that of Davis Lucas, Esq.; Acton House, of Conway R. Dobbs, Esq.; Harrybrook, of R. Harden, Esq.; Cooley Hill, of R. hardy, Esq.; Orange Hill, of J. Creery, Esq.; and Derryallen, of J. Behan. Esq. Fairs are held in the town on July 5th and Nov. 5th, and on the first Wednesday in every month; and at Clare on May 12th, for horses, cattle, and sheep. Courts leet and baron are also held, the former twice in the year, and the latter on the third Thursday in every month, for the recovery of debts under 40s. Petty sessions are held in the town every Tuesday. The living is a rectory, in the diocese of Armagh, and the corps of the prebend of Ballymore in the cathedral church of St. Patrick, Armagh, in the patronage of the Lord-Primate the tithes amount to £1000. The church is a spacious and handsome structure, in the early English style, with an embattled tower crowned with pinnacles, and was erected in 1812, at an expense of £2200, of which £1500 was a loan from the late Board of First Fruits, and £700 a gift from Lady Mandeville; the Ecclesiastical Commissioners have lately granted £144 for its repair. The glebe-house is a handsome residence, and the glebe comprises 520 acres. In the R.C. divisions the parish is the head of a union or district, called Tanderagee, which comprises also the parishes of Acton and Mullaghbrack, and contains three chapels, one in each parish; that of Ballymore is situated at Poyntz Pass. There are meeting-houses at Tanderagee and Clare for Presbyterians in connection with the Synod of Ulster, the former of the third and the latter of the first class; another at Clare in connection with the Seceding Synod, and of the first class; and places of worship for Primitive and Wesleyan Methodists. The parochial school is supported by the rector, the Dean of Tuam; five schools are supported by Lord Mandeville, two are aided by annual donations from Lord Gosford and the Rev. Mr. Bell, and there are three others, altogether affording instruction to about 580 boys and 440 girls; there are also three pay schools, in which are about 80 boys and 180 girls, and four Sunday schools. The interest of a bequest of £100 by some member of the Montagu family is divided in equal shares among the poor of the parishes of Ballymore and Seagoe. There are some very slight remains of the ancient church, where are two extensive cemeteries nearly adjoining each other, one exclusively for Protestants, and the other for Roman Catholics; in the latter is interred the noted Redmond O'Hanlon, the Irish rapparee. Near Ballynaback are two chalybeate springs, which have been found efficacious in scorbutic diseases. – See TANDERAGEE and CLARE.

BALLYMOYER, a parish, in the barony of UPPER FEWS, county of ARMAGH, and province of ULSTER, 3 miles (N.E.) from Newtown-Hamilton; containing 2729 inhabitants. This place, formerly called Tahellen, was the site of a religious establishment founded by St. Patrick, who appointed St. Killian to preside over it, and of which the church was destroyed by fire in 670; the ancient cemetery may still be traced in the demesne of Ballymoyer Lodge. The parish is situated on the road from Newtown-Hamilton to Newry, and comprises, according to the Ordnance survey, 7381¹/₄ statute acres, of which about 40 acres are underwood, about 2605 are bog and waste land) and the remainder arable and pasture. The lands were heathy and barren previously to 1778, when Sir Walter Synnot erected a house and became a resident landlord; scarcely a tree or shrub was to be seen, and the agricultural implements were of the rudest kind. He constructed good roads in the vicinity, planted forest trees to a considerable extent, and by his example and liberal encouragement of every improvement both as to their habitations and system of agriculture, effected a great change in the habits of the peasantry, and in the appearance of the country, which is now in an excellent state of cultivation, yielding abundant produce; the cultivation of green crops has been introduced, and is practised with success. There are some good quarries of stone; and in the demesne of Ballymoyer Lodge are some lead mines, the ore of which is very pure and lies conveniently for working. The river Cusher has one of its sources within the parish. Among the gentlemen's seats are Ballymoyer Lodge, the residence of Marcus Synnot, Esq., proprietor of the parish under the see of Armagh, pleasantly situated in a demesne of 300 acres, embellished with thriving plantations and forest timber of excellent growth, planted by the owner; Ballintate, of Capt. Synnot; and Ballymoyer Cottage, of W. Reed, Esq. Petty sessions are held here every Wednesday. The living is a rectory and perpetual curacy, in the diocese of Armagh; the rectory is part of the union of Armagh; and the perpetual curacy was instituted under the provisions of an act of the 7th of Geo. III, cap. 17, and is in the patronage of the Rector of Armagh: the tithes amount to £200, the whole of which is payable to the rector of Armagh: the income of the curate arises from a stipend of £50 from the rector, £12.6.0 from the augmentation fund,

and £50 from the glebe, amounting in all to £112.6.0 per annum. In the report of the Ecclesiastical Commissioners, in 1831, it is recommended to separate this parish from the union, and make it a distinct benefice. The walls of the original church were erected in the reign of Chas. I, but the clergyman appointed having been murdered, it remained unroofed until 1775, when Primate Robinson caused the work to be finished. The present church, a large and handsome edifice with a lofty square tower, was built in 1822, by aid of a gift of £900 from the late Board of First Fruits. The glebe-house, within a few perches of the church, was built in 1825, at an expense of £500, of which £450 was a gift and £50 a loan from the same Board; the glebe comprises 32a. 2r. 28p. In the R.C. divisions the parish is one of the three forming the union or district of Loughgilly, and contains a chapel. There are male and female parochial schools, aided by subscriptions from the ladies of the neighbourhood, and two other schools, supported by subscription, in which are about 200 boys and 100 girls; and there are also two Sunday schools. The remains of the former church, with the exception of the roof, are in good preservation, and form a picturesque and interesting object. Near the eastern end is a remarkably large ash tree, beneath the shade of which are deposited the remains of Florence Mac Moyer, otherwise Mac Wire or Mac Guire, a Franciscan friar, upon whose evidence Primate Plunket was executed at Tyburn in 1680. Some years since, a cairn was opened here and found to contain two separate tombs, in one of which were two urns of elegant form and workmanship containing ashes; one of them is in the possession of Mr. Synnot, of Ballymoyer Lodge, who has also a variety of ancient coins found in the neighbourhood, and some curiously marked stones, found in the large cairn of Mullyash, in the county of Monaghan.

BLACKWATERTOWN, a post-town, in that part of the parish of CLONFEACLE which is in the barony of ARMAGH, county of ARMAGH, and province of ULSTER, 5 miles (N.N.W.) from Armagh, and 70 (N.N.W.) from Dublin; containing 103 houses and 528 inhabitants. This place is situated on the old road from Armagh to Dungannon, and on the river Blackwater, from which it takes its name; it is connected by a stone bridge of three arches with the old village of Clonfeacle, now forming part of the town. During the rebellion of the Earl of Tyrone, in the reign of Elizabeth, an English garrison was placed here to cheek the incursions of that chieftain, who, under a plea of some injuries done to his party by the English, in 1595, attacked and expelled the garrison, and obtained possession of the fortress, which he afterwards destroyed and abandoned on the approach of Sir John Norris. In 1596 the Earl covenanted to rebuild it, and to supply an English garrison to be then stationed in it with all necessaries, as one of the conditions upon which peace was granted to him by the queen. In the following year the English forces, under Lord-Deputy Borough, assaulted the place and easily took possession; but the insurgents soon reappeared, and commenced an attack; and though the further progress of the war was prevented by the death of the general, yet a strong English garrison was stationed here as a frontier post. Tyrone was once more compelled to agree to repair the fort and bridge, and to supply the garrison; but he shortly after attacked the former with the greatest vigour; and as the works were weak and imperfect, the assailants were repulsed only by the determined valour of the garrison. The earl afterwards attempted to reduce it by famine; and the besieged were driven to the last extremities, when Sir Henry Bagnall, with the English army of about 5000 infantry and cavalry, and some loyal Irish clans, marched to their relief. This force, however, suffered a total defeat between Armagh and the Blackwater, and the fortress was immediately surrendered to the enemy, though it was soon after recovered.

This town, from its situation on the Blackwater, carries on a considerable trade in the export of corn and potatoes, of which great quantities are annually shipped to Belfast and Newry, and in the importation of coal and timber. Sloops of 50 tons' burden can deliver their cargoes at the quay; and the Ulster Canal, which is now in progress, passes close to the town. There is an extensive bleach-green at Tullydoey, belonging to Messrs. Eyre; and the extensive spirit and corn stores of Mr. Hanna furnish an abundant supply for the neighbourhood. Fairs are held on the second Wednesday in every month throughout the year; and a constabulary police force is stationed here. Tullydoey, the seat of J. Eyre Jackson, Esq., and also the residence of T. Eyre, Esq., are within a short distance of the town. There is a place of worship for Wesleyan Methodists, also a dispensary. On the western side of the river is the ancient and extensive cemetery of Clonfeacle, the church of which being in ruins, another was erected at Benburb, which is now the parish church. Opposite to the town are vestiges of a fort, by some called the Blackwater fort, in the attempt to take which Sir Henry Bagnall lost his life; and by others supposed to have been the strong fortress of the Earl of Tyrone, and one of those for which he stipulated when he obtained a patent of favour from Queen Elizabeth. – See CLONFEACLE.

CAMLOUGH, an ecclesiastical district, in the barony of UPPER ORIOR, county of ARMAGH, and province of ULSTER, 3 miles (W.) from Newry; containing 5822 inhabitants. This was anciently part of the O'Hanlons' country, and at the general plantation of Ulster, 1000 acres, or 12 townlands, with the manor of Maghernahely, were granted to Henry Mac Shane O'Nial for life, and after his death to Sir Toby Caulfield, who built an extensive bawn of stone and lime at Maghernahely, on the site of an ancient church. At Corrinchigo, in this district, Sir John Davis had at the same time a grant of 500 acres; but neglecting to plant or tenant the allotment, it was resumed and granted to Sir Oliver St. John, and is now the property of Viscount Mandeville. Camlough was formerly part of the extensive parish of Killevey, which, for ecclesiastical purposes, was divided into two parts in 1773. It is situated on the road from Newry to Newtown-Hamilton, and on a lake called Camlough, or "the Crooked Lough;" and comprises 10,176 statute acres, of which 2415 are mountain and bog, and 144 lake and water. The greater portion of the land is remarkably good, and in an excellent state of cultivation. Much of the mountain land cannot be brought into cultivation, although in many places there is sufficient depth of soil for the growth of forest trees. Near the village is the lake from which it derives its name, a fine sheet of water comprising 90 acres, a stream issuing from which flows in a northern direction to the Newry water, and gives motion to the machinery of several corn and flour, flax, spinning, and scutch-mills, besides beetling-engines, spade manufactories, and bleach-greens. At Bessbrook are very extensive mills for spinning linen yarn, worked by steam and water, and furnishing employment to 180 persons. Here are also two spade-forges, and two extensive bleach-greens but only the beetling-engines of the last are at present employed. A fair is held on the third Monday in each month; and a constabulary police force has been stationed here. There are several large and handsome houses in the district, the chief of which are Divernagh House, the residence of J. White, Esq., and Bessbrook, of J. Nicholson, Esq.

The living is a perpetual curacy, in the diocese of Armagh, and in the patronage of the Precentor of the cathedral church of St. Patrick, Armagh: the curate's income is derived from the tithes of five-townlands, amounting to £146.2.10. The church is a small edifice, with a tower and low spire, and is one of the numerous churches built by Primate Robinson; it was erected in 1774, but not consecrated till 1785, and the Ecclesiastical Commissioners have recently granted £150.5.9 for its repair. The glebe-house is situated at Ballintemple, three miles from the church, on a glebe of 80 statute acres: it was built in 1805, for which the late Board of First Fruits granted £150. In the R.C. divisions this is the head of a union or district, also called Carrickcruppin, comprising Camlough and part of the parish of Killevey, and containing three chapels, two in Camlough, situated respectively at Carrickcruppin and Lisslea, and the third at Killevey. A school at Sturgan, under the trustees of Erasmus Smith's charity, is endowed with £30 per ann., and with two acres of land and a residence for the master. There are a school of 65 children at Maghernahely, and one of 80 at Divernagh; a school at Corrinchigo was built and is supported by Lord Mandeville; and a handsome school-house has been lately built in the village, in connection with the National Board, aided by the noble proprietor, the Earl of Charlemont. In the townland of Aughnacloghmullan there is an extraordinary cairn, 44 yards in length by 22 in breadth: it contains a chamber, 19 yards long, and divided into four compartments, and is formed of upright stones, about seven feet high, surmounted by very large stone slabs, the whole covered with loose stones and earth. The walls of the bawn erected by Sir Toby Caulfield remain almost entire, and exhibit many of the hewn stones of the ancient abbey of Killevey. A little eastward of these walls stands the shaft of an elegant cross, of which the rest lies in a ditch. Some of the mullions of the windows of the abbey are seen in the walls at Divernagh; and an elegant silver medal was found near its site, and is now in the possession of W. W. Algeo, Esq. The Rev. H. Boyd, translator of Dante's "Divina Comedia," was perpetual curate of this parish.

CARGINS or CARRAGANS, an extra-parochial district, in the barony of UPPER ORIOR, county of ARMAGH, and province of ULSTER, 6 miles (N.W.) from Dundalk; containing 355 inhabitants. This place is situated on the road from Newtown-Hamilton to Dundalk, and in the midst of a mountainous district: it comprises 503 acres, of which more than 100 are mountain, half of which is barren rock; the land in cultivation is of a light friable nature, producing good crops. The Irish language only is spoken. There is a pay school in which are about 35 children.

CHARLEMONT, an incorporated market-town and district parish (formerly a parliamentary borough), in the barony and county of ARMAGH, and province of ULSTER, 5 miles (N. by W.) from Armagh, and 68 miles (N. by W.) from Dublin; containing 3642 inhabitants, of which number, 523 are in the town. This place derives its name from Charles, Lord Mountjoy, who, while Lord-Deputy of Ireland in 1602, erected a castle here, and called it Charlemont, partly after his name, and partly after his title. It was built to prevent the incursions of the O'Nials into the English pale, and to guard the wooden bridge which then afforded the only passage over the Blackwater. In 1641 it was deemed a place of considerable importance, and was taken by stratagem by Sir Phelim O'Nial, on the 22nd of October. Lord Caulfeild, a brave officer, grown old in the royal service, had been made governor, and lived with his Irish neighbours in unsuspecting confidence, when Sir Phelim invited himself to sup with his lordship, and he and his followers being received, on a pre-arranged signal seized the family, made the garrison prisoners, ransacked the castle, and afterwards killed Lord Caulfeild in one of O'Nial's houses. That chieftain subsequently retiring before the English forces, made this castle his headquarters for a short time. Owen O'Nial, expecting to be besieged here, strengthened the defences; and when the Scottish General Monroe attempted to surprise it, he was repulsed with loss, but the castle was at length captured by Sir Charles Coote. In 1665 it was sold to Chas. II for £3500, since which time it has been vested in the Crown. It was garrisoned by the Irish for Jas. II, in 1690, under Sir Teague O'Regan, and invested by Duke Schomberg. Caillemote, a French officer, being posted on the Blackwater, and harassing the garrison, after some time the governor was summoned to surrender. O'Regan, a courageous Irish officer, determined to hold out to the last extremity, but the distresses of the garrison becoming intolerable, the governor proposed terms of capitulation on the 13th of May, and on the 14th the garrison marched out with the honours of war, to the number of 800 men. On taking possession of the castle, the duke found in it 17 pieces of cannon, one large mortar, 83 barrels of gunpowder, amid various munitions of war.

The town is situated near the confluence of the rivers Blackwater and Callen, and on the road from Armagh to Dungannon and Coleraine. In 1833 it contained 111 houses, and is connected with the post-town of Moy by a recently erected stone bridge. Charlemont castle is still a place of great strength, fortified with bastions, a dry ditch, and escarp and counterscarp; and there are two ravelins, one in front, the other in rear of the works, surrounded by a glacis which runs along the side of the Blackwater. It is the ordnance depot for the North of Ireland, and the headquarters of the artillery for the district of Ulster. Formerly it had a military governor, but on the death of Gen. Sir John Doyle, Bart., in 1835, the office was abolished, as being a sinecure. The barracks, which are occupied by two companies of the Royal Artillery, are constructed to accommodate 5 officers, 151 non-commissioned officers and privates, and 79 horses, with an hospital attached for 22 patients. The town is well situated for trade, the river Blackwater being navigable for vessels of 90 tons' burden to Lough Neagh; it is connected with Belfast by the Lagan canal, and with Newry by the canal of that name, and the great Ulster canal now in progress to Lough Erne will open a communication with the West of Ireland. The linen manufacture is carried on to a considerable extent. There is a good market held on Saturday; and fairs are held on the 12th of May, Aug. 16th, and Nov. 12th, for cattle, linen yarn, and provisions. The charter granted to the corporation a market on Tuesday and a fair on the 1st and 2nd of May, with the tolls; and a subsequent patent to Sir Toby Caulfeild, dated March 1st, 1622, granted to him a market on Wednesday and a fair on the 5th and 6th of August, with the tolls; but these charter and patent fairs and markets have long been discontinued.

The borough, which comprises the townland of Charlemont, containing above 200 acres, and the liberties, containing 20 acres, was incorporated by charter of Jas. I, dated April 29th, 1613. The corporation consists of a portreeve, 12 burgesses, and an unlimited number of freemen. The portreeve was to be elected annually, on St. John's day, by the portreeve and free burgesses, the latter of whom were to be elected for life out of the inhabitants; and the freemen were to consist of all the inhabitants, and as many other persons as the corporation might elect. The charter also conferred on the portreeve and free burgesses the right of returning two members to parliament, which was exercised until the Union, when Francis William, Earl of Charlemont received £15,000, as patron of the borough, for the abolition of its franchise. Since the Union, the regularly elected burgesses have not acted; but Mr. Livingstone, the last portreeve, some time before his death, summoned in his official capacity a "corporation jury," similar to that which existed in Armagh; and in the year 1821 the surviving members of that jury elected a portreeve. From that time meetings have been held annually, at which a portreeve, town-clerk, and other officers have been elected, and burgesses and freemen admitted; and since 1827, the lord-lieutenant has ratified the portreeve's election. The borough court, granted by the charter to be held weekly, under the presidency of the portreeve, with jurisdiction in personal actions not exceeding five marks, having fallen into disuse, has been renewed by the new corporation. Courts leet and baron for the manor of Charlemont are held by the seneschal in the town of Moy, in May and November, and their jurisdiction extends over a wide district.

The agriculture of the surrounding district is in a progressive state of improvement: there is some good peat bog, and coal also is said to exist. The principal seats in the vicinity are Church Hill, the residence of Col. Verner; the Argory, of W. McGeough Bond, Esq.; and Clonfeacle glebe-house and demesne, occupied by the Rev. H. Griffin, all of which can be seen from the town. The living, which was created in 1830, is a perpetual curacy, in the diocese of Armagh, and in the patronage of the Rector of Loughgall. The new parish or district comprises the townlands of Charlemont, Corr, and Donavally, with Anagh McManus, Keenahan, Ahinlig, Lishloshly, Kinnego, Mullaghmore, Termacrannon, Anasannery, and Clenmaine. The church is a handsome structure, resembling in front one of the grand altars of York Minster; it was built and consecrated in 1833, by His Grace the Lord-Primate, and contains a handsome monument to the late Mrs. Jackson. Divine service is performed in two school-houses in the district, and on every alternate Sunday in the barrack for the military, by the perpetual curate. There is neither glebe-house nor glebe; the income of the perpetual curate is an annual money payment from the rector of Loughgall. The Wesleyan Methodists have a chapel in the town. The male and female parochial school was built in 1821, near the churcht by the Board of Ordnance and the inhabitants; it is supported by subscription. Summer Island male and female school, with a residence for the master, has an endowment of £7.10.0 from Col. Verner. Clenmaine school is supported by subscriptions; and Kinnego school, built and supported by W. Parnell, Esq., is situated on the College lands. About 100 boys amid 90 girls are educated in these schools, besides which there are a barrack and a hedge school, in which are about 80 boys and 40 girls, and three Sunday schools. There are some remains of the fortifications at Legerhill, from which Duke Schomberg bombarded the town, arid of a Danish rath. A curious gold ring, and a gold cross, studded with gems, and said to have belonged to Sir Teague O'Regan, have been discovered here; also, a few years since, a body almost in a complete state of preservation, with the clothes and spurs perfect. In the museum of Messrs. W. & J. Jackson there is a rare collection of minerals, petrifactions, coins, and other relics found in and near the town. Charlemont gives the title of Earl to the family of Caulfeild.

CLARE, an ancient village, in the parish of BALLYMORE, barony of LOWER ORIOR, county of ARMAGH, and province of ULSTER, 2 miles (W.S.W.) from Tanderagee; the population is returned with the parish. It originally formed part of the extensive possessions of the O'Nials; after the attainder of Hugh, Earl of Tyrone, it was granted by Jas. I to Michael Harrison, from whom it passed to Henry Boucher, Esq., who, in 1619, erected a bawn of stone and lime, 100 feet long by 80 wide, and subsequently built a large stone edifice, which was the origin of Clare castle, and located many English and Scottish families here. These settlers soon afterwards erected a meeting-house, which was destroyed, together with the whole village, in the war of 1641. A patent for a weekly market on Tuesday, and a fair on the 12th of May and two following days, was obtained in the reign of Jas. I The market has not been held for many years, but the fair still exists, and is well supplied with horses, cattle, and pigs. The village is situated on the river Cusher, over which is an ancient stone bridge; and on the river are very extensive flour, meal, and flax-mills. Several important privileges were formerly exercised as belonging to the manor, but the estate having been sold by the Earl of Sandwich, in 1807, no manorial court has since been held. In the village is a meeting-house for Presbyterians in connection with the Synod of Ulster, occupying the site of that destroyed in 1641; and near it is one in connection with the Seceding Synod. There are also male and female schools. In the vicinity are the ruins of Clare castle, standing on an eminence which commands extensive prospects over one of the best cultivated districts in the North of Ireland: the castle is the property of Robt. Harden, Esq., of Harrybrook, who intends to rebuild it in the ancient style. – See BALLYMORE.

CREGGAN, a parish, partly in the barony of UPPER DUNDALK, county of LOUTH, and province of LEINSTER, but chiefly in the barony of UPPER FEWS, county of ARMAGH, and province of ULSTER, 8 miles (W.N.W.) from Dundalk, on the road to Newtown-Hamilton; containing 14,261 inhabitants, of which number, 1674 are in that part of the parish which is in the county of Louth. This parish comprises, according to the Ordnance survey, $24,815\frac{1}{4}$ statute acres, of which $21,823\frac{1}{2}$, including $419\frac{1}{2}$ of water, are in Armagh, and $2991\frac{3}{4}$ in Louth. Of these, 21,640 acres are applotted under the tithe act, and valued at £19,708 per ann.; and 1088 are mountain, bog, and lakes. The surface is irregularly broken and the general aspect bold: the soil is generally good, and the system of cultivation improving. Linen cloth and yarn are manufactured to a small extent by the farmers, whose principal dependence has been the breeding of cattle, but now most of the grazing land has been converted into arable, and even much of the mountainous district has been brought into cultivation. The river Creggan, which divides this parish into two nearly equal parts, turns several mills and contains fine trout. Near the village are several hundred acres of bog or moorland used for fuel; and here is a coarse kind of granite and also a coarse slate, which is very hard and durable: the quarries, however, are not much worked, except by the neighbouring farmers, who use the stone for building. The village is pleasantly situated, and the surrounding scenery is picturesque. A market is held on Friday at Crossmaglen for provisions, and fairs on the first Friday in every month for farming stock. Cullyhanna, also a village in this parish, is an improving place. Fairs are held in it on the second Tuesday in January, April, July, and October; and there are two at Ball's-Mills. There is a penny post to Dundalk; and petty sessions for the Crossmaglen district are held in the school-room at Creggan, on alternate Saturdays, or weekly if requisite. The principal seats in the parish are Urker Lodge, the property of T. P. Ball, Esq., to whom the parish principally belongs; Crossmaglen, of Capt. Ball; and Clohog Lodge, of R. G. Wallace, Esq.

The living is a rectory and vicarage, in the diocese of Armagh, and forms the corps of the treasurership in the cathedral of St. Patrick, Armagh, in the patronage of the Lord-Primate, The tithes amount to £1050: the glebe-house, which is near the church, is romantically situated on the river Creggan, which flows through a deep glen abounding with picturesque scenery, and ornamented with evergreens, rustic seats, and walks cut out of the solid rock: the surrounding grounds have been greatly improved by the Rev. Dr. Atkinson, the rector. The glebe, comprising 300 Irish acres, consists of the whole townland of Cregganban except 40 acres appropriated as a glebe for Newtown-Hamilton, when that parish was severed from Creggan, The church is a spacious and handsome edifice in the centre of the parish, built in 1758, and to which a lofty square tower was added in 1799. In the R.C. divisions the parish is the head of two unions or districts, called Upper and Lower Greggan; the former contains four chapels, situated at Crossmaglen, Glasdrummond, Mowbane, and Shela, of which that at Crossmaglen was built in 1834, on a site given by T. P. Ball, Esq., at an expense of £750; and the one at Glasdrummond is a large and handsome building. The part called Lower Creggan is united with the parish of Newtown-Hamilton, and contains a chapel at Cullyhanna and one in Newtown-Hamilton, both in that parish. At Free-duff is a meeting-house for Presbyterians in connection with the Synod of Ulster of the second class; and there is a place of worship for Wesleyan Methodists at Ball's-Mills. The parochial schools, in which are about 50 boys and 40 girls, are supported by the rector, who gives the house, which was built in 1822, and a garden and two acres of land rent-free for the master, besides books for the children. There is a female working school in the church-yard, and an infants' school super-intended by Mrs. Atkinson; also schools at Tullynavale and Anavachavarkey, built by the rector, aided by some subscriptions, and chiefly supported by him; in the former, which is a large and handsome edifice, divine service is performed by the rector, or his curate, on Sunday evenings. At Darsey is a national school; and there are thirteen private schools in the parish, in which about 460 children are educated. A dispensary was established at Crossmaglen in 1830. In the northern part of the parish are vestiges of an ancient intrenchment, which extended more than a mile in length and about one third of a mile in breadth; it is now intersected by roads.

CROSSMAGLEN, a village, in that part of the parish of CREGGAN which is in the barony of UPPER FEWS, county of ARMAGH, and province of ULSTER, 8 miles (N.W.) from Dundalk, on the road to Newtown-Hamilton; containing 545 inhabitants. It comprises about 100 houses, of which several are large and well built, and has a penny post to Dundalk: the surrounding scenery is strikingly diversified. In the vicinity is a small lake, called Lough Maglen, or Magherlin; and there are numerous others in the surrounding district. The slate quarries here were formerly worked to some extent, but they are now in a declining state. A market for provisions is held on Friday; and there are fairs on the last Friday in every month for black cattle, horses, sheep, and pigs. A constabulary police station has been established in the village and a spacious and handsome R.C. chapel has been recently erected, which is the parochial chapel of a very extensive district, called Lower Creggan. A dispensary was built by subscription, in 1830. – See CREGGAN.

DERRYNOOSE, DERRAGHNUSE, or MADDEN, a parish, partly in the barony of TURANY, but chiefly in that of ARMAGH, county of ARMAGH, and province of ULSTER, 2½ miles (N.N.W.) from Keady, on the road to Middleton; containing 8024 inhabitants. This parish was united to Tynan in 1663, and separated from it in 1709, when the first church was built at Madden, from which it is frequently called the parish of Madden. It comprises, according to the Ordnance survey, 15,049 statute acres, of which 9653¾ are in the barony of Armagh: about 716 are bog, and about 20 water. The land is light, but fertile, and in a high state of cultivation. Leslie Hill, the seat of David Leslie, Esq., is beautifully situated, and the avenue and plantations have been much improved of late years; there are also several good farm-houses in the parish. The living is a rectory and vicarage, in the diocese of Armagh, and in the patronage of the Archbishop: the tithes amount to £646.10.6. The glebe-house, which, as well as the church, is at Madden, was erected by the incumbent, the Rev. James Jones, and is large and handsome, and pleasantly situated on a fertile glebe of 460 acres. The church is a very commodious edifice, rebuilt in 1816, by aid of a loan of £1000 from the late Board of First Fruits, and recently repaired by aid of a grant of £157 from the Ecclesiastical Commissioners. In the R.C. divisions the parish is the head of a union or district, comprising also that of Keady, and containing three chapels, two in Keady and one at Derrynoose, near the ruins of the old church; it was built in 1824, at an expense of £500. There is a place of worship for Presbyterians in connection with the Synod of Ulster, which was rebuilt in 1834, at a cost of £800. Besides the parochial schools, there are others at Temple and Kilcreevy; a female school at Fargort, built by Capt. Singleton on two acres of land; and Derrynoose school, built by Lord Charlemont, and supported by his lordship, Col. Close, and Capt. Singleton; there are also five private schools. The old church is a picturesque object, situated in an extensive cemetery. Near Madden is a valuable chalybeate spring; and lead mines exist in the parish, but are not worked at present.

DRUMCREE,a parish, in the barony of O'NEILLAND WEST, county of ARMAGH, and province of ULSTER; containing, with the post-town and district parish of Portadown, 12,355 inhabitants. According to the Ordnance survey, it comprises 13,385¾ statute acres: there is a very large tract of bog, most of which is valuable. The weaving of linen and cotton is carried on to a great extent. The living is a rectory, in the diocese of Armagh, and in the patronage of the Lord-Primate: the tithes amount to £650. A large and handsome glebe-house was erected by the Rev. C. Alexander, in 1828, aided by a gift of £100 from the late Board of First Fruits: the glebe comprises 567 acres, of which 93 are bog. The parish church is a large ancient building, with a tower and spire; and a chapel of ease was built at Portadown, in 1826. The R.C. parish is co-extensive with that of the Established Church, and has a small chapel at Drumeree. There are places of worship for Wesleyan Methodists at Portadown and Scotch-street, and for Primitive Methodists at Derryanville, Scotch-street, and Drumnakelly. Two large and handsome schools have been erected and endowed by the Rev. C. Alexander, who also principally supports three others. The school at Mullantine was built and is supported by Lady Mandeville; and at Ballyworken, Sir F. W. Macnaghten, Bart., has endowed one with a house and four acres of land for the master. In these schools about 370 children are educated, and about 60 are educated in two private schools. Roger Marley, Esq., bequeathed £30 per annum to the poor, payable out of a farm at Drumanally; and Mrs. Johnston, in 1809, left for their use the interest of £100. At Battentaggart are considerable remains of an extensive mansion, erected by the Bolton family, in the reign of James I A very ancient bell was found some years since in the churchyard of Drumcree. – See PORTADOWN.

EGLISH, a parish, partly in the barony of ARMAGH, but chiefly in that of TURANEY, county of ARMAGH, and province of ULSTER, 4½ miles (N.W.) from Armagh, on the road from Caledon to Charlemont; containing 5419 inhabitants, and comprising, according to the Ordnance survey, 10,574¾ statute acres, of which 7146 are in the barony of Turaney; 9840 acres are applotted under the tithe act, of which about one-fifth is pasture; 526 are tithe free; and there is a small portion of wasteland. Agriculture flourishes, the land is excellent, and the country much ornamented by the plantations of Elm Park, Knappagh, and Glenaule. There are quarries of limestone, which is much used for building and burning for manure. The Ulster canal passes through this parish: the inhabitants combine with husbandry the weaving of linen cloth. The seats are Elm Park, that of the Earl of Charlemont; Knappagh, of James Johnston, Esq.; Glenaule, of Joseph Johnston, Esq.; the glebe-house, of the Rev. W. Barlow; and the modern residences of B. Eyre and R. Cross, Esqrs., bordering on the county of Tyrone. It is a rectory and perpetual cure, in the diocese of Armagh; the rectory forms part of the union of

Armagh, and the perpetual cure was instituted under the act of the 7th of Geo. III, cap. 17, and is in the patronage of the Rector. The tithes amount to £469.0.10: the income of the perpetual curate is £200 per ann. arising from £100 paid by the rector, and £100 derived from the glebe lands. The glebehouse is commodious, and is situated on a glebe of 64 statute acres, given for that use by the late Joseph Johnston, Esq., of Knappagh, to Primate Robinson, who built the house. The same benefactor also gave the ground on which the old church and parish schoolhouse were built, and six acres for the use of the schoolmaster. The church is a large handsome edifice, having a square tower with pinnacles; it was erected in 1821, 1½ mile south-east from the site of the old one, at a cost of £2000, partly by subscription, and partly from a loan of £1000 from the late Board of First Fruits. In the R.C. divisions the parish forms part of the union or district of Armagh, and contains a chapel. There is a parochial school on the glebe, aided by private subscriptions; two are supported by Lord and Lady Charlemont; one by endowment of seven acres of land and a house for the master, by Primate Robinson; one by the perpetual curate; Ballymartrum school, built and supported by Mr. Johnston, who has endowed it with an acre of land; and one, the school-house of which was built by Mr. Jackson. In these schools about 330 children are instructed. There is also a private school, the master of which has a house rent-free. The strongholds and palaces of the Hy Nials, Kings of Ulster, stood in this parish, mention of which is made in the 6th century by St. Fiech, and some traces exist on the townland of Crieve-Roe; they are called "the king's stables" by the country people. The extensive and nearly perfect fort of Navan, with its deep fosses and earthworks, occupies the entire summit of a hill. Not far from Navan is Lisdown, or "the city of forts," which gives name to the townland on which it stands. The ruins of the old church form a picturesque object on the summit of a hill near the western confines of the parish.

FORKHILL, a post-town and parish, partly in the barony of LOWER ORIOR, but chiefly in that of UPPER ORIOR, county of ARMAGH, and province of ULSTER, 4½ miles (N.N.W.) from Dundalk, and 44½ (N. by W.) from Dublin, on the road from Dundalk to Armagh; containing 7063 inhabitants, of which number, 152 are in the town. This was constituted a parish by act of council in 1771, by separating 12 townlands from the parish of Loughgilly, and 11 from Killevy. It comprises, according to the Ordnance survey, 12,590 statute acres, of which 11,910 are applotted under the tithe act, and valued at £5184 per annum; 8380 acres are arable, and 3519 bog and mountain; the state of agriculture has much improved. Among the many mountains is Slieve Gullion, on the eastern boundary, rising 1895 feet above the level of the sea; they all afford pasture, and some have been lately planted. There are quarries of excellent stone, used for building. The town consists of 36 houses and is a constabulary police station. Fairs are held on May 1st, Aug. 1st, Sept. 29th, and Dec. 8th. The linen and cotton manufacture are carried on to a limited extent, and within the parish are four cornmills, from which a considerable quantity of meal is ex ported through the port of Dundalk to Liverpool, The principal seats are Forkhill House, the residence of J. Foxall, Esq.; Forkhill Lodge, of Mrs. Dawson; Longfield, of Major Bernard; Bellmont, of the Rev. Mr. Smith, and of S. E. Walker, Esq.; and the Glebe-house, of the Rev. J. Campbell, LL.D. The living is a rectory, in the diocese of Armagh, and in the patronage of the Lord-Primate: the tithes amount to £650; the glebe comprises 164 statute acres. The church is a plain structure, erected in 1767. In the R.C. divisions the parish is the head of a union or district, comprising also a portion of that of Killevy, or Meigh, in which union are two chapels; the chapel at Mullaban, in this parish, is a plain commodious building. There is a Wesleyan Methodist meeting-house in the town. Seven schools were founded and are supported by the trustees of the late Richard Jackson, Esq., of Forkhill Lodge; another is aided by an annual donation from the same source, and one by the rector. In these schools about 600 children are instructed; and there are two private schools, in which are about 90 boys and 60 girls. A dispensary in the parish is also maintained by the trustees of Mr. Jackson, who by will dated July 20th, 1776, left a great portion of his extensive property to pious and charitable uses: in consequence of some litigation as to its division, it was determined by act of parliament that a portion of the rents of the estate of Forkhill, immediately from the decease of the testator, should be applied to the use of the poor children of his tenants, as directed in the will; the lands then assigned for this purpose yielding £375 per annum. After deducting £200 per annum for agency, &c., one-half of the residue of the net revenue was appropriated to the propagation of the Christian religion in the east, and the other half to his sister and her heirs: he made also many minor charitable bequests. Mrs. Barton, by deed in 1803, gave £40 per annum, to be equally divided among 20 poor women of this parish; and Mrs. Jackson bequeathed £10 per ann., payable out of the Killesandra estate, in Cavan, to the rector, for the benefit of the poor. On the top of the mountain of Slieve Gullion there is a large heap of stones near a cave, supposed to have been the burial-place of some Druid, or ancient chieftain; near which is a deep lake. Near this was formerly Rosskugh, or the fort of Carrick-Brand, a considerable military station, with extensive outworks.

GRANGE, a parish, partly in the barony of O'NEILLAND WEST, but chiefly in that of ARMAGH, county of ARMAGH, and province of ULSTER, 2 miles (N.) from Armagh, on the road to Belfast; containing 4132 inhabitants. This parish, which was formed out of the parish of Armagh in 1777, comprises, according to the Ordnance Survey, 6795$\frac{1}{4}$ statute acres, of which 2411$\frac{1}{2}$ are in O'Neilland West, and 4383$\frac{3}{4}$ in Armagh. The land is generally good, and well cultivated; there is a considerable quantity of bog. There are quarries of excellent limestone and freestone, from which latter the stone is raised for the restoration of Armagh

cathedral. A considerable quantity of linen cloth is woven here, and there is an extensive bleach-green at Alistragh. The principal seat is Castle-Dillon, the splendid residence of Sir Thomas Molyneux, Bart., near whose extensive and richly wooded demesne is an obelisk, 60 feet high, erected by the Right Hon. Sir. Capel Molyneux, Bart., in 1782, to commemorate the passing of some acts securing the independence of the Irish parliament. Here are also Drumsill, the residence of the Misses Mc Geough; Alistragh, of R. McBride, Esq.; the Grange, of M. Pringle, Esq.; and the glebe-house, of the Rev. C. W. Lyne. The living is a perpetual cure, in the diocese of Armagh, and in the patronage of the Dean of Armagh. The curate has a stipend of £100, paid by the dean, with the glebe-house, a large and commodious building surrounded by a fine plantation, and a glebe comprising 37$\frac{3}{4}$ acres, the two latter valued at £100 per annum. The church is a handsome edifice, built in 1779, of compact limestone, with a square tower and octagonal spire. In the R.C. divisions the parish forms part of the union or district of Armagh, and has a small plain chapel. The parochial school is situated near the church, and is aided by an annual donation from the incumbent; two schools for females are aided by the dean, the incumbent, and Miss McGeough; and a national school is aided by an annual donation of £20 from Lord Charlemont, who also built the school-house: they afford instruction to about 270 children. The late Rt. Hon. Sir Capel Molyneux, Bart. bequeathed a rent-charge of £30, on the Castle Dillon estate, to the poor Protestant housekeepers of this parish, which is distributed by the incumbent.

GRANGE O'NEILL, an extra-parochial district) locally in the parish of KILMORE, barony of LOWER ORIOR, county of ARMAGH, and province of ULSTER; containing 903 inhabitants, and more than 800 acres of excellent land. In ecclesiastical concerns it belongs to the lordship of Newry, and is under the jurisdiction of Lord Kilmorey, as abbot of Newry.

HAMILTON'S BAWN, a village, in that part of the parish of MULLAGHBRACK which is in the barony of LOWER FEWS, county of ARMAGH, and province of ULSTER, 1$\frac{3}{4}$ mile (S.) from Richhill, on the road to Market-Hill; containing 86 houses and 462 inhabitants. This district was granted by Jas. I to J. Hamilton, Esq., who, in 1619, built a strong bawn of lime and stone, 60 feet square, with flankers; settled 26 British families here, and armed 30 men for the king's service. The bawn was almost entirely destroyed in 1641, when great cruelties are said to have been perpetrated here. This place, which was formerly of considerable note, is the subject of a humorous poem by Dean Swift, entitled "the Grand Question debated whether Hamilton's Bawn shall be a Barrack or a Malt-House." Fairs are held on the 26th of May and November; and a court baron is held for the manor of Johnstown, on the first Monday in every month, for the recovery of debts under 40s. Here is a male and female school, assisted by the Rev. Dr. Blacker. On the hill above the town are the ruins of a castle, which, until recently, was regularly garrisoned.

JONESBOROUGH, a parish, in the barony of UPPER ORIOR, county of ARMAGH, and province of ULSTER, $4\frac{1}{2}$ miles (S.W.) from Newry, adjoining the post-town of Flurrybridge, and containing 1598 inhabitants, of which number, 174 are in the village. According to the Ordnance survey it comprises $2185\frac{3}{4}$ statute acres, including about 700 acres of bog and mountain. Clay-slate and good granite for building are obtained here. The village, which comprises 35 houses, is situated in a mountain pass at the foot of two lofty hills close to the confines of Louth, and was burnt in 1798. Here is a good inn; and a dispensary has been established, which is supported in the usual way. It has much traffic with Newry and Dundalk; and cattle fairs are held on June 4th, Aug. 15th, Oct. 21st, and Dec. 3rd. Near the village is Jonesborough House, the residence of Hamilton Skelton, Esq.; and the glebe-house, of the Rev. Robert Henry. Here were formerly barracks for the accommodation of a troop of infantry, but the building has been converted into a private residence. The parish was formed out of that of Killevy, or Ballymore, in 1760, and endowed with the tithes and glebe, in 1789, by Primate Robinson. It is a rectory, in the diocese of Armagh, and in the patronage of the Lord-Primate the tithes amount to £155. There is a glebe-house, which was built by aid of a gift of £450 and a loan of £80, in 1816, from the late Board of First Fruits, and has a glebe of 6a. 3r. 11p. The church is a plain neat building, erected in 1772, consecrated in 1785, and repaired in 1812 by a gift of £400 from the same Board. In the R.C. divisions it forms part of the union or district of Faughart, and has a large handsome chapel in the village. About 100 children are educated in two private schools. A little south of the village stands an upright single stone, with an illegible inscription; and not far distant are the ruins of Moyrath castle, erected in the 17th century to defend the mountain pass.

KEADY, a market and post-town, and a parish, partly in the barony of TURANEY, but chiefly in that of ARMAGH, county of ARMAGH, and province of ULSTER, 6 miles (S.S.W.) from Armagh, and $61\frac{1}{2}$ (N.N.W.) from Dublin, on the road from Armagh to Dublin; containing 9082 inhabitants, of which number 896 are in the town. It is advantageously situated on the river Keady, which issues from Clay Lake, about a mile and a half distant, and which, from its numerous falls, attracted the attention of some enterprising Englishmen, who formed a large bleaching establishment here about the year 1750, and laid the foundation of the linen trade, previously to which the whole of the surrounding country was little better than an uncultivated heath. The town contained, in 1831, 249 houses, of which many are very well built; but after the retirement of the parties who originally introduced the trade, it began to decline. In 1826, the Messrs. Sadler, of Leeds, erected a very extensive establishment at Dundrum, and were the first who attempted to make linen from millspun yarn, and who introduced the manufacture of fine linen into this neighbourhood. Since that period, the

increase of the trade has been very rapid. There are some very large mills for spinning flax at New Holland and Darkley, in which 780 persons (principally young females) are constantly employed; an extensive manufactory for fine linen has been established at Ballier, affording employment to 2500 persons; another for sheeting at Dundrum, and bleach-greens at Anvale, Greenmount, Dundrum, Ballier, Millview, Darkley, and Linenvale, where about 235,000 pieces of linen are annually finished, principally for the English market. There are three lakes in the parish, called Clay, Tullynavad, and Aughnagurgan, the waters of which are dammed up at a great expense by the proprietors, and an abundant supply is secured throughout the year. The market is on Friday, for linen yarn and general provisions; and fairs for live stock are held on the second Friday of every month. Here is a constabulary police station; a manor court is held monthly for the recovery of debts under £2, and petty sessions in the court-house every Friday. The court-house and the market-place are commodiously arranged.

The parish, including part of Armagh-Breague, comprises, according to the Ordnance survey, $15,351\frac{3}{4}$ statute acres, of which 208 are under water; the soil is generally light and stony, but in some parts loamy and rich; the system of agriculture is improving, and there is a considerable quantity of bog, affording a valuable supply of fuel; nearly the whole of the waste land has been enclosed and brought into a good state of cultivation. There are several quarries of good building stone. A lead mine was opened here and wrought, a few years since, by the Mining Company of Ireland, but has been discontinued: it is, however, about to be re-opened, preparations for working it having been made at a great expense, and are nearly completed. The surrounding scenery is in many places highly picturesque: in the vicinity of the town, and on the road from Armagh, more than 100,000 trees of different kinds have been planted within the last five years. The principal seats are Violet Hill, the residence of A. Irwin, Esq. Annvale, of W. Kirk, Esq.; Greenmount, of J. A. Kidd, Esq.; Dundrum, of S. Kidd, Esq.; Ballier, of J. B. Boyd, Esq.; Millview, of Jos. McKee, Esq.; Linenvale, of the Rev. S. Simpson; Tassagh, of F. Stringer, Esq.; Roan, of W. Girven, Esq.; Mountain Lodge, of H. Garmany, Esq.; New Holland, of Lieut. McKean, R.N.; the Lodge, of the Rev. P. Coleman; and Darkley, of H. McKean, Esq. The living is a rectory and vicarage, in the diocese of Armagh, and in the patronage of the Lord-Primate; the tithes amount to £323.1.6$\frac{1}{2}$. The church, a neat plain edifice, was erected in 1776, by Primate Robinson, and was enlarged and a tower added to it by aid of a loan of £200 from the late Board of First Fruits, in 1822. The glebe-house was built in 1779, by aid of a gift of £100 from the same Board; the glebe comprises 40 acres. In the R.C. divisions the parish is the head of a union or district, comprising also Derrynoose, and containing three chapels, situated at Keady (a plain cruciform edifice), Derrynoose, and Madden. There are places of worship for Presbyterians in connection with the Synod of Ulster, and the Seceding

Synod, of the third class, and for Wesleyan Methodists. About 320 children are taught in the four public schools in this parish, and there are nine private schools, in which are about 240 children. There is a dispensary, with an infirmary attached to it. At Tessagh is the cemetery of the ancient Culdean priory of Armagh, in which was found, in 1824, an antique ring containing a large emerald richly set.

KILCLUNEY, or KILCLOONEY, a district parish, partly in the barony of LOWER ORIOR, but chiefly in that of LOWER FEWS, county of ARMAGH, and province of ULSTER, 2 miles (S.W.) from Markethill, on the road from Newry to Armagh; containing 7627 inhabitants. It was constituted, in 1792, by disuniting 22 townlands from the parish of Mullaghbrack, and comprises, according to the Ordnance survey, 12,833$\frac{1}{4}$ statute acres, of which 3109 are heath and bog, and the remainder in a high state of cultivation. At Carricklane is a quarry of good clay-slate, from which was raised the stone for building Gosford Castle. Lead ore has been also found in considerable quantities, and there are indications of coal. The weaving of linen and cotton cloth is carried on. It is in the diocese of Armagh, and on its separation from Mullaghbrack, a perpetual curacy, in the gift of the Prebendary of Mullaghbrack, was instituted, under the provisions of an act of the 7th of Geo. III; and a church was built at Glassdrummond, a plain neat edifice, for the erection of which the late Board of First Fruits gave £500. The glebe-house, towards which the same Board granted £450 as a gift and £50 as a loan, is a handsome building, situated on a glebe of 22 acres. In the R.C. divisions the parish forms part of the union or district of Lisnadill, or Ballymacnab: the chapel is a large and handsome edifice at Clady. There are two places of worship for Presbyterians in connection with the Seceding synod, one of the first class at Redrock, the other at Ballylane. There are eight public schools, some of which are aided by donations from the Rev. Dr. Blacker, others by Lords Charlemont and Gosford, and the parochial school by the prebendary and perpetual curate: they afford instruction to about 680 children. Some vestiges yet exist of the old church of Kilcluney, which was burnt in 1641, and also of a bawn built in 1619 by H. Achison, Esq., which was destroyed at the same time. Cairnamnhanaghan, or "The Vicar's Cairn," which is noticed more particularly under the head of Mullaghbrack, is in this district.

KILLEVEY, or KILSLEVE, a parish, partly in the barony of LOWER ORIOR, but chiefly in that of UPPER ORIOR, county of ARMAGH, and province of ULSTER, 4 miles (W.) from Newry; containing, exclusively of Camlough and Meigh, 4259 inhabitants. Including the parishes of Camlough and Meigh (which are described under their own heads) it comprises, according to the Ordnance survey, 28,174 statute acres, of which 4191 are in Lower, and the remainder in Upper Orior. Of these, about 21,440 are arable amid pasture, 190 water, and 6300 mountain and bog. The mountain called Slieve Gullion separates this parish from Forkhill, and rises to the height of 1893 feet above the level of the sea. The system of agriculture has been much improved recently. Whinstone and grey granite are extensively worked for building, and porphyry is also found. There is a communication with Lough Neagh by the Newry canal, and the river Bann. The principal seats are Drumbanagher Castle, that of Lieut.-Col. Maxwell Close, a handsome residence recently erected in the Italian style, from a design by W. H. Playfair, Esq., of Scotch freestone, and situated in an extensive and richly planted demesne; Killevey Castle, built in the Gothic style, the seat of Powell Foxall, Esq.; and Ballintemple glebe, of the Rev. A. Cleland. The living is a rectory, in the diocese of Armagh, constituting the corps of the precentorship of Armagh cathedral, and is in the patronage of the Lord-Primate; the tithes, including those of the perpetual curacies of Camlough and Meigh, amount to £1417.12.10. This parish, prior to 1773, included the district which has since been formed into the parishes of Camlough and Meigh, and had four churches, situated at Cloughinny, Camlough, Meigh, and Drumbanagher. The church at Drumbanagher was used as the parochial church till 1832, when one was built at Cloughinny, by a grant of £2000 from the late Board of First Fruits: it is a spacious cruciform structure, in the later English style. The glebe comprises 1150 statute acres, which is mostly unimprovable mountain land. In the R.C. divisions it is partly in the union or district of Forkhill, but chiefly in that of Camlough, and has a chapel at Lispomanon. There are five public schools, in which about 340 children are educated, two of which are principally supported by Col. and Mrs. Close, and two by Mr. and Mrs. Hall; and one private school, in which about 120 children are educated. Near Drumbanagher Castle are the remains of a very extensive camp, which was the principal rendezvous of the Earl of Tyrone's army in the reign of Elizabeth; and near it is Tuscan's Pass, a most important station in early times, connecting the country of the O'Hanlons with that of the Maginnises. On the summit of Slieve Gullion is a very large cairn, which on recent examination was found to be one of the sepulchral monuments of the ancient Irish, and is supposed to have contained the remains of Cualgue, son of Breogan, a Milesian chieftain, who fell in battle on the plain beneath, and from whom the mountain and the surrounding district most probably derived their name. Near the cairn, and also on the summit of Slieve Gullion, is a pool called the Loch, about 60 yards in diameter, which, together with the cairn, forms the subject of a poem ascribed to Ossian, in which "Fionn-Mac-Cumhall," or Fingal, and his heroes make a conspicuous figure; it is called Laoi-na-Sealga, or "the Chace," and is among the translations of Irish poems by Miss Brooke.

KILLYLEAGH, a district parish, partly in the barony of TURANEY, and partly in that of ARMAGH, county of ARMAGH, and province of ULSTER, 5 miles (W.) from Armagh, on the road from that place to Caledon; containing 3452 inhabitants. It was formed out of the parishes of Armagh, Tynan, and Derrynoose, under the provisions of

Monument, parish of Killevey. Drawn by John Bell and engraved by Brocas. From James Stuart's Historical memoirs of the city of Armagh *(Newry, 1819).*

the act of the 8th of Geo. IV, cap. 43; and comprises 5635 statute acres of very fertile arable and pasture land, which is under an excellent system of cultivation. A great part of the parish and the whole of the village belong to Trinity College, Dublin. Here are some excellent quarries of freestone, clay-slate, and limestone, of which the last is extensively worked: coal also exists on the College estate, but is not much used. Linen-weaving is carried on to a considerable extent. The village, which is on the side of a hill near the Ulster Canal, consists of one long street of stone houses: it has a penny post to Armagh and Tynan, and a cattle fair on the last Friday in every month. A court for the manor of Toaghey and Balteagh is held monthly, for the recovery of debts under 40s. The principal seats in the parish are Elm Park, the residence of the Earl of Charlemont, which is in a beautifully planted demesne; Knappagh, of I. Johnston, Esq.; Woodpark, of A. St. George, Esq.; Fellows-hall, of T. K. Armstrong, Esq.; and Dartan, of Maxwell Cross, Esq. The living is a perpetual curacy, in the diocese of Armagh, and in the alternate patronage of the rectors of Armagh, Derrynoose, and Tynan, each of whom contributes to the perpetual curate's stipend. The church, which was erected by subscription in 1832, is a handsome building, with a lofty square tower, on an eminence. About 210 children are educated in the parochial and another public school, the latter of which is aided by an annual donation from – Close, Esq.; and about 140 in two private schools.

KILLYMAN, a parish, partly in the barony of O'NEILLAND WEST, county of ARMAGH, but chiefly in that of DUNGANNON, county of TYRONE, and province of ULSTER, 2 miles (N.) from Moy, on the river Blackwater and the road from Belfast to Dungannon; containing 7579 inhabitants. According to the Ordnance survey it comprises 10,559$^1/_4$ statute acres, of which 3154$^3/_4$ are in Armagh, and 7404$^1/_2$ in Tyrone, and of which 7729 are applotted under the tithe act and valued at £8534 per annum. The land is exceedingly fertile, and the system of agriculture improved; there is abundance of bog, and on the lands of Dungorman a quarry of red sandstone, which is chiefly used for building and for flags. The river Blackwater for nearly two miles forms here a boundary between the counties, and after separating those parts of the parish which are in opposite baronies, falls into Lough Neagh; it is crossed by Verner's bridge, a handsome structure of one arch, with others on each side, forming a continued causeway, which is frequently overflowed, leaving only the central arch visible above the river. The surface is marked by numerous elevations, the highest of which are Drumina, Roan hill, and Lowestown, the valleys between which are good meadow land. There are extensive meadows along the banks of the Blackwater and the Roan, and at Bernagh is an extensive wood of full-grown oaks, which, with the plantations of Roan hill and the other woods and plantations in the parish, has a very fine effect. Limestone, freestone, basalt, quartz, clay, and clay-slate are found in abundance; there are also indications of coal. In the sandstone near Roan hill are interesting specimens of fossil fish entirely perfect, with the fins minutely distinct. The gentlemen's seats are Bernagh, the residence of the Hon. Mrs. Knox, a handsome mansion on the great line of road; Church Hill, the seat of Col. Verner, a spacious and elegant residence, situated in an extensive and improved demesne, and commanding a fine view of the river Blackwater; the Grange, of Miss Thompson; Grange Park, of H. H. Handcock, Esq.; Brookfield, of H. Atkinson, Esq.; Rhone Hill, of T. Greer, Esq.; Tamnamore, of Jackson Lloyd, Esq.; and Crane-brook, of J. Cranston, Esq. The manufacture of linen and cotton is extensively carried on throughout this neighbourhood; and there are three large bleach-greens. At Twyford is a paper-mill, and at Lower Corr, a large manufactory for coarse earthenware, of which there are also others on a smaller scale in various parts of the parish. A manorial court is held monthly by the seneschal of the Lord-Primate, in which debts to the amount of £5 are recoverable. The living is a rectory, in the diocese of Armagh, and in the patronage of the Lord-Primate; the tithes amount to £484.12.4. The church, a neat structure, was erected in 1823. The glebe-house is a handsome edifice, and the glebe comprises 226 acres. In the R.C. divisions the parish forms part of the union or district of Dungannon: the chapel is a neat stone building, roofed with slate. There is a place of worship for Wesleyan Methodists. About 250 children are taught in four public schools, of which the parochial school is aided by £10 annually from the incumbent, and another is wholly supported by Col. Verner; there are also four private schools, in which are about 200 children, and a Sunday school. At Mullinakill is an ancient cemetery, which is still used.

KILMORE, a parish, partly in the barony of LOWER ORIOR, but chiefly in that of O'NEILLAND WEST, county of ARMAGH, and province of ULSTER, on the road from Armagh to Belfast; containing, with the post-town of Richhill (which is described under its own head), 14,037 inhabitants. This place, anciently called Kilmore-Aedhain, derived that name from the foundation of a church in the territory of Huadneth, by St. Mochtee, the founder of Louth, by whom it was dedicated to St. Aedan. The parish comprises, according to the Ordnance survey, 17,274$\frac{1}{2}$ statute acres, of which 4799$\frac{3}{4}$ are in the barony of Lower Orior, and 12,474$\frac{3}{4}$ in that of O'Neilland West. The soil is fertile; the system of agriculture is highly improving; there is no waste land and only a small quantity of bog. There are several quarries of whinstone, which is raised for building; and limestone is found in great abundance, and quarried both for building and for manure. The surrounding scenery is finely varied, and towards the south and east are some beautiful views extending to the sea, and comprehending the mountains of Mourne. The principal seats are Richhill Castle, the property and residence of Miss Richardson, situated in an extensive and embellished demesne; Wheatfield, of H. Clendining, Esq.; Bellview, of G. Langtrey,

Esq.; Killynhanvagh, of Major T. Atkins; Anna Hill, of H. Walker, Esq.; and Course Lodge, of J. Orr, Esq. The linen manufacture is carried on to a considerable extent, employing a great number of persons; and a court is held at Richhill on the first Friday in every month for the manor of Mullalelish and Legacony, in which debts under 40s are recoverable.

The living is a rectory, in the diocese of Armagh, constituting the corps of the chancellorship of the cathedral of Armagh, in the patronage of the Lord-Primate; the tithes amount to £1213.4.4. The glebe-house, towards which the late Board of First Fruits contributed a gift of £100, was erected in 1793; it is a spacious and handsome residence, situated in grounds tastefully disposed; the glebe comprises 679 acres of profitable land. The church, with the exception of the ancient tower, was rebuilt in 1814, at an expense of £2800, of which £2000 was a loan from the same Board; and in 1825 the massive square tower was surmounted by a lofty octagonal spire covered with copper, at an expense of £300, of Which half was defrayed by the rector and the remainder by subscription; it occupies a commanding eminence, and is seen to great advantage at a distance. A church was built in 1775 at Mullyvilly, for the accommodation of the parishioners in that part of the parish: the living is a perpetual curacy, in the patronage of the Rector. The R.C. parish is co-extensive with that of the Established Church; there are two chapels, both small buildings, situated respectively at Richhill and Mullavilly. There are places of worship for Presbyterians in connection with the Synod of Ulster, of the third class, and for the Society of Friends and Independents. About 550 children are taught in eight public schools, of which two are supported by the rector, two by the trustees of Erasmus Smith's fund, one by Miss Richardson, of Richhill Castle, and two are endowed with an acre of land each by the rector, who also built the school-houses. There are also two private schools, in which are about 70 children, and six Sunday schools in connection with the Established Church and the several dissenting congregations, two of which are aided by annual donations from the rector and Mr. Caulfield. A payment of £3.1.6 is annually made to the poor, arising from land near the village, called the Honey Pot field; and Mr. Atkinson, of Greenhall, in 1827, bequeathed £50, of which the interest is annually divided by the rector among the Protestant poor. There are a mendicity association and a voluntary poor fund. In the townland of Castle Roe are extensive ruins of the castle which gave name to the district, and which is said to have been founded by Rory O'Nial in the reign of Elizabeth; it occupied a lofty eminence, commanding the entire country. The former glebe-house was part of the ancient abbey, and contained several dormitories and cells with narrow lights and very massive walls; but the only vestige of the abbey is the holy well, enclosed in the rector's garden. On a high hill in the parish, Cromwell is said to have had an encampment.

LISNADILL, a parish, partly in the baronies of ARMAGH and UPPER FEWS, but chiefly in that of LOWER FEWS, county of ARMAGH, and province of ULSTER, 2 miles (S.E.) from Armagh, on the road to Newtown-Hamilton; containing 7699 inhabitants. This parish comprises, according to the Ordnance survey, 18,556½ statute acres, of which 4468½ are in the barony of Armagh, 5824 in Upper Fews, and 8264 in Lower Fews. The land is remarkably good, and the system of agriculture in a very improved state. Limestone of excellent quality is quarried in several parts of the parish, chiefly for agricultural purposes. The principal seats are Beech Hill, the residence of T. Simpson, Esq.; Ballyards, of J. Simpson, Esq.; and Ballier, of J. B. Boyd, Esq. The weaving of linen for the manufacturers and bleachers of the surrounding district affords employment to many of the inhabitants; and there are two very extensive bleach-greens, in which, on an average, 56,000 pieces are annually finished for the English markets. The living is a rectory and perpetual curacy, in the diocese of Armagh; the rectory forms part of the union of Armagh, and the perpetual curacy was instituted under the provisions of an act of the 7th of Geo. III The tithes amount to £650; and the stipend of the curate is £100, paid by the rector of Armagh, who is the patron; the curate has also the glebe-house, a handsome residence built by Primate Robinson, and 64 acres of glebe, purchased by the primate for the endowment of the living. The church is a spacious edifice in the later English style, with a square embattled tower erected by Primate Robinson in 1772, and has the arms of the founder over the entrance. In the R.C. divisions the parish is the head of a union or district called also Ballymacnab and Kilcluney, comprising the parishes of Lisnadill and Kilcluney, part of Mullaghbrack, and the district of Armaghbreague; there are chapels at Ballymacnab and Granemore, and a spacious and handsome chapel is now being erected in the parish. About 650 children are taught in six public schools, of which the parochial school is endowed with 7 acres of land by Primate Robinson, who also built the school-house; two are partly supported by the rector and curate, and one by Thos. Wilson, Esq.; there are also two private schools, in which are about 120 children, and five Sunday schools. The ancient church was destroyed in the war of 1641, but its extensive cemetery is still used. At Corran, in 1833, was found a cylindrical case of gold, containing many antique gems and ornaments, among which was a necklace of jet richly carved; it is now in the museum of J. Corry, Esq., of Armagh.

LOUGHGALL, or LEVALLEY-EGLISH, a post-town and parish, partly in the barony of ARMAGH, but chiefly in that of O'NEILLAND WEST, county of ARMAGH, and province of ULSTER, 4 miles (N.E.) from Armagh, and 70 (N.) from Dublin, on the great north road from Denny through Dungannon to Armagh; containing 5934 inhabitants, of which number, 325 are in the town. The parish, which is bounded on the north by the river Blackwater, comprises, according to the Ordnance survey (including the district parish of Charlemont), 10,924½ statute acres, of which 2449¾ are in the barony of Armagh, and the remainder in O'Neilland West; 59½ acres are water, and of the land about two-thirds are exceedingly rich and fertile, and the remainder of inferior quality. The system of agriculture is highly improved under the auspices of the resident gentry, and excellent crops are raised; there is some valuable bog, but no waste land. Limestone abounds and is extensively quarried for agricultural purposes and for repairing the roads. The weaving of linen cloth is still carried on here to a considerable extent, affording employment to more than 600 persons who are engaged by the manufacturers and bleachers of Banbridge. The principal seats are Drumilly, the residence of Mrs. Cope, an ancient mansion with two lofty square towers projecting from the front, and overlooking the village; Hockley Lodge, of the Hon. H. Caulfield; Andress, of G. Ensor, Esq.; Green Hall, of Mrs. Atkinson; Summer Island, of Col. Verner; Eden Cottage, of W. P. Newton, Esq.; Cloven Eden, of W. B. Picknoll, Esq.; Loughgall House, of J. Hardy, Esq.; and the glebe-house, of the Rev. Silver Oliver. The fine mansion and demesne of Castle Dillon, the seat of Sir Thos. Molyneux, which is described particularly in the account of Richhill, are partly in this parish and partly in that of Armagh. The village, though small, is beautifully situated in a fertile valley in the midst of a richly cultivated and picturesque country; and consists of 60 houses, of which the greaten number are large, well-built, and of handsome appearance. There is a large and handsome market-house, but the market, and also four fairs which were formerly held, have been discontinued. A constabulary police force is stationed here; and a manorial court is held monthly before the seneschal for the recovery of debts not exceeding 40s.

The living is a rectory, in the diocese of Armagh, constituting the corps of the prebend of Loughgall in the cathedral of Armagh, and in the patronage of the Lord-Primate: the tithes amount to £512.10.0. The glebe-house is a handsome residence, on which, in 1782, £220.17.6 was expended in improvements; the glebe comprises 139¾ statute acres, valued at £179 per annum, which, together with houses and gardens in the village, valued at £48.5.0, makes the whole value of the prebend £739.15.0 per annum. The church, a neat edifice in the early English style, with a square tower, was built in 1795 by subscription and assessments; a gallery was added to it in 1822, at an expense of £110.15.4½, and it has been recently repaired by a grant of £110 from the Ecclesiastical Commissioners: the building is of hewn marble, and the interior is elegantly arranged, and contains a handsome cenotaph to the late Bishop Cope, who was for some time curate of the parish. There is a district church at Charlemont, of which the living is a perpetual curacy. In the R.C. divisions the parish is the head of a union or district, comprising also that of Tartaragan, in each of which is a chapel. There is a place of worship for Presbyterians in connection with the Synod of Ulster, of the third class, and at Ballymagerney is a place of worship for Methodists. About 580 children are taught in six public schools, of which one, endowed with a school-house and two acres of land by Col. Cope, is supported by the trustees of Erasmus Smith's charity; three are supported by Mr. Cope, and one by donations from the incumbent and Sir T. Molyneux, Bart. There are also five private schools, in which are about 200 children, and seven Sunday schools. Nearly in the centre of the village are the ruins of the ancient church, of which the western gable and turret are nearly entire.

LOUGHGILLY, a parish, partly in the barony of LOWER FEWS, and partly in that of UPPER FEWS, but chiefly in the barony of LOWER ORIOR, county of ARMAGH, and province of ULSTER, 4 miles (E.S.E.) from Market-Hill, on the road from Armagh to Newry; containing, with the district parish of Baleek and the village of Mountnornis (which see), 10,198 inhabitants. This parish, which takes its name from the lake on which it is situated, comprises, according to the Ordnance survey, $16,029\frac{1}{2}$ statute acres, including $80\frac{1}{2}$ of water; of these, 5299 are in Lower Fews, $2289\frac{1}{4}$ in Upper Fews, and $8441\frac{1}{4}$ in Lower Orion. The lake extended several miles in length from Pointz-Pass to Mountnorris, forming a continued morass and fortified by a military post at the former, and at the latter by another erected by Gen. Norris, from whom that station had its name; but with the exception of about 5 acres of water near the glebe-house, the whole has been drained and brought into cultivation. The land is fertile; about three-fourths are under tillage and in a very high state of cultivation; the remainder, though in some parts rocky, affords good pasture. Slate is found in the parish, but the quarries are not at present worked. There are several substantial and some handsome houses, of which the principal are Glenaune, the elegant residence of W. Atkinson, Esq.; and the glebe-house, of the Rev. Dr. Stuart. In the southern part of the parish is a small lake, called Loughshaws, from which a small stream flowing through Glenaune affords a convenient site for some extensive mills that have been established here for spinning cotton and weaving calico, in which are 170 power-looms, affording employment to nearly 300 persons; and also for bleach-greens and other mills, in which the manufactured goods are finished for the English markets. Since the establishment of these works, the proprietor has planted a great portion of mountainous and rocky land, introduced a good practical system of agriculture, and greatly improved the entire neighbourhood. A manorial court for the district of Baleek is held here every month, in which debts to the amount of 40s. are recoverable. The district of Baleek was separated from this parish in 1826, and erected into a perpetual curacy. The living of Loughgilly is a rectory, in the diocese of Armagh, and in the patronage of the Lord-Primate; the tithes amount to £926.18.4. The glebe-house was built in 1782, at an expense of $£923.1.6\frac{1}{2}$, and subsequently enlarged and improved at a cost of £1819; the glebe comprises 500 statute acres, valued at £585.11.8 per annum. The church is a spacious and handsome edifice with a tower, originally built at an expense of $£1384.12.3\frac{3}{4}$, a loan from the late Board of First Fruits, and rebuilt in 1828

by aid of a gift of £830.15.0 from the same Board. In the R.C. divisions the parish is the head of a union or district, comprising also the parishes of Ballymoyer and Baleek, in each of which is a chapel. There are places of worship for Presbyterians in connection with the Synod of Ulster and the Seceding Synod, also for Covenanters. About 350 children are taught in four public schools, of which the male and female parochial schools are supported by the trustees of Erasmus Smith's fund, and one by Lord Gosford, who has endowed it with an acre of land. The parochial school-house was built on the glebe in 1813, at an expense of £250. There are also a private school, in which are about 60 children, and seven Sunday schools. A school-house is being built at Killycarran by the Education Society, who intend endowing it with £30 per annum from the surplus funds of the collegiate school at Armagh, which latter was founded by Chas. I, who granted seven townlands in this parish for the foundation of a school at Mountnorris, but which was some years afterwards established at Armagh. Four unendowed almshouses were built by Dean Dawson, in 1811, for four aged women; and the late Lord Gosford bequeathed a sum of money, of which the interest is annually distributed among the poor. During the rebellion of the Earl of Tyrone, the garrison of this place was put to the sword by the O'Donells; it also suffered greatly in the war of 1641, when a dreadful carnage took place. There are several remains of fortifications in the neighbourhood; the "Tyrone Ditches" are near the junction of the parish with those of Killevy and Ballymore; but of the extensive fortress of Port-Norris, or Mount-Norris, not a vestige can be traced.

LURGAN, a market and post-town, in the parish of SHANKILL, barony of O'NEILLAND EAST, county of ARMAGH, and province of ULSTER, $13\frac{1}{2}$ miles (N.E.) from Armagh, on the road to Belfast, and $67\frac{1}{2}$ (N.) from Dublin; containing, in 1831, 2842 inhabitants, since which period the population has very much increased. This place formed part of the territory of the O'Nials, and on the settlement of Ulster was, with the lands of Dowcorran and Ballenemony, together comprising 2500 acres, granted by Jas. I to William Brownlow, Esq., who erected a handsome house at Dowcorran, and shortly after built the town of Lurgan, in which, in 1619, were 42 houses, all occupied by English families. On the other parts of the estate were 45 families, and the colony continued to flourish till the war in 1641, when the town was burned by the insurgents, who converted the church into a garrison, and afterwards demolished it; they also destroyed the mansions of Dowcorran and Ballenemony. After the restoration the town was rebuilt, but was again destroyed by the army of Jas. II, and its proprietor declared an outlaw. It was, however, restored in 1690, when a patent for a market and fairs was obtained, and soon afterwards an important branch of the linen manufacture was established here, which has continued to flourish till the present time, The town is situated in the midst of a fertile and well-cultivated district, and consists of one spacious street, containing 482 houses,

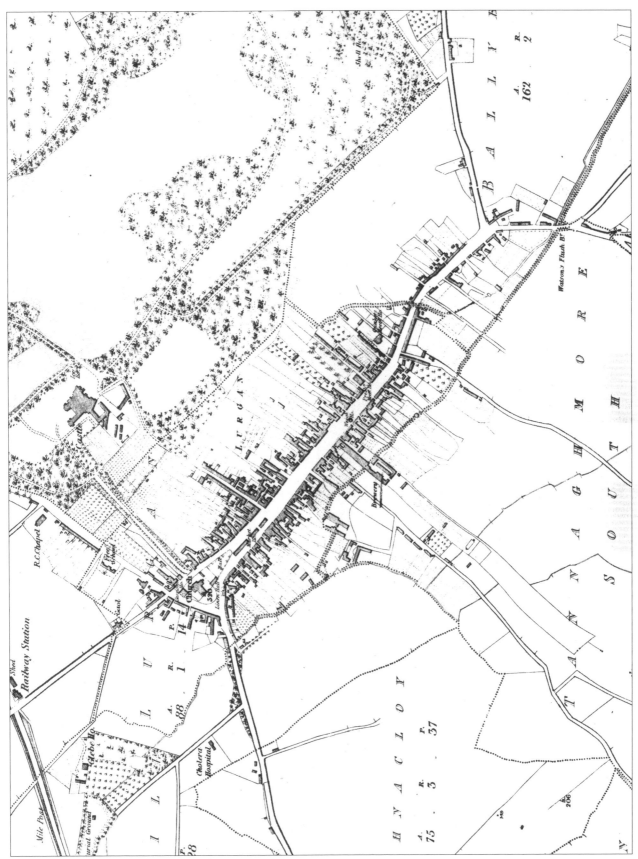

Lurgan. Part of 6 inch O.S. map of Co. Armagh, sheet 6, published 1836 (reproduced at 140%).

33

substantially built of stone and roofed with slate, many of which are large and handsome. The manufacture of diapers was introduced here by William Waring, Esq., M.P. for Hillsborough, during the whole of the reign of Anne; and the Lurgan and Waringstown manufacturers have always been eminent in this branch of the trade. Damasks of superior quality, and cambrics, are made here in large quantities, and sold in the market weekly, to the amount of from £2500 to £3000; and there is scarcely a family in the district that is not more or less connected with the linen trade. There are two large tobacco-manufactories, two ale-breweries, and an extensive distillery, in which 15,000 tons of grain are annually consumed. A facility of intercourse with Belfast is afforded by Lough Neagh and the Lagan navigation, and the trade of the town is progressively increasing. The market is on Friday, and is abundantly supplied with provisions; and great quantities of linens are sold on the market days in the brown linenhall, a spacious building, erected by subscription in 1825. Fairs are held on Aug. 5th and 6th, and Nov. 22nd and 23rd. A chief constabulary police force is stationed in the town; a manorial court is held every three weeks, and petty sessions every Friday; the quarter sessions for the county are also held here. The court-house is a large, handsome, and well-arranged building; and there is a district bridewell, containing 7 cells, with day rooms and airing-yards, and well adapted for classification. The parish church, a handsome edifice with a tower surmounted by an octagonal spire; the R.C. parochial chapel, a neat Gothic building; and meeting-houses for Presbyterians and the Society of Friends, are in the town. A mendicity society and a voluntary poor fund have been established, to which Mr. Brownlow contributes £100 per annum. Near the town is Lurgan House, the residence of the Rt. Hon. Charles Brownlow, now being rebuilt on an extensive scale and in the Elizabethan style, with freestone brought from Scotland; the approach is by a handsome lodge and gateway of the same character, and the demesne, which is very extensive, is embellished with a profusion of stately timber, and with an artificial lake of 100 acres; there are various other seats in the vicinity, which, with the schools and other institutions, are noticed under the head of Shankill.

MARKETHILL, a market and post-town, partly in the parish of MULLAGHBRACK, and partly in the district of KILCLUNEY, barony of LOWER FEWS, county of ARMAGH, and province of ULSTER, 5½ miles (E.) from Armagh, on the mail coach road to Newry, and 60 miles (N. by W.) from Dublin; containing 1043 inhabitants, and comprising 195 houses. It consists of one principal street, from which two others diverge, and is situated in the midst of a fertile country, the extensive demesne and splendid castle of Gosford, the property of Viscount Gosford, adding greatly to its beauty. Two miles to the south-west is the Vicar's Cairn, or Carricktole, commanding a most extensive and beautiful view. Dean Swift in his writings notices a favourite spot here, which he named Draper's Hill; it is now within Lord Gosford's demesne. This is a thriving town, having more than doubled its inhabitants and houses within the last ten years; it has an excellent market on Friday, and a fair on the third Friday in each month for cattle and pigs: petty sessions are held every Friday, and quarter sessions for the county, alternately with Ballybot, in a neat sessions-house. The staff of the Armagh militia is at this town; among their muniments is deposited the stand of colours taken by them from the French at Ballynamuck, in 1798. It is a constabulary police station; and here is a small prison, with separate cells for males and females. There are large meeting-houses for Presbyterians of the Synod of Ulster and the Associate Synod, and one for Wesleyan Methodists, also a national school and a dis-pensary. – See MULLAGHBRACK.

MEIGH, an ecclesiastical district, in the barony of UPPER ORIOR, county of ARMAGH, and province of ULSTER, 4 miles (S.W.) from Newry, on the road from Dublin to Belfast; containing 7164 inhabitants. This district was formed in 1830, by separating some townlands from the parish of Killevey. Agriculture is improving, and the waste land consists of bog or mountain, which is well adapted for the growth of trees. A great part of the mountain was planted by Jos. Foxall, Esq., who was the first to commence the improvements on Slieve Gullion, which are still being carried on to a great extent by Powell Foxall, Esq., who has formed a road halfway up the mountain on an inclination of one in twenty feet. There are some quarries of a fine description of granite, also one of a hard flagstone, which is used for building; and from the existence of very strong chalybeate springs it is supposed that iron might be found. There are two corn-mills, and some linen, diaper, frieze, and drugget are manufactured. Petty sessions are held on alternate Mondays. The principal seats are Killevey Castle, the residence of Powell Foxall, Esq.; Heath Hall, of J. Seaver, Esq.; Carrick-brede, of A. Johnston, Esq.; and Hawthorn Hill, of Hunt Walsh Chambre, Esq. The living is a perpetual curacy, in the diocese of Armagh, and in the patronage of the Rector of Killevey, who receives the tithes of Meigh, which are included with those of Killevey: the curate's income is £75 per annum, paid by the rector. The church is a neat edifice, built of granite in the castellated style: it has a handsome porch, ornamented with minarets, and the battlements are coped with hewn stone; it was erected in 1831, at an expense of £1200, of which £900 was a gift from the late Board of First Fruits, and the rest was defrayed by subscriptions of the landed proprietors. In the R.C. divisions this district forms part of the two unions of districts of Meigh and Killevey, and has chapels at Cloghog, Drominter, and Ballinless. There are two schools under the Board of Education, a private school, and a dispensary. At the foot of Slieve Gullion are the extensive ruins of a nunnery, which is said to have been founded by St. Dareria, Or Monenna, sister of St. Patrick, and abbess of Kilsleve, who died in 517; her festival is celebrated on the 6th of July. At the dissolution, it and the twelve surrounding townlands were granted to Sir Marmaduke Whitchurch, ancestor of the Seaver, Foxall, and Chambre families, who are now in possession of the lands of the manor of Kilsleve or Killevey. Near it is a cave, or subterraneous passage, communicating with the abbey.

MIDDLETOWN, a market-town and district parish, in the barony of TURANEY, county of ARMAGH, and province of ULSTER, 2 miles (S.S.W.) from Tynan, to which it has a penny-post, and on the high road from Armagh to Monaghan; containing 5145 inhabitants, of which number, 735 are in the town. This place owes its present prosperity to Dr. Sterne, a former bishop of Clogher, who in the latter part of the last century bequeathed the then village of Middletown, eight townlands in this parish, and five in the adjoining parish of Donagh, in the county of Monaghan, to trustees (incorporated by an act of the Irish parliament passed in 1772), who have expended considerable sums for the benefit of the tenantry in general, and in the erection of a market-house, school-house, dispensary, and fever hospital at Middletown. The town consists of two streets crossing each other at right angles, and contained, in 1831, 160 houses, which number has been since increased to 187: several of the houses are large and well built. An extensive distillery, with machinery on an improved principle, was established here in 1831, by Mr. Matthew Johnston: it produces annually about 80,000 gallons of whiskey, and consumes on an average 1500 barrels of malt, and 12,000 barrels of raw grain. The distillery has caused the establishment of markets for grain on Wednesday and Saturday, and there is a market on Thursday for provisions. Fairs are held on the first Thursday in each month, for horses, cattle, and pigs. Here is a station of the constabulary police, and petty sessions are held on alternate Wednesdays. The district parish, which was formed in 1792, by disuniting 33 townlands from the parish of Tynan, comprises 7339 statute acres; it contains a considerable portion of bog, that supplies abundance of fuel; coal is supposed to exist, and there is a quarry of good stone, the produce of which is applied to building purposes. The land on one side of the town is low, flat, and marshy, and on the other hilly and tolerably good; and there are several lakes, which discharge their waters into that of Glaslough, in the county of Monaghan. The Ulster canal, now in progress from Lough Erne to Lough Neagh, will pass through the parish. The principal seats are Ashfort, the residence of H. Harris, Esq., and Chantilly, of the Rev. James Mauleverer. The living is a perpetual curacy, in the diocese of Armagh, and in the patronage of the Rector of Tynan, who allows a stipend of £50 to the curate, together with the glebe, comprising 54 statute acres, and valued at £56.5.3 per annum, The glebe-house, a neat mansion called Chantilly, was built by aid of a gift of £450, and a loan of £50 from the late Board of First Fruits, in 1812. The church, a plain but commodious building, was erected in 1793. In the R.C. divisions the parish forms a separate district under the name of Upper Tynan: the chapel, a plain building, is at Ashfort, about a quarter of a mile from the town. There are two places of worship for Presbyterians of the Seceding Synod, one of the third class in the town, and one of the second class at Drumhillery. The school at Middletown was founded in 1820, by the trustees of Bishop Sterne's charity, who have endowed it with about £70 per ann.; and the school at Drumhillery was built and is chiefly supported by the Earl of Caledon: in these, and in the parochial school at Crossdall, about 250 children are educated. There are also six private schools, containing about 160 children; and six Sunday schools. Bishop Sterne's trustees are now establishing schools at Feduff and Tullybrick; also an infants' school in the town. The fever hospital is a neat edifice, built in 1834, containing 4 wards with accommodation for 16 patients; and the dispensary, with a residence for the physician, is a handsome building in the Elizabethan style: both are entirely supported by the bishop's trustees. Midway between Middletown and Keady are the ruins of the ancient castle of Crifcairn, of which the western portion only remains: the walls are 9 feet thick and about 66 feet high, and there are the remains of some arches that appear to have been turned on wattle or basket work. Several traditions respecting this castle prevail among the peasantry. Ardgonnell castle, the ruins of which also exist, was built by the O'Nials, and its last occupant was Sir Phelim O'Nial, the first commander of the Irish at the breaking out of the war of 1641.

MOUNT-NORRIS, or PORT-NORRIS, a village, in the parish of LOUGHGILLY, barony of UPPER ORIOR, county of ARMAGH, and province of ULSTER, 5 miles (S.S.E.) from Markethill (to which it has a penny post), on the road to Newry: the population is returned with the parish. The village is situated at the southern extremity of a morass extending from Pointz-Pass, a distance of five miles, and at the foot of the Balleek mountains; it derives its name from an important fortress erected in the reign of Elizabeth by Gen. Norris to protect the pass between Armagh and Newry; and on the plantation of Ulster by Jas. I received a charter of incorporation and a grant of 300 acres of land. In the reign of Chas. I it was one of the strongest fortresses in this part of the kingdom. That monarch conveyed to Primate Ussher six townlands, comprising 1514 acres, for the purpose of founding a college here for the classical education of Protestants: this college was afterwards founded in Armagh, which was considered a more eligible situation: the income arising from these lands is £1377 per annum. The village contains 10 houses, mostly well built. Fairs are held on the second Monday in every month, for the sale of live stock, which are well attended.

MOYNTAGHS, or ARDMORE, a parish, in the barony of O'NEILLAND EAST, county of ARMAGH, and province of ULSTER, 4 miles (N.W.) from Lurgan, on the road to Stewartstown, by way of the Bannfoot ferry; containing 2891 inhabitants, This parish is situated on the southern shore of Lough Neagh, and is bounded on the south-west by the river Bann; it comprises, accord. ing to the Ordnance survey (including islands), 18,098$\frac{1}{4}$ statute acres, of which 12,178 are in Lough Neagh, 305$\frac{1}{2}$ in Lough Gullion, and 83 in the Bann. About one-half of the land is arable, and the remainder bog, which C. Brownlow, Esq., has attempted to drain and reclaim. For this purpose he erected a windmill, which was soon destroyed by a storm, and was replaced by a steam-engine, which proved ineffectual. An extensive embankment was formed across Lough Gullion, and the steam-engine long employed in draining it; but all these efforts were defeated, as the water seemed to return by subterranean springs. Agricultural pursuits, fishing, weaving linen, and working the turf bog, are the principal employments of the inhabitants. Raughlin, the seat of J. Forde, Esq., is surrounded by plantations, gardens, and pleasure-grounds of a luxuriant character, and commands splendid views of the lake and the counties of Tyrone, Derry, Antrim, Down, and Armagh: in the lake is an island, beautifully planted with fruit-trees and evergreens, the whole forming a beautiful spot in the midst of a boggy and unproductive tract. On the opposite shore is the glebe-house, the residence of the Rev. D. W. Macmullen. Moyntaghs was formerly part of the parish of Seagoe, but in 1765 it was erected into a separate parish. By charter of Jas. I, the rectory was made one of the five parishes constituting the union of Donaghclony and corps of the archdeaconry of the diocese of Dromore, to which it remained united until 1832, when, by act of council, the union was dissolved, and it was united and consolidated with the vicarage, and the living is now a rectory and vicar-age, in the diocese of Dromore, and in the patronage of the Bishop. The tithes amount to £54.2.6, besides which, the Ecclesiastical Commissioners grant £71.2.0 out of Primate Boulter's fund. The glebe-house was erected by aid of a gift of £415.7.8$\frac{1}{2}$, and a loan of £55.7.8$\frac{1}{4}$, British currency, from the late Board of First Fruits, in 1820; the glebe comprises 13 acres, valued at £16.5.0 per annum. A small church was built in 1765, close to the shore of Lough Neagh, but it was blown down in a storm on Nov. 4th, 1783; after which accident the new one was built, in 1785, on a more eligible site; its elevated situation and tapering spire, render it an interesting object when viewed from the lake or any of the neighbouring shores: the late Board gave £276.18.5$\frac{1}{2}$, British currency, towards its erection. In the R.C. divisions the parish forms part of the union or district of Seagoe. About 60 children are educated in the parochial school, which is principally supported by the incumbent; the school-house is large and commodious. There are also three private schools, in which are about 130 children, and a Sunday school. C. Brownlow, Esq., the proprietor of the parish, built a village near the Bannfoot ferry, naming it Charlestown; he obtained a patent for a fair on the first Monday in every month, but it has not yet succeeded. This village is seven miles from Lurgan, Portadown, and Stewartstown, being intentionally equidistant from each of these towns.

MULLAGHBRACK, a parish, partly in the baronies of O'NEILLAND WEST and LOWER ORIOR, but chiefly in the barony of LOWER FEWS, county of ARMAGH, and province of ULSTER; containing, with the district parish of Kilcluney, the posttown of Markethill, and the village of Hamilton's-Bawn (all of which are separately described), 16,099 inhabitants, of which number, 7627 are in the district parish of Kilcluney. This parish is of great antiquity; mention is made of it in Pope Nicholas's Taxation in 1291, at which time the rectory and several townlands belonged to the Colidei, or Culdees, of Armagh. At the plantation of Ulster, Jas. I granted 1000 acres of land here and the manor of Coolemalish to H. Acheson, Esq., who built a stone bawn at Carrickbane, 140 feet long and 80 feet wide, defended at the angles by four towers; and settled there 19 Scottish families, who, with their servants and retainers, furnished 30 armed men for the service of the king. Soon after, Sir James Douglas obtained a grant of 2000 acres and the manor of Cloncarney, on which his successor, Sir Archibald Acheson, built a strong castle and placed 36 British families, who furnished 148 armed men. He also built a town round his castle of Cloncarney, in which he placed 30 more British families, who provided 30 soldiers for the king. This town was the origin of the present flourishing town of Markethill, and the family of the Achesons were ancestors of its present proprietor, the Earl of Gosford.

The parish is situated on the road from Armagh to Newry, and comprises 24,296 statute acres: the land in the northern part is of good quality, but that in the south-eastern portion is mountainous and poor. The system of agriculture is rapidly improving; there is no waste land, and very little bog, not at all sufficient for a due supply of fuel for the population; lime, which is brought from Armagh, is the chief manure. Lead ore of rich quality is found in the townland of Cavanaghgrough or Cavanagrove, but no attempt has been made to work it; and near the R.C. chapel at Drumlack is a thin seam of excellent coal. Gosford Castle, the seat of the Earl of Gosford, is a sumptuous and stately structure in the Norman style, built of granite from the Mullaglass quarries: the castle has been 17 years in progress of erection, and is not yet completed; it is situated in an ample and highly improved demesne, about a quarter of a mile to the east of the former mansion, which was built on the site of the castle originally erected by Sir A. Acheson in 1617, and destroyed in the insurrection of 1641. The other seats in the parish are Drumart, that of J. Hardy, Esq.; Marlacoo, of R. Boyd, Esq.; and Ballynewry, of B. Atkinson, Esq. A court for the united manors of Coolmahish and Cloncarney is held on the first Wednesday in every month, for the recovery of debts under 40s; and a court for the manor of Johnstown is held at Hamilton's-Bawn on the first Monday in every month, for the recovery of debts to the same amount. Part of the parish is within the manor of Armagh, and part also in that of Clady, for which courts are occasionally held at Cambough and Clady. Courts leet are also held twice in the year. Several townlands are tithe-free, and the townland of Derrynaught was given by Primate Robinson to the Armagh Observatory. The living is a rectory and vicarage, in the diocese of Armagh, constituting the corps of the prebend of Mullaghbrack in the cathedral of Armagh, and in the patronage of the Lord-Primate. The tithes amount to £671.4.6½; the glebe-house, a handsome residence beautifully situated, was erected in 1829, by the Rev. S. Blacker, LL.D., the present incumbent, at an expense of £4651.8.0; the glebe, which consists of five townlands, comprises 1146 statute acres, valued at £1416 per annum. The church, a neat edifice near the castle, was rebuilt in 1830, at an expense of £1787, of which £1035 was defrayed by the incumbent, £200 by the Earl of Gosford, £100 by the Lord Primate, £32 by subscription, and £400 by parochial assessment. In the R.C. divisions the parish is partly in the union of Ballymore, and partly in that of Kilcluney: the chapel, situated about half a mile from the church, belongs to the Ballymore union; that for the Kilcluney district is at Clady, and is now being rebuilt; there are places of worship for Presbyterians in connection with the Synod of Ulster and the Seceding Synod, and Wesleyan Methodists. About 720 children are taught in six public schools: of these, the Cabra school, with a residence for a master and mistress, was built and endowed with £30 per ann. by the late A. McCreight, Esq.; the present incumbent has endowed the parochial school with £20 per ann.; and the Gosford school was built and is supported by Lady Gosford. There are also seven schools, each of which is in connection with some educational society, in which are about 240 children; and nine Sunday schools. On the estate of Lord Charlemont is a cairn, called Cairnamnhanaghan, or "the monk's cairn," a conical heap of stones still covering more than two acres, though much reduced by the peasantry, who have carried away many of the stones for building, a practice now prohibited by the proprietor. There is a similar cairn about five miles distant. Parts of the walls of the bawn built by H. Acheson, Esq., are still remaining, and in Gosford demesne are five Danish forts.

MULLAVILLY, or MULLAGHVILLY, an ecclesiastical district, in the barony of LOWER ORIOR, county of ARMAGH, and province of ULSTER, 2 miles (N. by W.) from Tanderagee, on the road from Newry to Portadown; containing 6593 inhabitants. This district comprises 6880 acres, generally remarkably good, and under an excellent system of agriculture: the Brachy bog, containing about 350 acres, is very valuable for fuel. The manor court of Tannybalton was formerly held here, but it has been for some time discontinued, The principal proprietors are Viscount Mandeville and the Count de Sahis. Near the church is Mullavilly House, the residence of J. Atkinson, Esq.; the glebe-house is the residence of the Rev. Maxwell Carpendale; and there are several other very good houses, the residences of farmers. The living is a perpetual curacy, in the diocese of Armagh, and in the patronage of the Chancellor of Armagh. The income of the perpetual curate amounts to £94.4.7½, of which £69.4.7½ is paid by the rector of Kilmore, and £25 out of Primate Boulter's Augmentation Fund. The glebe-house was built by aid of a gift of £450, and a loan of £50, in 1812, from the late Board of First Fruits: the glebe consists of 10 acres, valued at £12. 8. per annum. Prior to the year 1755, this formed part of the parish of Kilmore, but in that year seventeen townlands were set apart to form the district of Mullavilly, shortly after which the church was erected, at the cost of Primate Robinson, but it was not consecrated till 1785; it was considerably enlarged in 1820, at an expense of £738 British, of which sum £387 was a loan from the late Board of First Fruits; it has lately been repaired by aid of a grant of £137 from the Ecclesiastical Commissioners, and is a handsome cruciform building, with a square embattled tower at the west front, surmounted by a low spire. In the R.C. divisions this parish forms part of the union or district of Kilmore: the chapel is a small building, at Mullavilly. At Vinecash there is a place of worship for Presbyterians in connection with the Synod of Ulster, of the third class; and another at Ahoney, belonging to the Seceding Synod, of the second class. About 650 children are educated in seven public schools, of which one at Mullavilly is on Erasmus Smith's foundation, and has a large and handsome school-house, erected by the Count de Salis at an expense of £600, on two acres of land with which he endowed it; one at Mullahead was built and is supported by Lord and Lady Mandeville, and conducted on the moral agency system; and those at Ballintaggart, Derryhall, and Ballyloghan are supported by the Misses Richardson. There are also two private schools, in which about 80 children are educated; and six Sunday schools, one of which is supported by Miss Richardson. Attached to the school at Mullahead are a lending library, and a loan and clothing fund, of the benefits of which every necessitous tenant on the estate partakes.

NEWTOWN-HAMILTON, a post-town and parish, in the barony of UPPER FEWS, county of ARMAGH, and province of ULSTER, 9 miles (S.E.) from Armagh, and 52¼ (N. by W.) from Dublin; containing 7253 inhabitants, of which number, 1020 are in the town, This place, which is situated on the roads leading respectively from Dundalk to Armagh, and from Newry to Castle-Blayney and Monaghan, in the midst of the Fews mountains, owes its origin and importance to the late Mr. Hamilton, who laid the foundation of the present town about the year 1770, previously to which time, the whole district was a dreary, wild, and uninhabited waste. About the beginning of the last century, an attempt was made to establish a town at Blackbank, and a castle was erected for the protection of the new settlers but the undertaking failed, and soon after an attempt was made for the same purpose at Johnston Fews, which resulted only in the erection of a few mud cabins. After the failure of both enterprises, Government erected barracks at those places, and troops were regularly stationed there till the establishment of the present town, when they were removed to this place; the ruins of the castle and barracks of Blackbank, and also of those of Johnston, within a few miles of this town, are still remaining. The whole face of this extensive district was completely changed after the

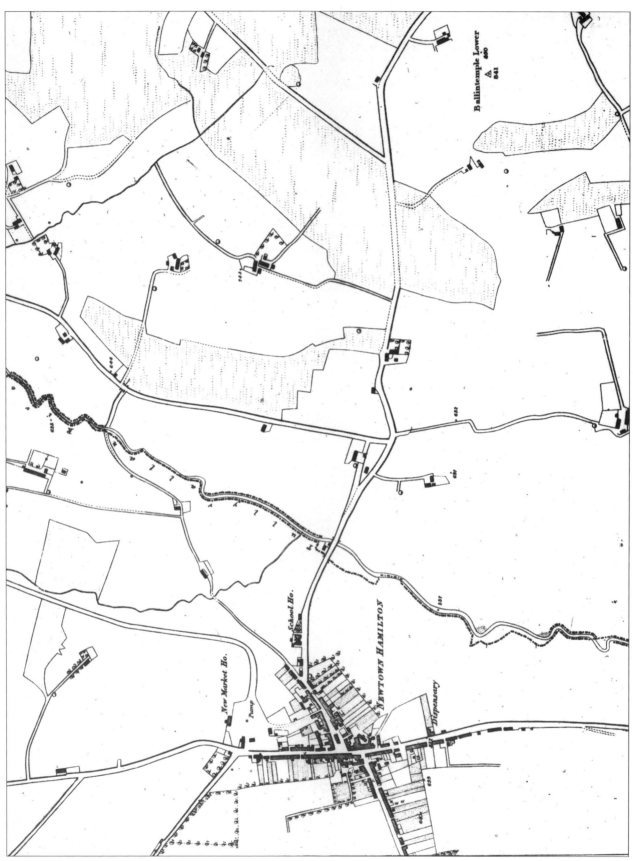

Newtownhamilton. Part of O.S. map of Co. Armagh, sheet 24, published 1836 (reproduced at 140%).

establishment of the town; the lands were rapidly brought into cultivation, several roads were opened, and great numbers of persons were induced to settle here under the advantageous leases granted by Mr. Hamilton; the town gradually increased in extent and importance, and the surrounding district was erected into a parish by Primate Robinson, who severed it from the parish of Creggan, built a church, and endowed the living. The present town contains about 60 houses, many of which are large and well built of hewn stone and roofed with slate found in the parish; it has a sub-post-office to Castle-Blayney and Newry. There is a large market every Saturday for provisions; and fairs are held on the last Saturday in every month for cattle, horses, pigs, and butter, and are numerously attended. A constabulary police force is stationed here; also a body of the revenue police, since the establishment of which, the depot for two companies of the regiments stationed at Armagh, which were quartered in this town, has been broken up and the military withdrawn. Petty sessions are held on alternate Fridays; there is an excellent court-house, in which the quarter sessions for the county were held till 1826, since which time they have been removed. Near the town were formerly mills for smelting lead ore, which continued in operation so long as wood lasted for fuel.

The parish comprises, according to the Ordnance survey, 12,404$\frac{1}{2}$ statute acres, of which 10,397 are applotted under the tithe act, and valued at £6320 per annum. The land in some parts is very good, but better adapted for oats than for wheat; the soil is light and friable, and the system of agriculture improving. There is abundance of bog for fuel; stone of good quality for building is extensively quarried; there are some quarries of excellent slate, not now worked; and in the mountain district is lead ore of rich quality, which might be worked with advantage. There are many good houses in the parish, of which the principal is Harrymount, the residence of Henry Barker, Esq. The living is a rectory and vicarage, in the diocese of Armagh, and in the patronage of the Lord-Primate: the tithes amount to £537.18.7. The glebe-house, towards the erection of which the late Board of First Fruits contributed a gift of £100, is a handsome residence; it was built under the old acts in 1806, at the cost of £592 British, defrayed by the above grant and by £500 supplied out of the private funds of the then incumbent; in 1830 the sum of £316 was expended on improvements. The glebe comprises 31 acres of arable land, valued at £38.15.0 per annum. The church, for the repair of which the Ecclesiastical Commissioners have recently granted £106, is a plain edifice, erected by Primate Robinson, in 1775, out of funds provided by the late Board of First Fruits. In the R.C. divisions the parish forms part of the union of Lower Creggan: the chapel, in the town, is a spacious and handsome edifice. There is a place of worship for Presbyterians in connection with the Synod of Ulster, of the first class; and there are two for those in connection with the Seceding Synod, both also of the first class. A school in the town is supported from the funds of Erasmus Smith,

under the patronage of the Lord-Primate; a parochial school is supported by the rector; and a school, built on his own estate, is supported by W. McGeough Bond, Esq. There are also five private schools, in which are about 180 children. There are some remains of an extensive encampment at Cloghamether, said to have been the chief residence of O'Nial of Ulster, between whom and Baldragh, Prince of Louth, a battle is said to have taken place near the town. In this fort, which is nearly two miles in circuit, the army of Cromwell encamped in the winter of 1645, and was severely harassed by the Irish forces, who hemmed them in on every side, and cutting off their supplies, reduced them to such distress that many perished through hunger.

PORTADOWN, a market and post-town, and district parish, in the barony of O'NEILLAND WEST, county of ARMAGH, and province of ULSTER, 9 miles (N.E.) from Armagh, and 69 (N. by W.) from Dublin, on the road from Armagh to Belfast; containing 4906 inhabitants, of which number, 1591 are in the town. This place, anciently called Port-ne-doon, or "the port of the fortified eminence," derived that name from an ancient castle of the McCanns or McCanes, who were tributaries of the O'Nials and occupied this very important station, commanding the pass of the river Bann. The adjoining lands were, under the name of the manor of Ballyoran, granted by Jas. I to William Powell, Esq., and afterwards by Chas. I, in the 7th of his reign, to Prudence Obyns and John Obyns, Esq., who erected a large mansion in the Elizabethan style for their own residence, and built 14 houses, in which they settled fourteen English families. Of the ancient mansion there is scarcely a vestige, except the gardens, and the avenue, which is still tolerably perfect. The town, which has been greatly extended, and the manor, are now the property of Viscount Mandeville. The former is very advantageously situated on the river Bann, over which is a stone bridge of seven arches, connecting it with the small suburb of Edenderry, in the parish of Seagoe. It consists of one spacious and handsome street, with several smaller streets branching from it in various directions; and contains 315 houses, of which those in the principal street are large and well built. The town has been greatly improved within the last 40 years, previously to which it was comparatively of little importance; it is paved and cleansed by a committee appointed under the act of the 9th of Geo. IV, which raises money for that purpose by an assessment on the inhabitants. The river, which falls into Lough Neagh about seven miles below the town to the north, and communicates with the Newry canal about one mile above it to the south, is navigable for vessels of 80 tons burden; but from a bar at its mouth, and from want of depth in the canal, the vessels generally navigating it seldom exceed 60 tons. The bridge, which is the only one across the river between Knock and Toome, a distance of full 30 miles, was built in 1764, hut has suffered so much from the winter floods, that it has become necessary to rebuild it, and the expense is estimated at £8000. The chief trade is in corn, pork, cattle, and agricultural pro-duce, and is greatly

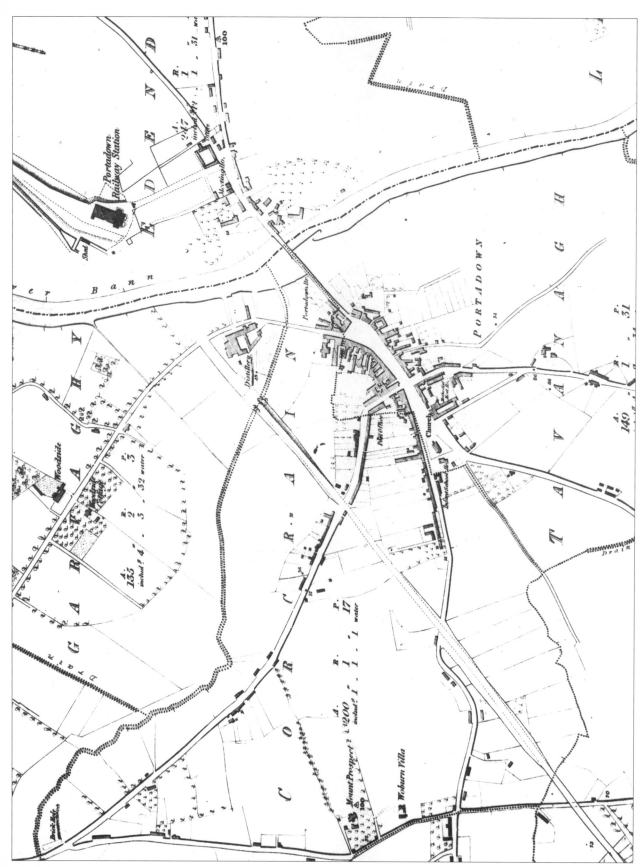

Portadown. Part of O.S. map of Co. Armagh, sheet 9, published 1836 (reproduced at 140%).

promoted by the situation of the place in the centre of an extensive and fertile district. The corn trade is particularly brisk during the winter; on an average, from £10,000 to £15,000 is laid out weekly in the purchase of grain, which is shipped to Newry and Belfast for exportation to England, the vessels returning with cargoes of timber, coal, slates, iron, and articles for inland consumption. The manufacture of linen, lawn, cambric and sheeting is extensively carried on, chiefly for the bleachers and factors of Banbridge; and the weaving of cotton goods for the merchants of Belfast also affords employment to a great number of persons. A very large distillery has been established, consuming annually more than 3000 tons of malt, bere, and oats; there is also a very extensive porter brewery; and since the Tyrone collieries were opened, brick-making has been extensively carried on. The market is on Saturday, and is abundantly supplied with provisions of all kinds, and with linen yarn, which is sold in great quantities. Fairs are held on the third Saturday in every month, and also on Easter-Monday and Whit-Monday, for cattle, pigs, and pedlery, and during the winter great quantities of pork are sold. A large and commodious market-place, with shambles and every requisite, has been recently erected by subscription, and is under the regulation of a committee. A chief constabulary police force is stationed in the town; petty sessions are held every Saturday; and courts for the manors of Ballyoran and Richmount, at which debts to the amount of 40s. are recoverable, every third Monday, before a seneschal appointed by Viscount Mandeville.

The district parish comprises 3836 statute acres, mostly in a profitable state of cultivation; the demesne attached to the ancient mansion of the Obyns family, with the exception of a tract of woodland, has been parcelled out into farms. The principal seats are Ballyworkan, the residence of G. Pepper, Esq.; Carrick, of Lieu. Col. Blacker, a fine old mansion, embellished with some stately timber; Clowna, of J. Woolsey, Esq.; Eden Villa, of W. Atkinson, Esq.; and Fair View, of T. Carleton, Esq. The living is a perpetual curacy, in the diocese of Armagh, and in the patronage of the Rector of Drumcree, who pays the curate a stipend of £150. The church, a handsome edifice in the early English style, with a tower at the east end, and for the erection of which the late Board of First Fruits contributed a gift of £831, and a loan of £461, was built in 1826; and the Ecclesiastical Commissioners have lately granted £173 for its repair. In the R.C. divisions the parish gives name to a union or district, including also the parish of Drumcree, where is the chapel. There are two places of worship for Wesleyan Methodists. About 550 children are taught in seven public schools, of which two are supported by the rector, four by Lord and Lady Mandeville, and one partly by Mrs. Henry; there are also five private schools, in which are about 100 children, and two Sunday schools. A dispensary for the tenants of the Portadown estate is wholly supported by Lord Mandeville, by whom also a lending-library and a loan fund have been established.

POYNTZ-PASS, or FENWICK'S PASS, a small town, partly in the parish of AGHADERG, barony of UPPER IVEAGH, county of DOWN, but chiefly in the parish of BALLYMORE, barony of LOWER ORIOR, county of ARMAGH, and province of ULSTER, $2\frac{3}{4}$ miles (S.W.) from Loughbrickland, to which it has a penny post; containing 660 inhabitants, of which number, 88 are in the county of Down. This place was formerly an encumbered pass through bogs and woods, from the county of Down into that of Armagh, and from the O'Hanlons' to the Magennises' country: it derives its present name from this important military position having been forced, after a desperate action, by Lieut. Poyntz, of the English army, with a few troops, against a numerous body of Tyrone's soldiers, for which service he was rewarded with a grant of 500 acres in this barony: there are some remains of the castle which formerly commanded the pass. At Drumbanagher are vestiges of the intrenchment surrounding the principal strong hold of the Earl of Tyrone, during his wars with Queen Elizabeth, called Tyrone's Ditches. Poyntz-Pass is now one of the most fertile and beautiful spots in this part of the country. To the south is Drumbanagher Castle, the handsome residence of Lieut.-Col. Maxwell Close, built in the Italian style, with a large portico in front; on an eminence above the town is Acton House, the elegant residence of C. R. Dobbs, Esq.; not far from which is Union Lodge, that of W. Fivey, Esq., in a beautiful demesne, bounded by the extensive waters of Lough Shark. That portion of the town which is in the county of Armagh was built about 1790, by Mr. Stewart, then proprietor, who procured for it a grant of a market and fairs; the former was never established, but the latter, held on the first Saturday in every month, are large and well attended, great numbers of cattle and sheep being sold. The town comprises 116 houses in one principal street, intersected by a shorter one. It contains the church for the district of Acton, a small neat edifice in the early English style, with a tower at the east front, built in 1789, and considerably enlarged and improved in 1829; a R.C. chapel, a school, and a constabulary police station.

RICHHILL, a post-town, in that part of the parish of KILMORE, which is in the barony of O'NEILLAND WEST, county of ARMAGH, and province of ULSTER, 4 miles (E. by N.) from Armagh, and 64 (N. by W.) from Dublin, on the old road from Armagh to Belfast: containing 937 inhabitants. This town is situated on the river Tallwater, in the heart of a rich agricultural and populous manufacturing district, and from its elevated situation has an interesting appearance. It consists of two principal streets and contains 189 houses, of which several are handsome and well built; its chief commercial importance arose from its extensive linen market, in which the average weekly sales amounted to £2600, and the supply of which afforded constant employment to a great number of persons in the neighbourhood. But since the construction of a new line of road from Armagh to Belfast, which in shortening the distance between those places avoids this town, the market has declined, except for the sale of a little linen yarn, and the trade has been greatly diminished. Fairs are held on Shrove-Tuesday, July 26th, and Oct. 15th, principally for cattle; and a constabulary police force is stationed in the town. The market-house, a substantial and commodious building, was erected in 1753 by W. Richardson, Esq. There are places of worship for Presbyterians in connection with the Synod of Ulster, the Society of Friends, and Wesleyan Methodists; a school on Erasmus Smith's foundation, for which a handsome house was built in 1819, at the expense of the late Lord-Primate, and W. Richardson, Esq., who endowed it with two acres of land; a dispensary, and a clothing society. The neighbourhood is beautifully varied, and the scenery pleasingly picturesque. The ancient mansion of the Misses Richardson, proprietors of the town, with its castellated turrets, embosomed in a highly cultivated tract of country, chiefly in demesne, and richly wooded, forms an interesting feature; and within two miles is Castle Dillon, the seat of Sir Thos. Molyneux, Bart., in a demesne abounding with stately forest trees and embellished with a fine sheet of water, and an obelisk 60 feet. high, erected by the late Rt. Hon. Sir Capel Molyneux, in commemoration of Irish legislative independence obtained in 1782 by the volunteers of Ireland; the same baronet also erected a column to commemorate the foundation of the order of the Knights of St. Patrick. Adjoining Castle Dillon is Hockley Lodge, the seat of the Hon. Henry Caulfield, brother of Lord Charlemont, an elegant modern residence, containing some stately apartments and an extensive and valuable library. The poor of the neighbourhood of Richhill derive great benefit from the munificence and philanthropy of the Hon. Mrs. Caulfield and the Misses Richardson.

SEAGOE. or SEGOE, a parish, in the barony of O'NEILLAND EAST, county of ARMAGH, and province of ULSTER, 1 mile (N.N.E.) from Portadown, extending along the river Baun, and intersected by the great roads leading from Arinagh to Belfast, and from Portadown to Banbridge; containing 9736 inhabitants. This place, which is said to have derived its name from Seagh-Gabha, "the smith's seat," was allotted to Nial Gabha, one of the sons of the great O'Nial. It is traditionally said that, in 836, a battle was fought here, in which Blacar, a Danish chief, ancestor of the family of Blacker, defeated Ail, or O'Nial, and his sept; and the place, adjoining Carrick demesne, is pointed out, called Lis-na-grilly, signifying "the fort of the dagger," where there are still faint traces of a circular intrenchinent, The parish is bounded on the west by the river Bann, along which it extends for about $4\frac{1}{2}$ miles: it contains three manorial districts, subdivided into 47 townlands, comprising, according to the Ordnance survey, $10,982\frac{1}{4}$ statute acres: $1236\frac{1}{2}$ are in Lough Neagh, and $49\frac{1}{2}$ in the river Bann; the rest are chiefly arable, though, along the banks of the river, there is an extensive tract of low meadow and pasture ground, which is inundated about Christmas, and the water does not disappear till March, when it leaves behind a light

deposit of mud, enriching the soil and producing nutritious, though coarse, herbage: there is very little bog. Agriculture is considerably improved; the crops are corn, flax, and potatoes; onions are cultivated to a great extent. The fuel used is turf, cut and saved in the months of July and August, great quantities of which are conveyed up the Bann from the large bogs in Moyntaghs. The trade is principally confined to the produce of the land, and a considerable quantity of butter, which finds a market in Portadown; though there is scarcely a house or family which is not, in one way or other, connected with the linen trade, of which there are extensive manufacturers throughout the parish. On the townland of Balteagh and Kilfergan there is a quarry, the stone of which has been discovered to be highly valuable as marble, and for lithography, for which it is said to equal the best German stone; and at Killycomain a superior hard blue stone is found. On the hill of Drumlin, in the southern angle of the parish, are fine pits of gravel, particularly adapted for roads and walks. The surface of the parish is a gentle undulation of hill and dale; the highest point is the hill of Drumclogher, whence is obtained a full view of the parish and the rich scenery on the banks of the Bann, Lough Neagh, and the Mourne mountains; the river, here navigable for vessels of 60 tons, cannot be surpassed for its majestic appearance as it winds beautifully along the western boundary. It was crossed at Portadown by a bridge of seven arches, built in 1764, but which having given way in several places, a new bridge is now in progress of erection, at an expense to the county of £8000; it will be a very fine building of three arches, each more than 50 feet in span. The parish is well intersected with roads, there being also a new line of road between Armagh and Belfast, which is carried through it for nearly three miles, besides several minor roads communicating with the county of Down. The farm-houses exhibit much appearance of com-fort, particularly those on the Carrick estate, which are remarkable for their neatness. Manorial courts are held, in Kernan, for the estate of Viscount Mandeville; Carrowbrack, for that of Col. Blacker; and the Derry, for that of C. Brownlow, Esq.: the respective senesehals hold their courts every three weeks, for the recovery of debts under 40s, and courts leet are held once in the year. The principal gentlemen's seats are Seagoe House, the residence of the Venerable Archdeacon Saurin; and Carrick, of Lieut. Col. Blacker, a large edifice, built in 1692, but much improved since that time: the gardens and pleasure grounds retain many specimens of the taste of that age; in the sheep-walk of the demesne, on the summit of a low ridge or knoll is a curious excavation of an elliptic form, about 80 yards in circumference, sloping gradually inwards on all sides with great regularity; whether intended as a place of justice, or worship, there is no tradition; in the demesne are numerous fine old oaks, and well-grown beech and ash. Silverwood House is the seat of T. Cuppage, Esq.

The living is a rectory and vicarage, in the diocese of Dromore, forming the corps of the archdeaconry, and in the patronage of the Bishop: the tithes (chiefly of corn and hay) amount to £330, and the glebe comprises 500 acres, valued at £652.7.7 per ann., making the gross income of the archdeacon £982.7.7. The glebe-house is a commodious residence contiguous to the church; the latter is a large handsome edifice in the early English style, with a square tower, built at an entire cost of £2200, of which £1000 was a loan from the late Board of First Fruits; the Ecclesiastical Commissioners have recently granted £319 for its repair: the interior is fitted up in a very superior manner. In the R.C. divisions the parish is united with that of Moyntaghs; there are two chapels, at Derrymacash and Bluestone. At Edenderry, which forms a suburb to Portadown, there is a meeting-house for Presbyterians in connection with the Synod of Ulster, of the third class. There is also a place of worship for Wesleyan Methodists at Bluestone; and a dispensary has recently been established. There are male and female schools at Balteagh and Bluestone, with houses for the master and mistress, chiefly supported by Lord and Lady Mandeville, and conducted on the principles of the Moral Agency System, with a lending library attached to each: the loan and clothing fund of Tanderagee, and the dispensary of Portadown, are connected with these schools, and open to the free use of parents and children. There are also schools at Levaghery and Hacknahay, the former built by Col. Blacker, the latter considerably aided by Mrs. Cope; other schools are aided by annual donations from Archdeacon Saurin and Col. Blacker, and a girls' school at Carrick is superintended by Mrs. Blacker: in all these schools about 550 children are taught. There are also two private schools, in which about 180 children are educated; and a very extensive Sunday school at Bluestone. Near the spot where the battle was fought, in which O'Nial was defeated, several brazen swords and spear-heads of superior workmanship have been dug up; two nearly perfect are in the possession of the Earl of Charleville, to whom they were presented by Col. Blacker, who has in his possession a curious battle-hammer head of stone, found in the same place, the handle composed of osier withes, much resembling a smith's punch of the present day, which, from its elasticity, must have been a deadly weapon in close combat.

SHANKILL, a parish, partly in the barony of LOWER IVEAGH, county of DOWN, but chiefly in that of O'NEILLAND EAST, county of ARMAGH, and province of ULSTER, on the mail coach road from Belfast to Enniskillen containing, with the post-town of Lurgan, 7758 inhabitants. This parish comprises, according to the Ordnance Survey, 6584 statute acres, of which 4931½ are in the county of Armagh, and 1652½ in Down; of these, 59½ acres are in lakes at Lurgan, and 362 in Lough Neagh. The lands are of good quality and chiefly under tillage; the system of agriculture is greatly improved, and the parish is generally in an excellent state of cultivation; there are some quarries of whinstone, which is chiefly used for building, and for repairing the roads. The principal seat is Lurgan House, the splendid residence of the Rt. Hon. Charles Brownlow

(proprietor of the parish), a spacious structure in the Elizabethan style, beautifully situated in a richly wooded demesne with two fine artificial lakes, and embellished with timber of luxuriant and stately growth; the approach is by a handsome lodge and gateway of corresponding character, the whole of freestone brought from Scotland. The other seats are Woodville, the residence of G. Greer, Esq.; Silverwood, of Thos. Cuppage, Esq.; and Grace Hall, of C. Douglas, Esq.: there are also numerous handsome residences in the town of Lurgan. The linen manufacture is carried on to a great extent throughout the parish, in connection with the large establishments in the town; and diapers, lawns, and cainbricks of very superior quality are made in great quantities. The Lagan navigation from Belfast joins Lough Neagh in that part of the parish which extends into the county of Down. Fairs are held at Lurgan on Aug. 5th and 6th. and Nov. 22nd and 23rd. There is a chief constabulary police station, and manorial courts and petty sessions are held in that town, as noticed in the article on Lurgan, which see.

The living is a rectory and vicarage, in the diocese of Dromore, and in the patronage of the bishop: the tithes amount to £210. 16. The glebe-house, a handsome edifice, occupied by the Rev. Edw. Kent, was built in 1821, at an expense of £1384.12.3¾, of which £92.6.1¾ was a gift, and £969.14.7½ a loan from the late Board of First Fruits; and the glebe comprises 170 statute acres, valued at £325 per annum. The church, situated in the town of Lurgan, a handsome Grecian edifice with a lofty tower and octagonal spire, was built in 1712 and enlarged and repaired in 1828, for which purpose the late Board of First Fruits granted a loan of £800, and the Rt. Hon. C. Brownlow gave £100; it has recently been further repaired by a grant of £282 from the Ecclesiastical Commissioners: the congregation averages 600. In the R.C. divisions the parish is the head of a union or district, comprising also parts of the parishes of Donaghcloney and Maralin: the chapel, a handsome edifice in the later English style, is situated in the town. There are places of worship for Presbyterians in connection with the Synod of Ulster, of the second class, for the Society of Friends, and for Wesleyan and other Methodists. About 500 children are taught in five public schools, of which the parochial male and female schools are in connection with the trustees of Erasmus Smith's charity, who allow a salary of £20 to the master and £14 to the mistress; in the former are 120 boys and in the latter 100 girls, who are also clothed by a collection made at a charity sermon, and the incidental expenses of firing, &c., are defrayed by a subscription from the resident gentry. There are seven private schools, in which are about 230 children; and five Sunday schools. A inendicity society and a voluntary poor fund have been established, towards the support of which Mr. Brownlow contributes annually £100; and there are various other charities for the relief of the poor, to which Mr. Brownlow also contributes. The Rt. Hon. William Brownlow, ancestor of the present proprietor, and for more than 30 years a

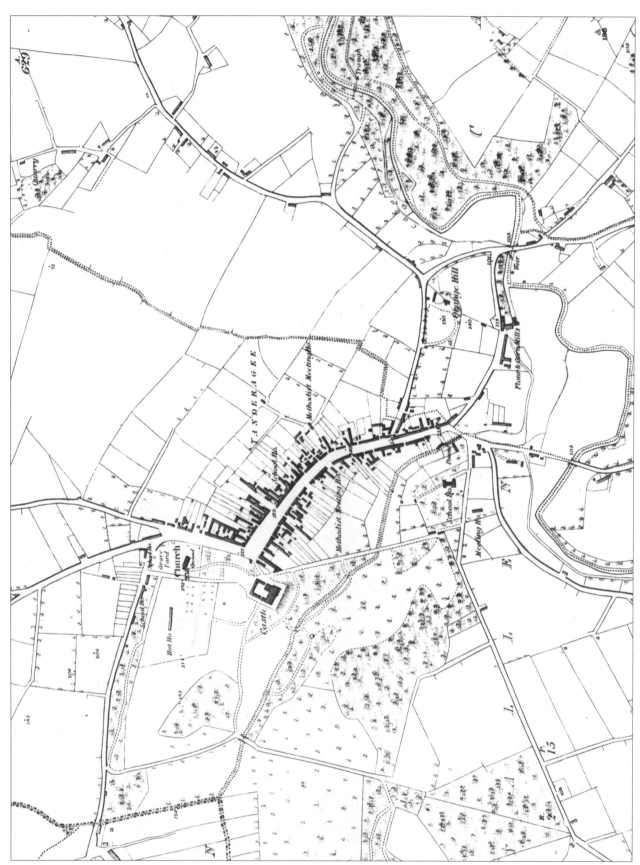

Tanderagee. Part of O.S. map of Co. Armagh, sheet 14, published 1836 (reproduced at 140%).

44

distinguished member of the Irish House of Commons till the Union, was a native of this place.

TANDERAGEE, or TAWNATELEE, a market and post-town, in the parish of BALLYMORE, barony of LOWER ORIOR, county of ARMAGH, and province of ULSTER, $4\frac{1}{2}$ miles (N.W.) from Loughbrickland; containing 1559 inhabitants. This town appears to owe its origin to the erection of a baronial castle here by the O'Hanlons, proprietors of the surrounding territory, on whose participation in the Earl of Tyrone's rebellion, in the reign of Elizabeth, the estates became forfeited to the crown, and were on the plantation of Ulster granted by Jas. I, in the 8th year of his reign, to Sir Oliver St. John, who rebuilt the castle and laid the foundation of the present town, which he peopled with English inhabitants. Sir Oliver, in 1622, also built the church, which afterwards became the parish church of Ballymore; and it appears to have been the intention of the King to make the town a free borough and to incorporate the inhabitants; but this design was never carried into effect; the only privileges they received were those of a market, fairs, and courts leet and baron. The town is beautifully situated in a richly cultivated part of the country, on the confines of the county of Down; within a mile of the Newry canal, which opens a communication between that town and Belfast; and on the estate of Lord Mandeville. It consists of two principal and three smaller streets, and in 1831 contained 253 houses, most of which are handsome and well built; its general appearance is prepossessing, and as seen from a distance, ascending from a beautiful vale, through which the river Cusher winds between its lofty and richly wooded banks at one extremity, the demesne of Tanderagee crowning the hill at the other, forms a strikingly picturesque feature in the landscape. Several coaches pass and repass through it to and from Bristol. The linen manufacture is carried on extensively in all its various branches: there are two large establishments in the town, and one at Derryallen, in all which linens, sheetings, damasks, diapers, drills, and other articles are manufactured in large quantities. There are also several extensive flax-mills, and in the various departments of the linen trade carried on here and in the immediate neighbourhood, more than 6000 persons are employed. The manufacture of damask was first introduced here in 1805, by Mr. J. Davis, who is now the only manufacturer of that article in the county. On the river Cusher, near the town, is a very extensive flour and meal-mill, the property of John Creery, Esq., in which more than 2000 tons of wheat and 1000 tons of oats are annually ground. This river and the Newry navigation join the Bann at about two miles distance from the town, affording facilities of conveyance and a supply of coal from Newry. The market is on Wednesday, and is largely supplied with flax, the weekly sale of which has amounted to £7000; besides linen, butter, and pork, averaging nearly £3000 weekly; much pork is bought in this market for Belfast. Fairs are held on the first Wednesday in every month, and also by charter on the 5th

of July and Nov. A constabulary police force is stationed in the town; courts leet are held twice in the year, and courts baron, at which debts under 40s. are recoverable, every third Thursday; petty sessions for the division are held once a fortnight. Adjoining the town is Tanderagee Castle, the splendid seat of Viscount Mandeville, erected on the site of the ancient castle of O'Hanlon, which, after it was rebuilt by Sir Oliver St. John, was surprised and completely destroyed by the O'Hanlons in the war of 1641: the present structure, which is still in progress, is spacious and of elegant design, and is situated in an ample demesne, richly embellished and pleasingly diversified with bold eminences clothed with stately timber. In the immediate neighbourhood is also the glebe-house, the elegant residence of the rector, the very Rev. Thos. Carter, Dean of Tuam, situated on a hill overlooking the town.

The church, originally built by Sir Oliver St. John, was nearly demolished during the war of 1641, and rebuilt in 1684; having fallen into decay it was taken down in 1812, and the present handsome structure built upon its site. In removing the materials of the old church, the skull of its founder, who was shot by an assassin on his return to the castle, was discovered, perforated by a bullet. A very extensive and important charitable establishment has been founded on the moral agency system by Lord and Lady Mandeville, upon the estate of Tanderagee, the benefits of which are open to the whole of their numerous tenantry, in the improvement of whose moral, intellectual, and social condition, it has, though comparatively in its infancy, already produced the most beneficial effects. The establishment includes a loan fund, a clothing fund, three dispensaries, an orphan asylum, a circulating library, and 25 public schools, to each of which is attached a lending library. The loan and clothing funds are conducted by the moral agent resident at the castle; the dispensaries are in the towns of Tanderagee, Portadown, and Tullahappy, and are open one day in every week, under the care of a physician, who devotes the whole of his time in dispensing medicines and in visiting the poor tenants at their own dwellings. The orphan asylum, at Tanderagee, is open to the female orphans of the Protestant tenantry, who are boarded, clothed, and educated for service in respectable families. The schools, for which spacious and handsome buildings, with houses for the master and mistress, have been erected, are scattered over the whole estate; those in this parish are at Tanderagee, Corvernagh, Cargans, and Ballymore, in which are about 260 children and 100 infants. There are also schools at Portadown and Mullantine, in the parish of Drumcree, and also in the parishes of Seagoe, Kilmore, and Killevy; to each is attached a Sunday school, and the aggregate number of children in all the schools exceeds 2000. An annual festival takes place at the castle, where all the children assemble and are hospitably entertained by Lord and Lady Mandeville; on the last occasion more than 2000 children attended. To the south-east of the town is the pass of Scarva from the county of Down into that of

Armagh, which was formerly defended by the strong and ancient castle of Glan Flusk, erected by Col. Monck, afterwards Duke of Albemarle, and of which there are considerable portions remaining.

TARTARAGHAN, or the LOW PARISH, a parish, in the barony of O'NEILLAND WEST, county of ARMAGH, and province of ULSTER, 3 miles (N.E.) from Loughgall, on the road from Lurgan, by Verner's-Bridge, to Dungannon; containing 6321 inhabitants, This parish is bounded for a short distance on the north-east by the river Bann, and on the north-west by the river Black water: it formerly was part of the parish of Drumcree, from which it was separated by act of parliament in the 8th of Queen Anne, and erected into a distinct parish, comprising, according to the Ordnance survey, 11,612 statute acres, of which 2122^3/$_4$ are in Lough Neagh, and in small lakes. The lands are chiefly under tillage; the soil is light, but fertile; and the system of agriculture is progressively improving, In the lower extremity of the parish, bordering on Lough Neagh, is a large tract of valuable bog; and there is a quarry of whinstone, which is raised chiefly for building. The principal seats are Crow Hill, the residence of J. Atkinson, Esq.; and Clantileu, of E. Obrie, Esq. About one-sixth of the population are employed in the linen manufacture. A manorial court is held at Clantileu, every third Thursday, for the recovery of debts to the amount of 40s.

The living is a rectory, in the diocese of Armagh, and in the successive patronage of the Lord-Primate, the Earl of Charlemont, and Chins. Brownlow, Esq.: the tithes amount to £276.18.6. The glebe-house was erected in 1775, at an expense of £523, of which £100 was a gift from the late Board of First Fruits, and the remainder was defrayed by the incumbent; the glebe comprises 40 statute acres, valued at £50 per annum. The church, originally built in 1712, on land given by Francis Obrie, Esq., who also endowed it with the tithes of eight townlands and gave 40 acres of land for a glebe, is now in ruins: the present church was built in 1816, for which purpose the late Board of First Fruits granted a loan of £800. Divine service is also performed every Sunday in summer, and on alternate Sundays. in winter, in a building formerly used as a place of worship for Wesleyan Methodists. The R.C. parish is co-extensive with that of the Established Church; the chapel, a very neat edifice, is at Eglish. There is a place of worship for Presbyterians of the Seceding Synod, of the second class, and also for Wesleyan Methodists. About 260 children are taught in five public schools, of which two are supported by the rector and Mr. Obrie, and one by Col. Verner; and there are four private schools, in which are about 160 children, and four Sunday schools. Adjoining the village of Moghery, and close on the shore of Lough Neagh, are the ruins of the old church; and in the townland of Eglish is an ancient cemetery, still used as a place of sepulture. In the townland of Derrycorr is a curious ancient road, formed of large oak trees placed longitudinally with planks of cleft oak laid over them transversely, and covered with sand and gravel about a foot

deep, forming a road across the bog at a considerable depth below the surface, and in an excellent state of preservation, though, from the accumulation of superincumbent bog, the timber must have remained there for many centuries. The sand and gravel were evidently brought from Lough Neagh, from portions of petrified wood and chalcedony being intermixed with them; and the road, which was recently discovered while cutting turf, is traceable for nearly two miles to the Lough, and is supposed by the peasantry to have been constructed by St. Patrick, for the purpose of conveying sand for the building of Armagh cathedral. In the year 1815 a golden gorget, weighing 12 oz and richly chased, was found in one of these bogs, and was purchased by the Rev. F. Gervais, rector of the parish.

TYNAN, a post-town and parish, partly in the barony of ARMAGH, but chiefly in that of TURANEY, county of ARMAGH, and province of ULSTER, 6^1/$_2$ miles (W. by S.) from Armagh, and 72 (N. by W.) from Dublin, on the road from Armagh to Monaghan; containing with the town of Middleton and the village of Killyleagh (both separately described), 11,542 inhabitants, of which number, 243 are in the town of Tynan. This was formerly a parish of great extent and importance: it is noticed in Pope Nicholas's Taxation in 1291 as belonging to the Colidei or Culdees of Armagh, who are said to have retained possession of it for some time after the Reformation. It was united with Derrynoose in the 14th and 15th of Chas. II, but the union was severed by an act of the 8th of Anne, c. 13, and lately the district parishes of Killyleagh and Middleton have been separated from it. It contains 17,646 statute acres, of which 80^3/$_4$ are under water, being the small lakes of Portnelligan, Houslough, and Kiltubrit, which discharge their superfluous waters into Glaslough, in the county of Monaghan, The soil is generally a rich loam of considerable depth: tillage is carried on to a great extent and under an excellent system: flax of the best quality is grown in very large quantities. There is no wasteland; bogs were numerous, but they are now mostly cut out or reclaimed: there are several quarries of limestone and freestone. Though the coal formation extends over a considerable district, little advantage has been derived from it, as the veins hitherto discovered are too thin to be worked with profit. Here was formerly an extensive forest, known by the name of the Bondville wood, consisting chiefly of oak, ash and fir, and extending over several hundred acres, but it was all cut away during a period in which the estate was under litigation. At Doogary and at Belteagh are large flour-mills. The Ulster canal, designed to connect Loughs Neagh and Erne, passes through the parish. The town, situated on an eminence, contains 40 houses; it has a dispensary, and petty sessions are held in it every second Wednesday and at Middleton on the alternate Wednesdays. The lands of the parish are divided among several proprietors in fee. Ten townlands belong to the Provost and Fellows of Trinity College, Dublin; eight to the trustees of Bishop Sterne's charities; the remainder to Lord Gosford, Lord Caledon, Sir James Strong, Bart., and several others. The great number of resident gentlemen who spend their incomes in the improvement of their property and in the diffusion of comfort and useful information through-out the district has tended much to the prosperity of all classes, the existence of which is apparent in the highly improved culture of the land, the exterior of the farm-houses and cottages, and the general appearance and demeanour of the population. The most remarkable seats are Tynan Abbey, the residence of Sir J. M. Stronge, who is proprietor of the village of the same name; Woodpark, of Capt. Acheson St. George; Fellows Hall, of T. Knox Armstrong, Esq.; Mount Irwin, of W. Irwin, Esq.; Darton, of Maxwell Cross, Esq.; Portnelligan, of Alex. Cross, Esq.; Ashfort, of Hugh Harris, Esq.; Bondville, of H. Coote Bond, Esq.; the glebe, of the Rev. W. Mauleverer; and Chantilly glebe, of the Rev. J. W. Trew.

The living is a rectory and vicarage, in the diocese of Armagh, being the corps of the prebend of Tynan in the cathedral of Armagh, and in the patronage of the Lord Primate: the tithes amount to £800.1.7, out of which the curates of Killyleagh and Middleton are paid: the townland of Cortaynan, comprising 564 acres, is tithe-free: the incumbent of Tynan has the appointment of the curate of Middleton and every third turn of that of the curate of Killyleagh. The glebe-house was built in 1777, at an expense of £1108 British, and has been since improved at a cost of £1442: the glebe contains 217a. 3r. 6p., statute measure, valued at £190.12.0, of which the incumbent holds 58 acres in his own hands, and the remainder is let to tenants. The church, situated in the village of Tynan, two miles from the church of Middleton and one and a half from that of Killyleagh, was built in 1784 and considerably enlarged in 1822, by the addition of a north and south transept and chancel, by which it has been made a commodious cruciform edifice, at an expense of £646, which was a loan from the late Board of First Fruits. In the R.C. arrangements the parish is divided into the Upper and Lower parishes, each having a chapel, one of which is in the village of Tynan, and the other at Ashford near Middleton: the former, erected in 1810 at an expense of £1800, has a very fine altar: the latter, built in 1828 at an expense of £1250, and to which two galleries were added in 1834, at a further expense of £300, has also an altar of very superior workmanship, which cost £100. At Lisdooney there is a place of worship for Presbyterians in connection with the Synod of Ulster, of the second class; and there are two for Seceders, one at Middleton of the third class, the other at Drumhillary of the second: they are all neat and commodious buildings. A female school on the glebe was built and is supported by the rector; a large school-house in the village of Tynan, with a residence for the master and an endowment of an acre of land, established by the trustees of Erasmus Smith's charities, affords instruction to 45 boys and 20 girls; and at Derryhaw is also a male and female school: in all these schools about 240 children are educated. There are also three private schools, in which are about 100 pupils; and five Sunday schools. A considerable tract of land, comprising 1312 acres, was bequeathed by Dr. Sterne, Bishop of Clogher, for supporting hospitals and schools, and for other charitable purposes; the management of this charity was vested in trustees by act of parliament in 1772. The remains of an ancient and highly ornamented stone cross, which originally stood in the churchyard, but was thrown down and defaced by Cromwell's soldiers, have been built into the wall of the churchyard for their better preservation.

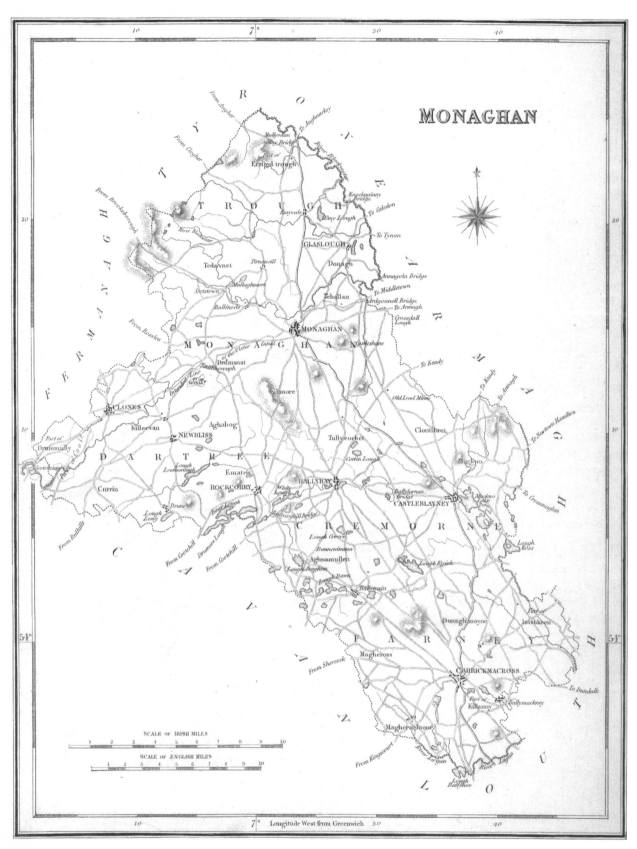

Monaghan. Drawn by R. Creighton and engraved by I. Dower. From Lewis's Atlas (London, 1837).

COUNTY MONAGHAN

A

TOPOGRAPHICAL DICTIONARY

MONAGHAN (County of), an inland county of the province of ULSTER, bounded on the east by Louth and Armagh, on the north by Tyrone, on the west by Fermanagh and Cavan, and on the south by Meath. It extends from 53° 53′ to 54° 25′ (N. Lat.), and from 6° 33′ to 7° 18′ (W. Lon.); and comprises an area, according to the Ordnance survey, of 327,048 statute acres, of which 9236 are unimproved mountain and bog, 6167 are under water, and the rest cultivated land. The population, in 1821, amounted to 174,697; and in 1831, to 195,536.

According to Whitaker, this county was inhabited in the time of Ptolemy by the Scoti, who then possessed all the inland parts of Ireland: it afterwards formed part of the district of Uriel, Oriel, or Orgial, which also comprehended Louth and part of Armagh; but it was more generally known by the name of Mac Mahon's country, from the powerful sept of that name. Its present name is derived from its chief town, Monaghan or Muinechan, "the Town of the Monks," although no trace of an ecclesiastical establishment can now be discovered there. Immediately after the English invasion, when De Courcy entered Ulster, he was joined by a chieftain named Mac Mahon, who ingratiated himself so much with him that he was entrusted with the command of two forts, which, on the first change of fortune, Mac Mahon utterly destroyed; and when questioned on his breach of faith, answered, "that he had not engaged to keep stone walls; and that he scorned to confine himself within such cold and dreary enclosures, while his native woods were open for his reception and security." Hugh de Lacy, some time after, invaded Monaghan and burned the town and abbey, but soon after erected a castle there and restored the monastic institution. In the reign of Hen. IV, Lord Thomas of Lancaster, his son, having gone to Ireland as Lord-Lieutenant, received the homage of several of the native chieftains, among whom was Mac Mahon, who then submitted so far to the rules of English law as to accept an estate for life in that part of the county called the Ferney, for

which he paid ten pounds a year chief-rent. This state of acquiescence, however, was not permanent; for, in the very next reign, Lord Furnival, who was then Lord-Deputy, found it necessary to undertake a military expedition against the Mac Mahons and other insurrectionary septs in Ulster; but, though he succeeded so far as to make them sue for the king's peace, he was unable to reduce them to the obedience of subjects.

The county remained in the same state until the time of Elizabeth, in the 11th of whose reign, the parts of Ulster that had not previously acknowledged the Queen's authority, were reduced into seven shires, of which Monaghan was one; and afterwards the Lord-Deputy Fitzwilliam, during a progress through this part of Ulster, caused Mac Mahon to be attainted and executed for high treason, and the county to be divided according to the baronial arrangement which it still retains, the lands to be allotted among the Irish occupiers and English settlers, and to be held according to the tenures of the law of England. According to this arrangement, the particulars of which are still extant in the original document, the five baronies contained one hundred "ballibetaghs," a term applied by the Irish to a tract of land sufficient to maintain hospitality, each ballibetagh containing 16 tathes of 120 English acres each; thus making the area of the county 86,000 acres, exclusively of church lands. All the grants then made contained a clause of forfeiture, in case of the re-assumption of the name of Mac Mahon, of failure in payment of rent, or of attainder on rebellion. The subsequent insurrection of the Earl of Tyrone, however, prevented the plan from taking effect. The chief of the Mac Mahons still continued to arrogate the title of supreme lord, and the whole county was occupied by three or four families only, namely, those of the chieftain, and of Mac Kenna, MacCabe, and O'Conally. So little had the progress of civilisation been forwarded by the measures of the English government, that in the succeeding reign of Jas. I, when the lord-deputy made a progress thither to inspect and settle the province, he was forced on entering the county to encamp in the open field. On investigating the titles by which the lands were held, it was found that the patents were all void in consequence of the non-observance or breach of some of the conditions; new grants were therefore made, and the country being reduced to a state of perfect submission, partly by intimidation and partly by concession, continued tranquil till the war broke out in 1641, when it followed the example of the rest of the north of Ireland in joining with the Irish against the lately established government, and the Mac Mahons again vainly endeavoured to recover their supremacy.

The county is wholly within the diocese of Clogher and province of Armagh. For purposes of civil jurisdiction it is divided into the baronies of Cremorne, Dartree, Farney, Monaghan, and Trough. It contains the disfranchised borough, market, and assize town of Monaghan; the market and post-towns of Carrickmacross, Castle-Blayney, Ballybay, Clones, and Newbliss; and the post-towns of Emyvale and Glaslough: the principal villages are Smithsborough (which has a penny-post), Ballytrain, Ballinode, Glennon, and Rockcorry. Prior to the Union it sent four members to the Irish parliament, two for the county at large, and two for the borough of Monaghan: since that period the two returned for the county to the Imperial parliament have been its sole representatives: the election takes place at Monaghan. The constituency, as registered at the close of the October sessions, 1836, consisted of 269 £50, 216 £20, and 1946 £10 freeholders; 4 £50 and 21 £20 rent-chargers; and 36 £20 and 602 £10 leaseholders; making in the whole 3094 registered electors. The county is included in the north-eastern circuit: the county court-house and gaol are in the town of Monaghan, where the assizes are held; general quarter sessions are held four times in the year at Monaghan and Castle-Blayney, which latter town has a sessions-house and bridewell. The local government is vested in a lieutenant, 11 deputy-lieutenants, and 50 other magistrates, besides the usual county officers, including two coroners. There are 21 constabulary police stations, having in the whole a force of an inspector, a stipendiary magistrate, a paymaster, 5 chief officers, 24 constables, 140 subconstables and 6 horses. The district lunatic asylum is at Armagh, the county hospital at Monaghan, and there are dispensaries at Ballytrain, Farney, Scotstown, Castle-Shane, Smithsborough, Ballybay, Clones, Newbliss, Drum, Rockcorry, Monaghan, Carrickmacross, and Glaslough; half of the expenses of the dispensaries is raised from the baronies in which they are situated, while in every other county it is assessed on the county at large. The amount of Grand Jury presentments for 1835 was £17,071.8.1$\frac{1}{2}$, of which £801.1.3 was for roads, bridges, &c., of the county at large; £7045.17.0$\frac{1}{2}$ for roads, bridges, &c., of the baronies; £5001.3.4 for public buildings, charities, officers' salaries and incidents; £2537.10.3$\frac{1}{2}$, for the police; and £1676.16.2$\frac{1}{2}$ for repayment of advances made by Government. In military arrangements the county is in the

northern district, and contains a barrack at Monaghan for cavalry, which has accommodations for 3 officers, 54 privates and 44 horses, and hospital accommodation for 4 patients, but is generally occupied by a detachment of infantry from Londonderry or Newry.

Monaghan is described by old writers as being very mountainous, and covered with wood: it is, however, rather hilly than mountainous, and is now entirely stripped of its forests. The Slievebeagh or Slabbay mountains form an uninterrupted ridge of high land along the north-western boundary, separating the county from, and exhibiting an uninteresting waste, with none of the romantic features that often atone for the want of fertility. The next mountain in point of extent is Cairnmore, whose summit commands a very expanded prospect, comprising the whole of this county, and parts of those of Armagh, Fermanagh, Cavan, Leitrim, Down, Louth, and Meath; Lough Erne, studded with beautiful islands, is also in full view, as are the numerous lakes scattered throughout the county. Crieve mountain, towards the south, though not of such extent as Cairnmore, is more elevated, commanding views far more extensive and varied. It is about six miles in circumference, and the waters flow from it in opposite directions, on one side towards Dundalk and on the other towards Ballyshannon. The lakes are numerous and highly interesting. On Cairnmore is one of considerable size and very deep: it has no apparent outlet for its waters, is always agitated, and is surrounded by a very wide strand. Another, called Lough Eagish, covers about 50 acres and is very deep: its waters are extremely useful for the supply of the neighbouring bleach-greens, fourteen of which are worked by the stream flowing from it, the tail race of one mill forming the head of the next in succession; the lake is under the care of an engineer, whose duty it is to regulate the flow of the water, so as to allow every claimant his fair proportion. But the largest and most interesting of all the lakes is that of Castle-Blayney, also called Lough Muckno: it is about 3 miles in length, covers upwards of 600 acres, and is embellished with numerous beautifully wooded islands; the shores are exceedingly romantic, and the demesne and woods of that mansion entirely surround its fertile banks. Glaslough, which gives name to a flourishing and beautiful town, and is situated near the northern boundary of the county, is somewhat less than that of Castle-Blayney; but the fertility and gentle undulations around its banks, the extensive demesne, the fine old timber, and the numerous plantations combine to form a delightful landscape. Near Mount Louise is a beautiful lake: the land rises suddenly and boldly from its shores, presenting an unusual inland scene, but the absence of wood considerably diminishes the effect. The town of Ballybay is situated between two lakes of considerable beauty. At Dawson Grove is a peculiarly interesting lake, around which is some sylvan scenery, rarely found in the North: there are also other very pretty lakes, particularly those of Emy, Leesborough, Creeve, and White

Lough, besides upwards of 180, upon a smaller scale, scattered over every part of the county. The climate is damp, but not unwholesome; the humidity is owing to the situation of the county, which is placed at the inner extremity of a very broad valley, for the most part forming the county of Fermanagh, through which pass the waters of Lough Erne to their influx into the Atlantic ocean at Ballyshannon; and as the wind from this quarter prevails for nine months in the year, the vapours are driven up the vale with great force, and rushing against the Slievebeagh mountains cause frequent showers or mists: this humidity is also much increased by the numerous lakes, whose exhalations, even in summer, are sensibly felt, particularly by strangers; the inhabitants, however, are in general very healthy.

The undulating surface of the county produces a great variety of soil. The low lands are generally wet, sour, and moory, particularly near the foot of Slievebeagh; yet even in this district are some exceptions, for amid the very poorest tracts several gentle elevations of limestone are found, and in the valleys are extensive deposits of marl; this moory soil is everywhere reclaimable, though the subsoil is stiff, and the shallow and mossy loam on its surface imbibes the moisture like a sponge, so that after a fall of rain it is nearly impassable for cattle, and a few dry days harden the surface so as to render it nearly impenetrable to a plough; this character pervades the greater portion of the barony of Trough. The central district, comprehending the depressed land between the Slievebeagh and Crieve mountains, is far superior to any other part of the county in point of fertility; it is interspersed with beautiful lakes, well watered with streams, has a sufficiency of bog, and in richness and natural capability may vie with some of the best improved lands in the north of Ireland. A vein of excellent land runs from Glaslough, by Tyhallon, Monaghan, Scotstown, and Clones, into Fermanagh at Corren. The southern extremity of the county consists for the most part of a rich and highly productive soil, based on a substratum of limestone, and in some places a deep loam highly improveable by calcareous manure. The soil in the intermediate district varies much in quality, and is disposed very irregularly: even in several parts of the same field it is seen sometimes to vary extremely, being deep and argillaceous at one spot, a gravelly grit at another, exhibiting at a third a stiff clay, and at a fourth a party-coloured mixture of red and greenish gravel; yet in general character it approximates nearly to that of the northern part. The western side of the county is a rich but shallow loam, in its natural state spongy, wet, and overspread with rushes, but capable of a high degree of improvement by manuring.

The large estates of the county vary from £20,000 to £1000 per ann., but a very considerable portion of the land is held in grants producing from £20 to £500 per ann.: the former are not resided on by the proprietor in fee, but the latter almost uniformly; many of them are held from the crown by the descendants of the Scotch colony introduced here after the settlement of the county by James I; a considerable portion were grants to Cromwell's soldiers, many of whose posterity now possess farms so small as not to yield an annual income exceeding £20. Few of the farms on the larger estates are tenanted in perpetuity: the usual term is 21 years, and a life, or 60 years and three lives. The mountainous districts form an exception to this observation, as they are divided into extensive portions, and mostly depastured by young cattle. An extraordinary mode of tenure formerly existed on some estates, of letting several townlands in one lease to all the occupying tenants, who might be from 20 to 30 joint lessees; by which practice part of the legal expenses for drawing the lease was saved by the tenants, but it gave the landlord a powerful control over them, as any one of the tenants is liable to have his goods seized for the rent of the whole: the rent paid by each is acknowledged by a receipt on account, and he who pays last obtains a receipt for the total amount. The farms throughout the county do not average 25 acres; the smaller, which are much more numerous, not six: so that ten acres may be adopted as the general average. Great improvements have been made within the last few years in almost every department of agriculture, both as to the treatment of the land and the implements. The principal manure is lime and the produce of the farmyard, together with composts of various kinds. Limestone in a state of decomposition is found in several districts; when first raised, it has a compact slaty appearance, but on exposure to the atmosphere forms a kind of paste; no benefit is derived from it as a manure for the first year; but for several years after the crops are most abundant. Marl, though found in several parts, is little used except in the southern districts, where it has been found very beneficial to the corn crops: but in general, land is seldom manured for any crop but the potato. In the northern districts, in consequence of the smallness of the farms, and the wetness of the soil, the manure is mostly carried to the fields in baskets, here called "bardocks," slung across the back of an ass, and very often on the shoulders of the women. There is no county in Ireland where manual labour is more employed in farming than in Monaghan. The spade which is generally used in tilling the land, working the manure, raising potatoes, &c., resembles the English spade in having a footstep on each side, but differs from it in having the blade made hollow and filled with timber, to which the handle is made to fit in a sloping form. In some parts, where the soil is heavy and adhesive, the blade tapers nearly to a point, and is much curved in the middle, to prevent the mould clogging upon it. The principal crops are wheat, oats and potatoes. Flax has been a favourite and beneficial crop for the last few years: the quantity sown is constantly increasing. Clover and green crops are every year becoming more common. The pasturage in the mountainous districts is mostly formed of rushes and sprit grass, neither of which affords much nutriment; in the other parts it is very rich and close, the grass heavy and exceedingly nutritious. In some parts white clover is produced spontaneously, though too often choked with rushes; in others it is sown with grass seeds and mowed twice or thrice a year: oats are also mixed with the clover seed, and cut green for fodder, by which management the farmers estimate that one acre is more productive than four of common pasture. The tops of furze, here called whins, are used for fodder; they are prepared by being pounded in a stone trough with a wooden mallet, which makes them very juicy; they are greedily eaten by horses, and answer the double purpose of food and medicine.

In some parts much attention is paid to the fences, which are generally quicksets of white thorn, often mixed with sallows that are afterwards applied to many purposes of country work; in some parts the only fence is a small mound of earth, apparently raised more as a boundary mark than as a means of security against trespassing. The chief breed of horned cattle is a cross of the Old Leicester with the Roscommon cow, which grows to a large size and fattens rapidly. Butter is made in great quantities in the north and west: for though there are no large dairies, every farmer makes some, the greater part of which is sent to Monaghan, Newry and Dundalk, where it is bought up for the English market. Sheep are very numerous in the north and north-west, and of great variety of sorts. The native horses are not of a good kind; those worthy of notice are brought in from other counties: a small strong breed called Ragheries, imported from Scotland by carriers who are inhabitants of the island of Rathlin, (whence the name) are in great request; they are cheap, durable, serviceable, well calculated for a hilly country, and live to a great age. Asses are also numerous: they are found to be extremely useful and very easily fed, being particularly fond of the green tops of furze, on which the Raghery horses also feed. Pigs are more numerous here than in any other county; they are slaughtered in great numbers for the provision merchants of Belfast, Newry and Drogheda, and are also exported alive to Liverpool. The lakes abound with fish, particularly trout and pike, which grow to a great size: the pearl muscle is found in some of the larger streams.

Of the extensive forests mentioned by early writers, no vestiges can be traced, except in the stunted underwood so frequent at the foot of the hills, and the numerous trunks of forest trees, found deeply imbedded in almost every bog. The mountains and hills present no remains of timber, and the only woods now found in the county are those belonging to the mansions and demesnes of the nobility and gentry. Those of Dawson Grove and Anketell Grove are more especially worthy of notice. At Glaslough are some of the finest ash trees in Ireland; near Monaghan are several remarkably large beech trees, and some few venerable oaks are to be seen in different parts, so that Monaghan may be said to produce timber nearly sufficient for its own consumption. Sycamore is in much repute for the shafts of

bleach-mills, round which the webs of cloth are rolled and beetled: it never splinters during the operation of the machinery, whereas when other timber is used for the same purpose, it must be cased with horse skins, which do not last long. In the moory bottoms at the foot of hills, groves of sallow and osier are planted, which thrive vigorously, and the wicker-work made of the twigs yields a return which forms no inconsiderable portion of the rent. Fuel is procured in the greatest abundance from the numerous bogs, which are so dispersed in every part that the carriage adds but little to the expense.

The county forms part of the northern extremity of the great limestone field of Ireland; and, except in its northern districts, the rock is well distributed and lies very advantageously for working. The limestone is of great variety and of excellent quality; at Glenmore it is raised in large blocks, and, when polished, exhibits all the varieties of fine marble. Freestone of beautiful and valuable quality is found in various parts. Part of Slievebeagh is formed of a fine white sandstone extensively used for architectural purposes. The south side of this mountain is formed altogether of jasper, in some places very pure, but mostly in a state of decomposition, much resembling clay-slate and of a bright vermillion hue: the mountains of Crieve are entirely formed of greenstone and basalt. Escars can be traced in several parts, particularly in the neighbourhood of Tyhallon, which, in one respect, are unlike all others in Ireland, being entirely formed of jasper, quartz, agates and argillaceous sand. Coal has been found in thin seams at the foot of the Slievebeagh mountain near Emyvale, and at Glennon in large blocks; but the most extensive beds are near Carrickmacross, where pits were opened a few years since, but after a few tons had been raised, the workings were discontinued. Iron-stone of inferior quality is frequently found; slate quarries are worked at the Crieve mountains, and flags in three quarries in Dartree. Large lead-works were erected in the Crieve mountains for the smelting of lead-ore, but they have been long since abandoned: the ore has also been found near Castle Blayney, both in large blocks and in thin veins: some promising veins can be traced in the limestone near Carrickmacross. Indications of copper have been discovered near Castle-Blayney, and ochres, potters' clay and soft unctuous earth in the same neighbourhood. Potters' clay found near Glaslough is wrought into glazed earthenware; brick clay, and oxyde of manganese, are distributed over all the country. The bones and antlers of the moose deer and the bones of several other kinds of animals, long since extinct in the island, have been discovered. Four teeth of extraordinary size were discovered on the Slievebeagh mountains, which on an examination by the Royal Society of London, were pronounced to be those of an elephant; two of them weighed $2^3/_4$ lb each; the other two, 6oz each.

The linen manufacture was established here at a very early period, and several towns and villages owe their origin to this branch of national industry. Both spinning and weaving declined considerably until the last two years, within which period the trade has revived. A large linen factory is now in process of erection at Glaslough, and great quantities are made and bleached in various parts: the yarn is spun by the women. A very good description of woollen cloth is manufactured in considerable quantities at Carrickmacross. At Stonebridge and Emyvale are iron-mills, which are chiefly employed in the manufacture of agricultural implements. Tanning is extensively carried on at Glaslough and Castle-Blayney.

The county has within it no stream of water deserving the name of river. The Blackwater, which bounds it on the side of Tyrone, receives several of its smaller tributaries; and a very rapid stream separates the county from Armagh. The Finn, which falls into Lough Erne, rises in the centre of Monaghan, but is not navigable for boats until it has quitted the county. The Lagan forms its southern boundary and afterwards joins the Glyde in the county of Louth. The canal from Lough Neagh to Lough Erne, now in progress, enters the county near Middleton and proceeds thence by Tyhallon, Bessmount and Monaghan, near to which town the works are almost finished; it is intended to carry it round this town and thence towards Clones, but some disputes having arisen respecting the lands through which the line was originally laid down, another line is now under survey.

There are two ancient round towers in the county, one at Clones, the other at Inniskeen. Contiguous to the former is a rath of large dimensions, and near the latter a circular mount enclosed with a wall of stone and mortar. At Freamount is another large rath, and another also of very considerable dimensions, but now nearly concealed by plantations, at Fort Singleton near Emyvale. Near Carrickmacross are the ruins of a Druidical temple, consisting of an oblong mound of earth enclosed by a circuit of large upright stones. Wicker hurdles of very curious workmanship have been found in the bogs, in a high state of preservation: they appear to have been carried thither by parties on a marauding expedition, for the purpose of crossing the bog, and having been left behind in the hurry of advance or retreat, were gradually imbedded in the bog. A curious relic is preserved at Knockbuy, near the town of Monaghan: it is called the "Balaghdthownagh," and consists of a box, about the size of a thick folio volume, containing a crucifix and some relics: it is kept with the greatest veneration as a kind of heirloom in the Bradley family, and is used as an attestation of innocence for imputed crimes which do not admit of the usual kind of evidence; when let out on an occasion of this kind, valuable security is always required for its restoration.

No county in Ireland has so few vestiges of monastic buildings: the abbey of Clones is the only one of which any remains exist: that of Monaghan is utterly destroyed, and a castle was erected on its site: the wealthy abbey of Tyhallon is known only by name. The castle of Monaghan is noticed by Sir John Davies, in his account of the lord-deputy's tour through the county, as being then in a state of ruinous neglect: the ruins of the old mansion-house of Castle-Blayney still standing are so close to the modern building as to injure the appearance of both: there are also the ruins of an old building in the same demesne, bearing no resemblance to a religious structure; the walls are very massive, but it is so overgrown with trees as to render its inspection very difficult. At Vicar's Dale, in Donaghmoyne, are the ruins of a castle; and near Dawson Lodge, those of another, called Maghernacligh.

The residences of the great landed proprietors are not remarkable for architectural splendour; they are rather good family houses, and are noticed in their respective parishes. The farm-houses are better than those of the same class in Leinster; those of the class that combines manufacture with farming are comfortable in appearance, but the habitations of the cottiers and journeymen weavers are miserably poor. Such tenants hold their hovel, with a small plot of ground for a garden, either by a "dry cot take" or a "wet cot take," the former implying an agreement by which the tenant pays a rent for his tenement and works at taskwork or for daily pay at the loom for his landlord; the latter signifying that he has also the grass for a cow in winter, for which he pays an additional amount of rent, but finds his own hay and grass in summer: these tenures are merely from year to year. The clothing of the peasantry is frieze, or a coarse light blue cloth manufactured at home and dyed with indigo: the women wear cottons more generally than stuffs: all are tolerably well supplied with linen and with shoes and stockings. Their food is potatoes, meal, milk, and butter; though in the poorer parts, where the population depends wholly on the produce of the soil, the cottiers are seldom able to procure anything better than salt to their potatoes; while in the neighbourhood of the county town the luxury of animal food is occasionally enjoyed. Irish and English are indiscriminately spoken in the intercourse of the peasantry with one another. An attempt was made some years ago to diminish the pressure of mendicancy, which is very prevalent, by compelling the paupers to wear badges, but it had no permanent effect. An extraordinary custom of annually electing a mayor, with power to decide all disputes, long prevailed in the village of Blackstaff, near Carrickmacross, which was composed of about 200 wretched hovels in the centre of 500 acres of bog, heath, and rock, so barren as never to have been cultivated, and on which the inhabitants supported themselves by holding each a very small portion of land at a considerable distance from the village. But the inconvenient distance of their habitations from their farms, and the dangers apprehended from this irregular union of a number of families during the disturbed period of 1798, caused the community to be broken up, and its members established on their separate plots of land; yet for years after they met annually at Blackstaff to commemorate the bygone pleasures of their former state of social intercourse. A chalybeate spring rises in Cairnmore, at a place called Drumtubberbuy, or "the ridge with the yellow spring," from which flows a stream of pellucid water covered with a strong scum of ochre; it is not noted for any medicinal qualities. At Tullaghan is a spring, the water of which, though tasteless and perfectly pellucid, forms an incrustation on all the substances it passes over near its source. This county gave the title of Baron to Sir Edw. Blayney, who was ennobled by Jas. I, in 1621, for his services against the Irish.

AGHABOG, a parish, in the barony of DARTRY, county of MONAGHAN, and province of ULSTER, 1 mile (W.) from Newbliss, on the road from Clones to Ballybay; containing 7442 inhabitants. It comprises, according to the Ordnance survey, 11,543$\frac{1}{2}$ statute acres, of which 222$\frac{1}{2}$ are covered with water, and 10,484 are arable and pasture land, applotted under the tithe act; there are also from 16 to 20 acres of woodland, and about 243 of bog. The soil is a rich but shallow loam on a deep, stiff, and retentive clay, which renders it wet unless drained and manured with lime and marl, but it produces naturally an abundant herbage: the inhabitants are nearly all engaged in the linen manufacture. Within the limits of the parish are five lakes, of which that near Leysborough demesne is the largest. Drumbrain is the neat residence of T. Phillips, Esq. The living is a rectory and vicarage, in the diocese of Clogher, and in the patronage of the Bishop: the tithes amount to £331.3.3. The church is a plain edifice, built in 1775, for which purpose the late Board of First Fruits gave £390. There is a glebe-house, with a glebe of 40 acres. In the R.C. divisions this parish forms part of the union of Killeevan: the chapel is a neat modern building, situated on the townland of Lathnamard. At Drumkeen there is a Presbyterian meeting-house, in connection with the Seceding Synod, and of the second class. There are seven public and two private schools in the parish. James Woodwright, Esq., of Gola, bequeathed £10 per ann. for the poor.

AUGHNAMULLEN, a parish, in the barony of CREMORNE, county of MONAGHAN, and province of ULSTER, 3 miles (S. by W.) from Ballybay, on the road to Dublin; containing 18,032 inhabitants. It comprises, according to the Ordnance survey, 30,710 statute acres (including 1643$\frac{1}{4}$ under water), of which 26,468 are applotted under the tithe act and valued at £19,323 per annum: there are large tracts of mountain and bog. The mountain of Bunnanimma is an isolated mass about six miles in circumference, and its summit, which, according to the above survey, rises 886 feet above the level of the sea, is the highest point of land in the county: the waters flow from this mountain on the south-east to the sea at Dundalk, and on the west-north-west to Ballyshannon. On the south-east part of it is Lough Eagish, or Crieve Lough, partly supplied by springs and partly by rainwater, which descends from the heights by which it is flanked on the east and west. A stream issuing from it presents by its rapid fall and constant supply,

together with the abundance of fuel furnished by the bogs in the neighbourhood, such favourable sites for bleaching-mills that not less than fourteen mills are situated on its short course northward to Ballibay water, the tail race of one serving as the head of the next below it: the lake is under the care of an engineer, or waterman, to regulate the flow of water, so that a deficiency is seldom experienced even in the driest seasons. There are many other lakes in the parish, the principal of which are Lough Avean, Lough Chantinee, and Lough Ballytrain, besides several of smaller size. A battle is said to have been fought on an island in the lough opposite the glebe-house, where many large bridles and battle-axes have been found: this island comprises several acres of very excellent land, mostly in pasture. Of the entire extent of the parish, 25,008 acres are arable and pasture, and 1503 are bog and waste land. The soil is of an average quality, and the system of agriculture is capable of great improvement: flax of good quality is cultivated to a great extent, and wheat, oats, barley, and rye are also grown. There are very extensive bleach-greens at Crieve, near Ballibay, the property of Messrs. S. Cuningham and brothers; also similar establishments at Drumfaldra and Cremorne, respectively belonging to Messrs. Cuningham and Mr. Jackson; and at Chantinee, to Mr. Forbes. There are flax-mills at Crieve and Laragh, the latter, in which machinery for spinning has been recently erected, the property of Messrs. Davison, and, with a weaving factory and bleach-green, affording employment to more than 300 persons; a large corn-mill at Rea, and two others at Derrygooney, all well supplied with water from the lakes. Some slate quarries of an inferior description, and a lead mine, were formerly worked, but have been discontinued. The principal seats are Mountain Lodge, situated in a beautiful demesne, that of Lieut.-Col. Ker; Lough Bawn, of W. Tenison, Esq.; Chantinee, in the demesne of which are some flue waterfalls, of J. Tilly Forbes, Esq.; the glebe-house, the residence of the Rev. R Loftus Tottenham; Cremorne Green, of J. Jackson, Esq.; Crieve House, of S. Cuningham, Esq.; Drumfaldre, of John Cuningham, Esq.; Carnaveagh, of Jos. Cuningham. Esq.; Derrygooney, of R. A. Minnitt, Esq.; Laragh, of A. Davison, Esq.; Bushford, of R. Thompson, Esq; Corfada, of J. McCullagh, Esq.; and Milmore, of the late T. Brunker, Esq.

The living is a rectory and vicarage, in the diocese of Clogher, and in the patronage of the Bishop: the tithes amount to £900. The church is a plain neat edifice, with a tower surmounted by four turrets, and occupies a picturesque situation: a grant of £185 has been recently made by the Ecclesiastical Commissioners for its repair. Near Ballytrain is a chapel of ease, a very neat modern structure, for the eastern division of the parish. The glebe-house is handsome and commodious, and the glebe comprises 40 acres. In the R.C. divisions this parish is divided into two districts, east and west, having separate parochial clergy: there are five chapels, of which one at Luttin, to which is attached a burial-ground, was built in

1822, at an expense of £800; and another at Loughbawn, a spacious slated edifice, was built in 1833 at an expense of £1000. There are two places of worship for Presbyterians; one at Ballytrain, in connection with the Synod of Ulster, and of the third class; and the other at Crieve, in connection with the Seceding Synod, of the second class. There are four public schools, in which about 360 boys and 180 girls are taught; and there are fifteen hedge schools, in which are about 600 boys and 360 girls; and five Sunday schools. On the summit of a hill overlooking Lough Eagish, about 23 years since, an urn was found in a rude tomb covered with a stone which weighed about two tons, supposed to be the burial-place of some prince or chief. The townland of Cremorne gives the title of Baron to the family of Dawson, of Dawson's Grove, in this county

BALLIBAY, a market and post-town, and a parish, partly in the barony of MONAGHAN, but chiefly in that of CREMORNE, county of MONAGHAN, and province of ULSTER, 8 miles (S. by E.) from Monaghan, and 50 miles (N.W. by N.) from Dublin; containing 6685 inhabitants, of which number, 1941 are in the town. This place, which is situated at the intersection of the roads from Castle-Blayney to Cootehill and Clones, and from Carrickmacross to Monaghan, derives its name from a pass between the lakes at the southern extremity of the town. A battle was fought in the vicinity, at a place called Ballydian, between De Courcy, first Earl of Ulster, and the Mac Mahons and O'Carrols. Prior to the introduction of the linen manufacture the town was of very little importance; but since the establishment of its linen market about the middle of the last century, it has rapidly advanced, and now contains about 400 houses, many of which are respectable and comfortably built, and has become the principal mart for the inhabitants of the surrounding country. The manufacture of linen, of a texture from nine to fourteen hundreds, is extensively carried on throughout the parish. The market is on Saturday, and is amply supplied; great quantities of butter are sold, and from October to February inclusive not less than from 8000 to 12,000 stone of flax is sold weekly: there are also extensive markets for grain on Tuesday and Friday. Fairs are held on the third Saturday in every month, and are remarkable for large sales of horses, horned cattle, and pigs. A reading society was established in 1816, and is supported by a proprietary of annual subscribers; the library contains nearly 1000 volumes. Petty sessions are held in the market-house irregularly: and here is a constabulary police station.

The parish comprises, according to the Ordnance survey, 8741¼ statute acres, of which 181 are in the barony of Monaghan, and 8560¼ in that of Cremorne; 180 acres are under water. It was formed by act of council in 1796, by separating from the parishes of Tullycorbet and Aughnamullen several townlands, applotted under the tithe act and valued at £6957 per annum. Its surface is studded with lakes and boldly diversified with hills and dales. About four miles from the town is the mountain of Bunnanimma,

at the base of which are bleach-greens and mills. The approach to the town opens upon an extremely beautiful and picturesque tract of country. To the east are seen, at the distance of 20 miles, the deep blue summits of the lofty Slievegullion, with the village, about a quarter of a mile beneath, apparently embosomed in hills and situated on the margin of a lake a mile in diameter, which forms its boundary on the east and south, and is itself bounded by a rich amphitheatre of woods. The soil is of a fair average quality, but agriculture is not in a very forward state: the growth of flax has been much encouraged, and large quantities of very good quality are raised. There is no waste land. Very extensive tracts of bog supply the inhabitants and the various works with abundance of fuel; so great is the quantity consumed that many of the manufacturers employ from 60 to 100 persons for three months every year to dig and prepare it. The draining of these bogs, and the numerous population around the works, have caused a great change in the climate of the Bunnanimma mountain, which formerly was liable to be enveloped in thick fogs for ten or twelve days successively; but now the drying of the turf is seldom interrupted for a single day. The mountain lands, though naturally very poor, have on this side been nearly reclaimed. The prevailing substratum is whinstone; slate also exists, and was formerly quarried for roofing; and there are extensive quarries of greenstone, called "Ribbil," of which the town is built. A lead mine was opened at Laragh, about half a mile from the town, but it has not been worked since 1826; it is very rich in ore, and from silver found in it has been manufactured some plate in the possession of Col. C. A. Leslie. About half a mile from the town is Ballibay House, the seat of that gentleman, on whose estate the town is built; it is a handsome and spacious mansion beautifully situated on the border of a lake, and backed by some extensive plantations. The other principal residences in the parish are Derry Valley, the seat of T. McCullagh, Esq.; Aghralane, of T. Lucas, Esq.; and Lake View, the residence of the Rev. Hercules Langrishe, the incumbent.

The living is a rectory and vicarage, in the diocese of Clogher, and in the patronage of the Bishop: the tithes amount to £383.5.0. The church is a neat edifice occupying a romantic situation on an eminence rising abruptly from the lake; the east window is embellished with stained glass, and there are some tablets to the memory of the Leslie family. The glebe-house is a handsome residence, towards the erection of which the late Board of First Fruits gave £100: the glebe comprises 25 acres. In the R.C. divisions this parish forms part of the union or district of Tullycorbet the chapel is situated at Ballintra, about a mile and a half from the town; and there is a small chapel of ease in the town, connected with the clergyman's residence. There are two places of worship for Presbyterians in connection with the Synod of Ulster; one of which, in the town, is a handsome building in the later English style, and is of the second class; the other is about a mile distant, and nearly adjoining it is a

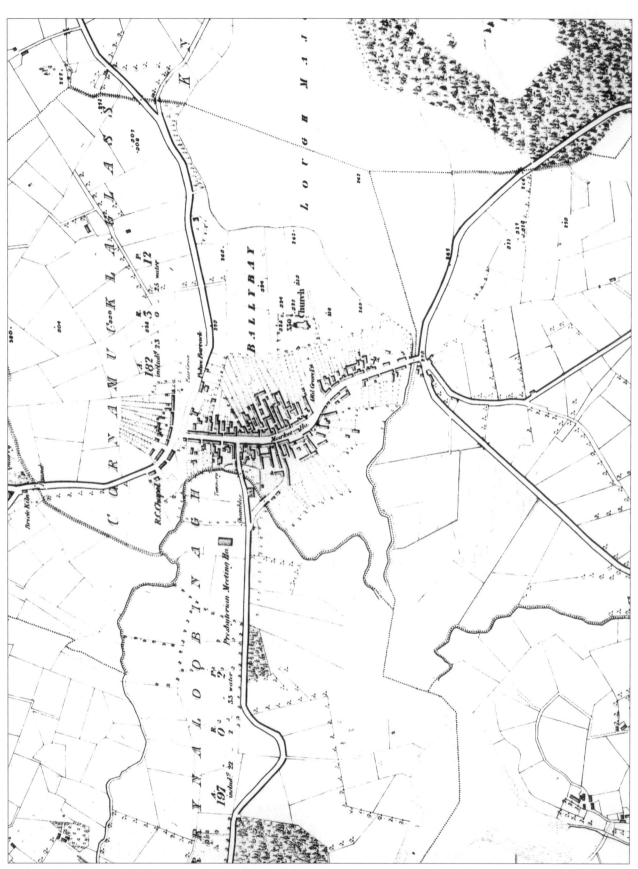

Ballibay. Part of the O.S. map of Co. Monaghan, sheet 107, published 1836 (reproduced at 140%).

place of worship for Seceders. About 150 boys and 110 girls are taught in four public schools; and there are also six hedge schools, in which are about 140 boys and 70 girls; and two Sunday schools. A dispensary is open two days in the week for the gratuitous aid of the poor.

BALLINODE, a village, in the parish of TYDAVNET, barony and county of MONAGHAN, and province of ULSTER, 3 miles (N.W.) from Monaghan; its population is included in the return for the parish. This place is situated on the road from Monaghan to Enniskillen, by way of Brookborough, and on a small river, over which there is a good stone bridge; and contains the parochial church and school, the former of which is a neat edifice with a steeple, and a dispensary. It has a patent for a fair for cattle on the first Saturday in every month, but no fairs are now held.

BALLYTRAIN, a village, in the parish of AUGHNAMULLEN, barony of CREMORNE, county of MONAGHAN, and province of ULSTER, 5 miles (S.) from Ballibay, on the old road to Shercock; containing 44 houses and 220 inhabitants. It is a station of the constabulary police; and fairs, chiefly for pigs, cattle, and sheep, are held on Feb. 1st, March 17th, May 1st, June 11th, Aug. 1st, Sept. 29th, Nov. 1st, and Dec. 23rd. In 1834, a R.C. chapel was built, at an expense of £100. The lake of Ballytrain is an extensive sheet of water supplying several mills, particularly one belonging to R. A. Minnett, Esq. Near the village is Lake View, the residence of the Rev. E. Mayne. In the vicinity are several forts, one of which is of great extent and commands a view of some picturesque scenery, embracing twelve lakes.

CARRICKMACROSS, a market and post-town, and a parish, in the barony of FARNEY, county of MONAGHAN, and province of ULSTER, 20 miles (S.E. by S.) from Monaghan, and 40 (N.W. by N.) from Dublin; containing 12,610 inhabitants, of which number, 2970 are in the town. This place derives its name from its situation on a rock and from one of its early proprietors, and is the only town in the barony. The barony was granted by Queen Elizabeth to the Earl of Essex, who resided in the castle here, part of the walls of which are still standing in the garden of W. Daniel, Esq. It was leased by the earl to Mr. Barton, whose wife and children were burnt, with the castle, by the insurgents of 1641, while he was attending his parliamentary duties in Dublin, as representative of the county of Monaghan. The town is situated on the mail coach road from Dublin to Londonderry, and consists of one principal street, with some smaller streets or lanes branching from it; and contains about 560 houses, many of which are of respectable appearance. A considerable retail trade is carried on with the surrounding country; and soap, candles, brogues, and coarse hats, are manufactured in the town, in which there are also a tanyard, a brewery (employing 100 men), and a distillery. Distillation was carried on here to a considerable extent before the Union, for 20 years, after which it very much declined; but, in 1823, a large distillery was erected, which makes 200,000 gallons of spirits annually, consuming in the manufacture about 25,000 barrels of grain, including malt, which is made in the town. The general market is held on Thursday, and one for corn on Wednesday and Saturday: the number of pigs exposed for sale at the market, during the season, is very great; they are principally purchased by dealers from Dundalk, Newry, and Belfast, for exportation. Fairs are held on May 27th, July 10th, Sept. 27th, Nov. 9th, and Dec. 10th; those in May and December, the latter of which is for fat cattle, are the largest. The market-house stands in the centre of the main street and was built out of the ruins of the castle. Petty sessions are held every alternate week; and here are a constabulary police station and a county bridewell on a small scale, but containing the necessary accommodation for the separation of prisoners.

The parish, which is also called Magheross, contains, according to the Ordnance survey, 16,702$\frac{1}{4}$ statute acres, including 299 of water; 15,068 acres are applotted under the tithe act, and there is a great quantity of bog. In the vicinity of the town are several limekilns, and the land has been greatly improved by the extensive use of lime as a manure. Mr. Shirley supplies his tenants at about half the usual price from his kilns, in which about 8000 barrels were burnt in 1835. The principal lakes are Loch Mac-na-ree, Lisdronturk, Corvalley, and Chantinee Loch, only part of which is in this parish. Coal exists, but is not worked at present; but good limestone and freestone are quarried for building. Lisinisk, the seat of Adam Gibson, Esq., is in this parish, which also includes part of the demesne of Loch Fea Castle, the seat of E. J. Shirley, Esq., although the castle is in Magheracloony. The living is a vicarage, in the diocese of Clogher, and in the patronage of the Bishop; the rectory is impropriate in Col. Willcox the tithes amount to £969.4.7$\frac{1}{2}$, of which £323.1.6$\frac{1}{2}$ is payable to the impropriator, and £646.3.1 to the vicar. The church is a neat stone edifice with a tower and spire, having a good clock with four dials. The remains of the old church are still standing: it was built in 1682, to replace the one that was destroyed by fire in 1641. There is a glebe-house, with a glebe of 112 acres. The R.C. parish is co-extensive with that of the Established Church, and is the benefice of the Bishop of Clogher, who resides in the town: there are three chapels, situated at Corduff mountain, Corcreagh, and Carrickmacross, the last of which is a handsome building, erected in 1783. There is also a Presbyterian meeting-house. A free grammar school was founded here by Lord Weymouth in 1711, and endowed with £70 per annum: it has been disused for some years, but the school-house is being rebuilt by the Marquess of Bath, a descendant of the founder. There are two national schools at Carrickmacross; six schools, situated at Mullaghcrogery, Cornasassinagh, Carrickmaclim, Corraghery, Corduffkelly, and Cargamore, aided by annual donations from E. J. Shirley, Esq.; a school supported by subscriptions, and two other schools, in which the pupils are taught gratuitously. About 780 boys and 670 girls are taught in these schools,

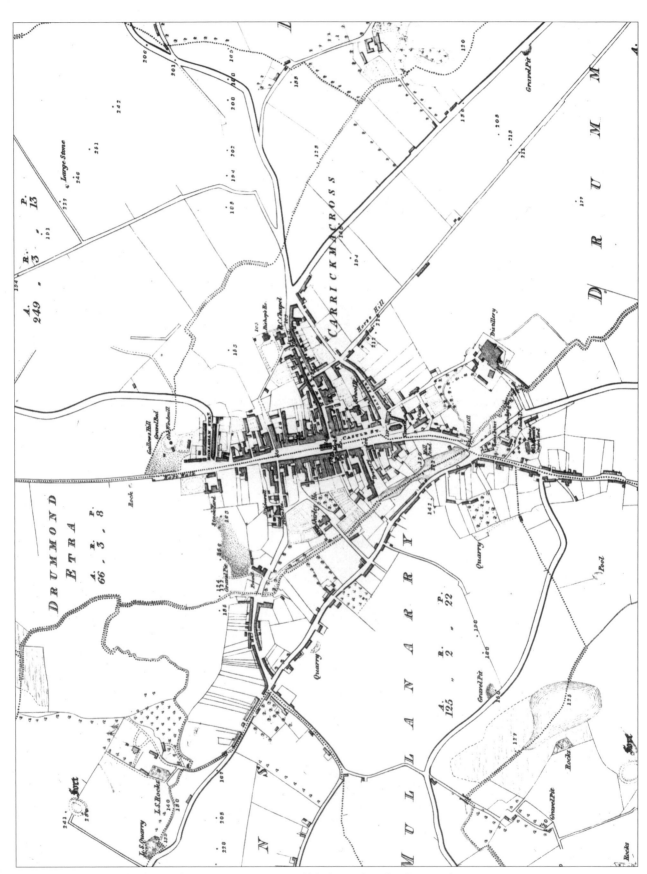

Carrickmacross. Part of the O.S. map of Co. Monaghan, sheet 29, published 1836 (reproduced at 140%).

Blaney Castle. Published by S. Hooper. 1791.

and about 470 boys and 230 girls in 13 private and hedge schools; there are also three Sunday schools. A dispensary was established in 1823; here is also a mendicity society; and a savings' bank was instituted in 1831 by the Marquess of Bath and Mr. Shirley: the amount of deposits, in November, 1835, was £1503.14.3, belonging to 81 depositors, the number of whom is rapidly increasing.

CASTLE-BLAYNEY, a market and post-town, in the parish of MUCKNOE, barony of CREMORNE, county of MONAGHAN, and province of ULSTER, 11 miles (S.E. by E.) from Monaghan, and 49 (N.N.W.) from Dublin; containing 1828 inhabitants. It derives its name and origin from Sir Edward Blayney, governor of the county of Monaghan in the reign of Jas. I, who, in consideration of the dependence of his garrison at Monaghan and Newry for a supply of provisions, which was rendered precarious by the hostility of the intervening country, received a grant of two ballybetaghs of land here) on condition of his erecting a fort between Monaghan and Newry; Castle-Blayney was accordingly erected, as a secure halting-place for the royal troops, and Sir Edward received this extensive estate, which his descendants still enjoy. The collection of habitations formed in the vicinity never, however, assumed the appearance of a town until the establishment of the linen market, and the rebuilding of the houses with stone, in the latter part of the last century, by the late noble proprietor. It is situated on the mail coach road from Dublin to Londonderry, and comprises 341 houses; is lighted by subscription, and has a respectable appearance. It consists of three streets meeting in the market-place, which is of a triangular form; and in the centre, on an elevated spot commanding every avenue, is the market-house, a very neat and ornamental building, with a spacious room on the second story, and a neat bell turret above the roof. Near the market-house are convenient shambles. The manufacture of linen, though not so extensive as formerly, furnishes employment to many persons in the surrounding districts; and there are three tanyards in the town. The principal market is on Wednesday, when considerable quantities of yarn and flax are sold: there are also markets for corn and butter on Tuesday and Friday; and fairs for live stock are held on the first Wednesday in every month. Here is a constabulary police station; also a neat sessions-house, in which the quarter sessions for the county are held four times in the year, and petty sessions every alternate week and a county bridewell, which affords the necessary accommodation for the classification of prisoners. The mansion of Castle Blayney, the seat of Lord Blayney, is

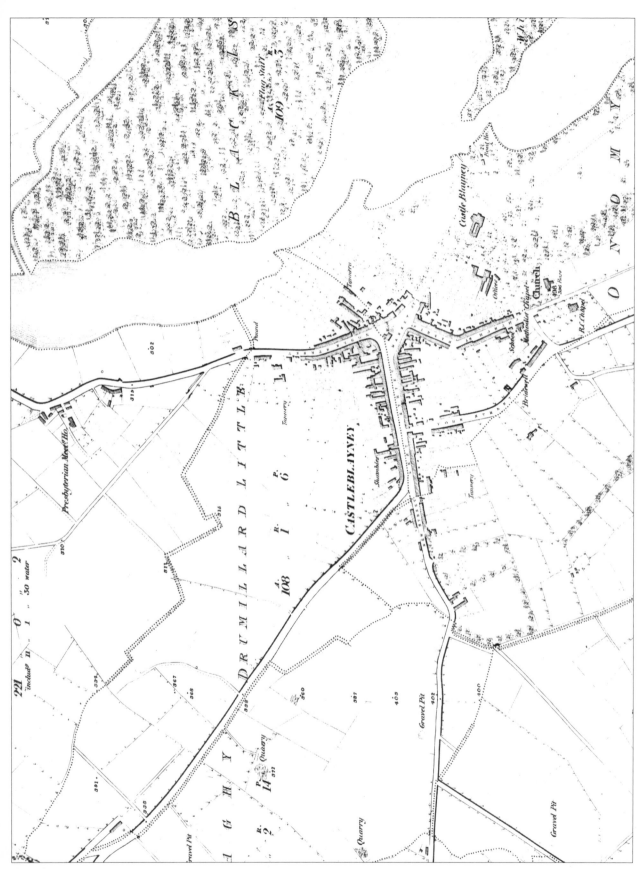

Castleblaney. Part of the O.S. map of Co. Monaghan, sheet 53, published 1836 (reproduced at 140%).

closely adjoining, and is encompassed by a demesne of great extent and beauty, which includes the Lake of Mucknoe and some fine woodland scenery: it is a handsome modern edifice, built near the site of the old castle. The ruins of an ancient fortress in Cornero wood, on the shore of the lake, are also within the demesne. The parish church of Mucknoe is in the town; it is very neat, with a handsome spire, and the interior has been comfortably fitted up by Lord Blayney, who has also planted the churchyard with trees and evergreens. There are also places of worship for Roman Catholics, Presbyterians, and Wesleyan Methodists. The parochial school, situated here, has an average attendance of 35 children; and there is a school for girls, supported by Lady Blayney, with an average attendance of 70 children. Here is also a fever hospital. – See CLONTIBRET and MUCKNOE.

CLONES, a market and post-town, and a parish, partly in the barony of CLONKELLY, county of FERMANAGH, and partly in the baronies of MONAGHAN and DARTRY, county of MONAGHAN, and province of ULSTER, 10 miles (W.S.W.) from Monaghan, and 62 (N.W. by N.) from Dublin ; containing 22,254 inhabitants. The ancient name of this place was Cluan Innis, "the Island of Retreat," it having formerly been nearly surrounded by water; and more recently it was called Cloanish or Clounish. An abbey, dedicated to St. Peter and St. Paul, was founded here in the early part of the 6th century, by St. Tigernach or Tierney, who, becoming Bishop of Clogher, removed that see to Clones, where he died of the plague in 550. The abbot was the Primus Abbas, or first mitred abbot of Ireland. In 836, the abbey was burnt; and in 929, Ceanfoile, comarb of Clones and Clogher, died here. The abbey was destroyed by fire in 1095, and, in 1184, the abbot Gilla Christ O'Macturan was elected Bishop of Clogher. In 1207, Hugh de Lacy destroyed the abbey and town; but five years after they were rebuilt by the English, who also erected a castle here. In 1316, and again in 1504, the abbot of Clones was elected Bishop of Clogher. In 1486 died the abbot Philip Mac Mahon, and, in 1502, the abbot James Mac Mahon, both relations of the Lords of Ergal. The abbey was dissolved by the act of Hen. VIII, and in the 29th of Elizabeth an inquisition was taken of its possessions. The manor of this abbey is still called "St. Tierney," and at the suppression was granted, together with the abbey, to Sir Henry Duke. The corbeship, or comorbanship, of Clones seems to have been held by the sept of Mac Mahon, the head of which, during the rebellion in Queen Elizabeth's reign, procured from the pope a grant of it for his eldest son, who was then a boy, with one of whose daughters it was conveyed in marriage to Sir Francis Rushe, whose daughter Elinor, in 1629, again conveyed it in marriage to Sir Robt. Loftus, eldest son of Adam, Lord Loftus, Primate and Chancellor of Ireland, and first Chancellor of Trinity College, Dublin. In 1640, Sir Robert and his son Henry died, and the manor came to Anne, only daughter of the former, who married the Hon.

Richard Lennard Barrett, whose son, Dacre Barrett, Esq., represented the county of Monaghan in the Irish parliament in 1692: it has since continued in this family, and is now the estate of Sir Thomas Barrett Lennard, Bart, In the settlement of Ulster, to assimilate the Irish to the English church, corbeships were abolished, and their possessions, commonly called termon lands, granted to the bishops. At the time of the dissolution of monasteries, there were three ecclesiastical estates belonging to Clones; viz., the abbey lands, Bow the property of Sir T. B. Lennard, which are tithe-free; the estate of the great church of Clones, belonging to the same proprietor, which pays one-third of the tithes to the incumbent; and the lands of the corbe, or the ternon lands, the property of the Bishop of Clogher, which pay the entire tithes to the incumbent.

The town is situated on the road from Monaghan to Belturbet, and contains 429 houses, of which those recently erected are slated, and the more ancient are thatched. There is a brewery in the town; and at Stonebridge is an extensive foundry for spades, ploughs, and other agricultural implements, established about ten years since; also large flour-mills at Analoar, on the river Finn. The Agricultural and Commercial Bank has a branch establishment in the town. A yarn market is held on Thursday, at which linen cloth to the value of £150 is sold weekly; and there is a fair on the last Thursday in each month, for cattle, pigs, horses, &c., which is well supplied; and a fair is held at Roslea, in this parish, on the 8th of each month. The market-place of Clones is of a triangular form, with a market-house in it, and a pump, also a very ancient stone cross, the shaft of which is about 12 feet high; it stands at the top of a flight of steps, and both the shaft and top are ornamented with figures in relief; the upper part is circular, and the whole has a very antique appearance. Here is a chief constabulary police station. A manorial court, called "St. Tierney's Manor Court," is held in the town monthly by the senesehal, for the recovery of debts under £2; and petty sessions are held every alternate Friday. Courts are also held in the parish for the manors of Roslea and Shannick.

The parish is of great extent, comprising, according to the Ordnance Survey, 42,877 statute acres, of which 27,581 are in Fermanagh, and 15,296 in Monaghan. About one-twentieth of the land is bog, 616 acres are water, and the mountainous tracts afford good pasture. Agriculture is in an improved state, and much of the land is of a superior quality; tillage is conducted on an extensive scale. Limestone of good quality is found in various places, and on the summit of Carnmore mountain is a quarry of fine white freestone, which is much used for building. A vein of coal was found near this mountain, but is not worked. That part of the parish which is in Dartry barony has no fewer than 32 lakes, of which, Loughs Oonagh, Camm, and Lisnaroe, and the lake near Smithsborough, are the largest. In that part of it which is in the barony of Monaghan is an extensive lake, near Watts-bridge, besides five smaller lakes, the waters of

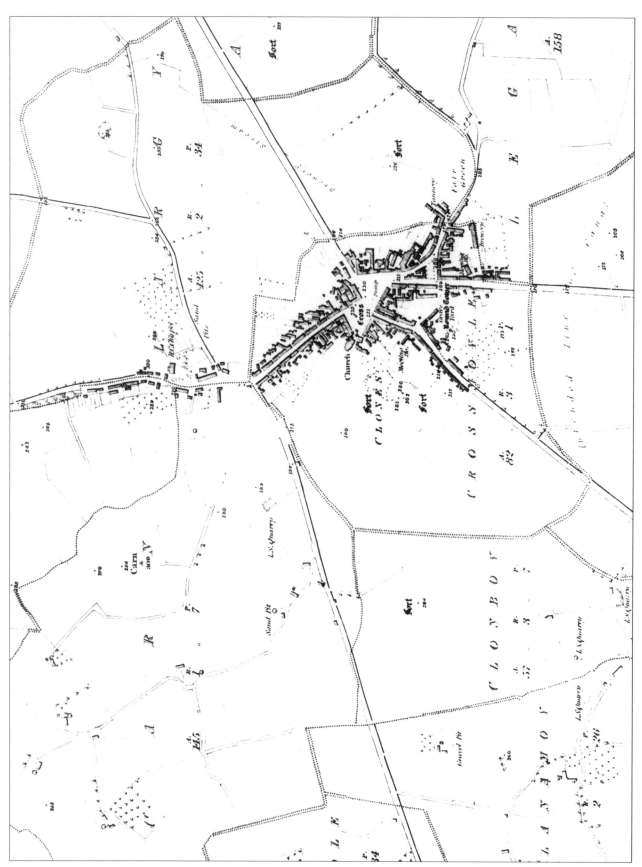

Clones. Part of the O.S. map of Co. Monaghan, sheet 71, published 1836 (reproduced at 140%).

which unite in their course towards Newbliss. The principal seats are Summerhill, of the Rev. J. Richardson; Lisnaroe, of Nicholas Ellis, Esq.; Lough Oonagh, of Mrs. Murray ; Spring Grove, of E. Madden, Esq.; Johnstown, of C. P. Irvine, Esq.; Scottsborough, of W. Scott, Esq.; Island Cottage, of Captain Ross; Carrowbarrow, of the Rev. M. F. Dudgeon; and the glebe-house, of the Very Rev. H. Roper, rector of the parish, and Dean of Clonmacnois.

The living is a rectory and vicarage, in the diocese of Clogher, and in the patronage of Sir T. B. Lennard, Bart.: the tithes amount to £950.3.11. The glebe-house was rebuilt in 1816, and towards defraying the expense, a gift of £100 and a loan of £1500 were granted by the same Board: the glebe comprises 700 acres. The parochial or mother church stands on the hill of Clones, at the upper end of the market-place, and has a handsome steeple, with a clock and bell: it was built at an expense of about £3500, of which £1022 was a loan and £900 a gift, in 1822, from the late Board of First Fruits. There are also two chapels of ease on the townlands of Clough and Aughadrumsee; the former was built by a loan of £1015 from the late Board of First Fruits, in 1828; to the repairs of the latter the Ecclesiastical Commissioners lately granted £136.2.11. In the R.C. divisions this parish forms two benefices, Clones East and Clones West: there are chapels at Clones and Drumswords for the former, and at Roslea and Magherarney for the latter; the chapel at Roslea is a spacious building, erected in 1834, with a bell tower and beautiful altar. There is a Presbyterian meeting-house at Stonebridge, in connection with the Synod of Ulster, and of the third class; at Smithsborough is one of the second class, connected with the Seceding Synod; and there are places of worship for Wesleyan and Primitive Methodists. There are male and female parochial schools at Cluigh, also schools at Clones, Carra-street, Smithsborough, Rossbrick, Larg, Granshaw, Magherarney, Aughnashalvey, Bruskena, Greaghawarren, Deer-Park, Clonkeen, Clononacken, Ahadrumsee, Clones, Spring-grove, Magheravilly, Gortinawing, Patenbar, and Knockavaddy. Each of these schools is aided by subscriptions, and at Salloo is one supported by J. Whittsit, Esq. The whole afford instruction to about 1200 boys and 700 girls; and in 11 private schools are about 180 boys and 90 girls, besides a considerable number in 12 Sunday schools. There are two dispensaries, one at Clones, the other near Roslea; a savings' bank, the deposits in which, belonging to 133 depositors, amounted to £3241.9.6 on the 20th of November, 1835: and a charitable loan fund.

On the south side of the town are the ruins of the ancient abbey to which it owes its early fame, and through which the road from Cootehill now passes. The walls of a small chapel still remain on one side of the road, and are built of square hewn freestone on the outside, and of limestone within; it is encompassed by an ancient burial-ground, enclosed by a strong wall. On the other side of the road is another burial-ground, similarly enclosed, in which

are many curiously decorated tombstones, and where there is yet standing one of the ancient round towers. The walls of this tower are four feet thick, and very rough on the outside, but composed of smooth limestone within. The internal diameter is 10 feet, and there are resting-places for the joists of five successive floors. The thickness of the walls diminishes towards the top, and there is a doorway about four feet above the ground; at the top were large embrasures. On the surface, in this burial-ground, is a large stone coffin: the lid is very heavy, and of an angular shape, like the roof of a house, with two small pillars rising from the ends, and an ancient inscription on each side, but so much defaced as to be illegible. It is supposed to be the coffin of a Mac Mahon. Near these cemeteries is an extensive artificial mound of earth, very steep and rather difficult of access, being on the summit of a considerable hill. In the parish are two wells, much celebrated among the peasantry for curing the jaundice; one, about three miles from Clones, on the road leading to Monaghan, is called the Grailabuy Well; the other, about a mile from Clones, on the road to Enniskillen, is called Clintiveran Jaundice Well. Near the fort is an excellent spring, called Tubbertierney.

CLONTIBRET, a parish, in the barony of CREMORNE, county of MONAGHAN, and province of ULSTER on the confines of the county of Armagh, 6 miles (N. by W.) from Castle-Blayney, on the road to Monaghan; containing 15,941 inhabitants, and comprising, according to the Ordnance survey, 26,553$\frac{1}{4}$ statute acres, of which 334 are part of Mucknoe lake, 198$\frac{3}{4}$ are in small loughs, 3920 bog, and the remainder, with the exception of a small portion of rough rocky pasture, good arable land, and all under tillage. Agriculture is improving; and the bog affords abundance of good fuel. Grauwacke slate is found in abundance, and is quarried for building and for repairing the roads. A mine of antimony was discovered on Lord Middleton's property, and was worked for some time, but not paying, it was discontinued. A lead mine has been recently opened in Carriganure, on the estate of E. Lucas, Esq. M.P., of Castleshane; and lead ore is also found in the townland of Killicrum. Millmount, the handsome residence of A. Swanzy, Esq., and Rockfield House, of H. Swauzy, Esq., are within the parish. The living is a rectory and vicarage, in the diocese of Clogher, constituting the corps of the archdeaconry of Clogher, and in the patronage of the Bishop. The tithes amount to £800; and the gross revenue of the dignity, including tithes, glebe, and lands, is returned at £852. The glebe-house was erected in 1752, by aid of a gift of £100 from the late Board of First Fruits; the glebe comprises 40 acres, besides which the lands of the archdeaconry, called the "Archdeacons Hill," situated in the parish of Clogher, contain 9a. 2r. 12p., let on lease at a rent of £16.16.0 per annum. The church is a plain old structure, with an ancient square tower surmounted by a spire; it is in a very dilapidated condition, and it is in contemplation to erect a new church. Divine service is also occasionally performed in a school-house at the southern extremity of the parish, In the R.C. divisions, part of the parish is included in the union or district of Mucknoe or Macrey, and the remainder forms a district of itself; the chapel is at Anyallow. There is a place of worship for Presbyterians in connection with the Synod of Ulster, and also one in connection with the Seceding Synod on the con-fines of the parish; and there is also a place of worship for Primitive Wesleyan Methodists. There are parochial and other schools aided by private subscription; in which about 520 children are instructed; and there are two pay schools, in which are about 120 children. There is a dispensary at Castleshane, close to the parish, in the benefits of which it partakes. Charitable donations to the amount of £500, and £15 per ann., have been bequeathed by various benefactors for the relief of the poor. Much pine or fir, with the roots frequently up-right, and the mark of fire on them, and much black and grey oak, are found in the boggy lands. In Cornero wood, on the shore of Mucknoe lake, are the ruins of an ancient castle.

CURRIN, a parish, partly in the barony of COOLE, county of FERMANAGH, but chiefly in the barony of DARTRY, county of MONAGHAN, and province of ULSTER, 3 miles (S.W.) from Clones, on the road to Ballyhaise and Stradone; containing, with the town of Drum and the village of Scotshouse (each of which is separately described), 7180 inhabitants, This parish comprises, according to the Ordnance survey, 11,372 statute acres, of which 10,987 are in Monaghan, and 385 in Fermanagh. The land is chiefly arable; there are about 200 acres of woodland, but little bog, and fuel is very scarce. There are several lakes in the parish, of which those contiguous to Drum, and to the Hilton demesne, are the most extensive. In addition to agricultural labour, the chief occupation of the inhabitants is the linen manufacture. Hilton Lodge, the beautiful residence of Col. Madden, is situated on the confines of Fermanagh, and commands a fine view of the neighbouring mountains; the demesne, which is several hundred acres in extent, is well furnished with fine timber, and has a well stocked deer park. The other seats are Minore, that of Captain Cottnam; and Laurel Hill, the property of George Moore, Esq.

The living is a rectory and vicarage, in the diocese of Clogher, united by episcopal authority to part of the rectory and vicarage of Drumkrin, together forming the union of Currin, in the patronage of the Bishop. The tithes amount to £400, and the gross tithes of the benefice to £584. The glebe, which was erected by a gift of £380.15.0 from the late Board of First Fruits, in 1828, comprises 60 acres of profitable land, valued at £100 per annum. The parochial church, at Scotshouse, is a neat modern structure in good repair; there is also a chapel of ease at Drum. On the next avoidance it is provided by acts of council, dated Jan. 7th, 1804, and March 6th, 1806, that the union be dissolved, when the part of Drumkrin will be attached to the parish of Drummully. The R.C. parish is co-extensive with that of the Established Church: the chapel is at Scotshouse. There are two

Presbyterian meeting-houses in Drum, one in connection with the Synod of Ulster, of the third class; and one for Seceders, of the second class. There are schools at Scotshouse, Tattenaghcake, Carnagarry, Aghrea, Mockla, Carne, Laurel Hill, Killefargy, and Drum, in which are about 530 boys and 330 girls. There are also three private schools, in which are about 40 boys and 20 girls; and six Sunday schools.

DONAGH, a parish, in the barony of TROUGH, county of MONAGHAN, and province of ULSTER, containing, with the post-towns of Glasslough and Emyvale (which are separately described), 11,068 inhabitants. This parish is supposed to derive its name from St. Dimpna, the patron saint of the district, who is said to have conferred the virtue of preventing or curing almost all diseases (which many of the peasantry yet believe is retained) on the waters of the celebrated spring, TubberPhadric: her silver staff is in the possession of Owen Lamb, of Knockboy, near Monaghan. In March, 1688, about 3000 of the Irish being garrisoned in the fort of Charlemont, and attempting to plunder the Protestants of the neighbourhood of Armagh, Lord Blayney had frequent skirmishes with them, in which he constantly prevailed, until the 13th of the month, when, on being informed that his castle of Monaghan was taken by the Rapparees, and that all the Protestant forces in that quarter had retreated to Glasslough, where they were closely besieged by the enemy; and hearing that Sir Arthur Rawdon had quitted Loughbrickland, of which the Irish army, under Gen. Hamilton, had taken possession, he marched to join his friends at Glasslough, where they were relieved by the valour of Matthew Anketell, Esq., a gentleman of considerable property in the neighbourhood (which is now possessed by his immediate descendant, W. Anketell, Esq., of Anketell Grove), who had collected two troops of horse and three companies of foot. The Irish, commanded by Major McKenna, with a force of 600 men, intrenched themselves in an old Danish fort, called the fort of Drumbanagher, in a commanding situation, and from this eminence kept up a heavy fire on the Protestants who advanced against them: but Mr. Anketell, who was of undaunted courage, burst into the fort, at the head of his troops, routed and pursued the enemy with considerable slaughter, but was himself slain in the hour of victory. Major McKenna and his son were both taken prisoners, and the former was destroyed, in the moment of excitement, in revenge of the death of the spirited leader of the Protestant force, The body of Mr. Anketell was interred in the aisle of Glasslough church with great solemnity, and a plain stone with an inscription has been set up to his memory.

This parish is situated on the roads from Monaghan to Belfast, and from Dublin to Londonderry, on a small river called Scamegeragh, or the "sheep ford river," (from which a small village in the neighbourhood takes its name), which is tributary to that of the Blackwater, which also intersects the parish. According to the Ordnance survey, it comprises

16,202$\frac{1}{4}$ statute acres, of which 241$\frac{3}{4}$ are under water; the land is principally arable, with a small portion of pasture; there is a considerable tract of bog, with some woodland. Agriculture is much improved, under the auspices of a Farming Society, which holds its meetings at Glasslough. Besides the great lakes of Glasslough and Emy, there are two smaller ones. There are excellent quarries of marble, used for monuments and for the ornamental parts of architecture, which is largely exported to England and to the United States; freestone quarries also abound, whence large quantities, superior to Portland stone, are procured, and the great entrance to Caledon House was constructed of this stone; there is also an extensive quarry of grey basalt. The corn and flax-mills belonging to Mr. Young, called the New Mills, about 1$\frac{1}{2}$ mile from Glasslough, employ about 20 persons, and at Emyvale are mills belonging to William Murdock, Esq. In addition to agricultural and other pursuits, the linen manufacture is carried on to a considerable extent. Manor courts for Castle Leslie are held on the third Saturday of each month; and petty sessions are held at Emyvale on alternate Thursdays. The seats and demesnes are Glasslough Castle, the beautiful residence of Mrs. Leslie; Anketell Grove, of W. Anketell, Esq.; Fort Johnston, of T. Johnston, Esq.; and Castle Leslie, of C. Powell Leslie, Esq.

The living is a vicarage, in the diocese of Clogher, and in the patronage of the Bishop, to whom the rectory is appropriate: the tithes amount to £465, of which £310 is payable to the bishop, and £155 to the incumbent. There is a glebe-house, with a glebe of about 40 acres. The church is a plain edifice at Glasslough, built about 1775. The R.C. parish is co-extensive with that of the Established Church, and contains chapels at Glennin and Corraghrin. There is a Presbyterian meeting-house, in connection with the Synod of Ulster, of the third class; also a small place of worship for Wesleyan Methodists. Five schools, supported chiefly by subscription, afford instruction to about 570 children; there are also nine private pay schools and one Sunday school. The only remains of antiquity are the old church of Donagh, and the Danish rath of Drumbanagher, where the battle was fought. Very ancient coins have been found on the estate of Mrs. Leslie; and numerous silver ornaments, helmets of brass, steel swords, druidical relics, and Gothic figures, found in the parish, are now in the possession of the Rev. H. R. Dawson, Dean of St. Patrick's.

DONAGHMOYNE, a parish, in the barony of FARNEY (called also, from this parish, DONAGHMOYNE), county of MONAGHAN, and province of ULSTER, 2$\frac{1}{2}$ miles (N.N.E.) from Carrickmacross; containing 14,070 inhabitants. It is situated on the mail coach road from Dublin to Londonderry, and comprises, according to the Ordnance survey, 25,604 statute acres, of which 102$\frac{1}{4}$ are in Lough Muckno, and 258$\frac{1}{4}$ in the smaller lakes with which the parish is interspersed. Nearly the whole of the land is in tillage; the soil is fertile and produces tolerably good crops, but the system of agriculture is in a very unimproved state.

Limestone abounds in the southern part of the parish, and is quarried for building and for agricultural purposes; and coal has been discovered on the townland of Corlea, but has not been worked. At Thornford there is an extensive corn-mill. The principal gentlemen's seats are Longfield, the residence of J. Johnston, Esq.; Rahens, of J. Read, Esq.; Donaghmoyne, of J. Bashford, Esq.; Cabragh Lodge, of J. Boyle Kernan, Esq.; Rocksavage, of J. Plunkett, Esq.; Broomfield, of W. Henry, Esq.; Thornford, of Hamilton McMath, Esq.; and Longfield Cottage, of R. Banan, Esq.

The living is a vicarage, in the diocese of Clogher, and in the patronage of the Crown; the rectory is impropriate in J. B. Kernan, Esq. The tithes amount to £1430.15.4$\frac{1}{2}$, of which £476,18.5$\frac{1}{2}$ is payable to the impropriator, and £953.16.11 to the vicar. The glebe-house is a comfortable residence, with grounds containing seven acres; the glebe comprises 50$\frac{1}{2}$ acres. The church, a neat modern structure, was erected on a site presented by Jas. Bashford, Esq., by aid of a loan of £1250 from the late Board of First Fruits. In the R.C. divisions the parish is partly in the union or district of Inniskeen, and partly a benefice in itself; there are three chapels, situated respectively at Donaghmoyne, Lisdoonan, and Tapla, belonging to the parochial benefice, and one at Drumcatton belonging to the union of Inniskeen. There are schools at Lisdoonan and Donaghmoyne, supported by subscription, in which about 70 children are instructed; and 13 pay schools, in which are about 460 boys and 170 girls, also a Sunday school. At Fincairn, in the northern part of the parish, are several large stones, supposed to be a druidical monument. On the townland of Cabragh was formerly an abbey dependent on the abbey of Mellifont; and on the townland of Mannon are the remains of an ancient castle, or Danish fort, which, from its elevated situation, and the remains of the buildings on its summit, appears to have been a strong and very important post; it commands an extensive view of the surrounding country.

DRUM, a market-town, in the parish of CURRIN, barony of DARTRY, county of MONAGHAN, and province of ULSTER, 2$\frac{1}{2}$ miles (N.) from Cootehill, on the road to Clones, from both of which it has a penny-post: the population is returned with the parish. It occupies rather an elevated situation near Leysborough lake. In the vicinity is a quarry, from which the stone used in building the chapel of ease was obtained. It is a constabulary police station, and has fairs on the first Tuesday in every month. A chapel of ease to Currin church was built by a grant of £830 from the late Board of First Fruits, in 1828. Here are two Presbyterian meeting-houses, a school, and a dispensary. – See CURRIN.

DRUMKRIN, or ST. MARY'S DRUMCRIN, a parish, in the barony of DARTRY, county of MONAGHAN, and province of ULSTER, 10 miles (N.) from Cavan; containing 3751 inhabitants, and comprising 7469 statute acres. It is a rectory and vicarage, in the diocese of Clogher, partly united by act of council, in 1804, to the rectory and vicarage of Galloon, and partly to that of Currin; on the avoidance of

Dawson Grove. Drawn by P. Sandy and engraved by W. Walker and W. Angus. 1780.

the latter benefice, that part of the parish which is not united to Galloon will, with the exception of Hermitage and Lisnadish, which will remain annexed to Currin, be incorporated with the parish of Drummully. The tithes amount to £184. In the R.C. divisions it is in the union or district of Drummully, and. has a chapel at Drumslow. About 130 children are educated in two public schools, and about 200 in five private schools.

DRUMSNATT, a parish, in the barony of MONAGHAN, county of MONAGHAN, and province of ULSTER, $4^3/_4$ miles (S.W.) from Monaghan, on the road from that place to Clones; containing 3411 inhabitants. According to the Ordnance survey it comprises $5019^1/_4$ statute acres, of which 4436 are applotted under the tithe act: the land is moderately fertile and chiefly under tillage. The principal seats are Thornhill, the residence of J. Johnson, Esq.; Brookvale, of Capt. Johnston; and the Glebe-house, of the Rev. A. Mitchell. The living is a vicarage, in the diocese of Clogher, and in the patronage of the Bishop; the rectory is impropriate in Sir T. B. Lennard, Bart, The tithes amount to £189.4.$7^1/_2$, of which £106.3.1 is payable to the impropriator, and £83.1.$6^1/_2$ to the vicar. There is a glebe-house, with a glebe of 22 acres. The church, for the repairs

of which the Ecclesiastical Commissioners lately granted £316, is a plain modern structure with a tower. In the R.C. divisions it is the head of a union or district, comprising the parishes of Drumsnatt and Kilmore, and containing two chapels, of which that for Drumsnatt is at Kilnaclay. About 450 children are educated in four public, and 190 in three private schools; and there is a Sunday school.

EMATRIS, a parish, in the barony of DARTRY, county of MONAGHAN, and province of ULSTER, 3 miles (N.E. by E.) from Cootehill, on the roads to Clones and Monaghan; containing 7541 inhabitants; and comprising, according to the Ordnance survey, 12,297 statute acres, of which 590 are under water, and 10,793 are applotted under the tithe act, and valued at £8985 per annum. The soil is a rich shallow loam, on deep stiff clay, very difficult of cultivation: there is some bog, and about 400 acres of underwood. The weaving of linen to a small extent is combined with agriculture. Petty sessions are held on alternate Wednesdays at Rock Corry. Damson Grove, the noble mansion of Lord Cremorne, stands in a demesne of more than 1000 acres, embellished with lakes adorned with islands, on which grows the finest timber; some of these islands embrace remarkable views, particularly that of Bellamont forest. In one of the woods is a temple containing a beautiful group of marble statuary to the memory of Lady Ann Dawson: on a rising ground in the demesne, and close to the public road, is a handsome column, erected by public subscription, to the memory of Richard Dawson, Esq., who represented the county of Monaghan in five successive parliaments. The other seats are Freame Mount, the residence of R. Mayne, Esq.; Glenburnie Park of C. Stewart Corry, Esq.; Tanagh, of Capt. C. Dawson; Dromore Lodge, of Lieut. Dawson, R. N.; New Park, of Dacre Hamilton, Esq.; and Cremorne Cottage, of the Rev. n. Devereux. The living is a rectory and vicarage, in the diocese of Clogher, and in the patronage of the Bishop; the tithes amount to £365. The church, picturesquely situated in the demesne of Dawson Grove, is a handsome building with a tower, and was recently repaired by a grant of £100 from the Ecclesiastical Commissioners. The R.C. church is co-extensive with that of the established church; there is a chapel at Edergole, and another at Coravockan, a neat slated building. There is a place of worship for Presbyterians in connection with the Seceding Synod, of the second class, and three for Weslyan Methodists. The parish school is aided by an annual donation from the rector, and £10 from Lady Cremorne, with grass for a cow and a house rent free; in this school about 60 children are instructed. There are seven other public schools, one of which is an infants' school with a sewing school attached, under the patronage of Mrs Devereux. There are also three hedge schools, in which are about 120 boys and 50 girls; and four Sunday schools. A Clothing Society, for supplying the poor with blankets,&c., is aided by Lady Cremorne, T.C.S. Corry, Esq., and the rector; and a lending library is supported by general subscription. Near Freame Mount is a very large rath, occupying an acre of land, and commanding a number of Toghers, or bog passes, flanked by two smaller ones.

EMY VALE, a post-town, in the parish of DONAGH, barony of TROUGH, county of MONAGHAN, and province of ULSTER, $5^3/_4$ miles (N. by W.) from Monaghan, and $71^1/_2$ (N.W. by N.) from Dublin, on the road from Monaghan to Aughnacloy; containing 123 houses and 571 inhabitants. This town, which is nearly on the confines of the counties of Armagh and consists principally of one street, and is skirted by a stream tributary to the river Blackwater, which, descending from the mountains on the west, frequently, becomes a rapid and dangerous torrent after heavy rains. On its banks is a large flour-mill, and in its bed above the town is a quarry of greenstone. There is a constabulary police station, and petty sessions are held every fortnight in the town, in which is also a branch of the Glasslough dispensary. In the vicinity are several gentlemen's seats, which are noticed in the account of Donagh, which see.

ERRIGAL-TROUGH, a parish, partly in the barony of CLOGHER, county of Tyrone, but chiefly in that of TROUGH, county of MONAGHAN, and province of ULSTER, 3 miles (S.S.W.) from Aughnacloy, on the road to Emyvale, and on the river Blackwater; containing 9321 inhabitants. It comprises $24,792^1/_4$ statute acres, according to the Ordnance survey, of which $21,174^1/_4$ are in Monaghan, and $102^1/_4$ are under water; 21,834 acres are applotted under the tithe act. About four-fifths of the land are arable and pasture, and there is a great deal of mountain land used for grazing, and some bog on the western boundary: agriculture is improving. There is abundance of limestone and sandstone; and coal is supposed to exist in the Sleabea mountains, though it has not been worked. On the north-western confines of the parish is Lough More. A small factory for weaving linen has been recently erected here. The gentlemen's seats are Fort Singleton, that of T. Singleton, Esq., situated in a well wooded demesne of 200 acres; Favour Royal, the handsome residence of J. Corry Moutray, Esq., erected near the site of the ancient house, which was destroyed by fire in 1823, and surrounded by a richly wooded demesne of 740 acres; and Laurel Hill, of W. H. Mayne, Esq. The living is a vicarage, in the diocese of Clogher, and in the patronage of the Bishop; the rectory is appropriate to the see of Clogher: the tithes amount to £400, of which $£2157.8^1/_4$ is payable to the bishop, and the remainder to the incumbent. The glebe-house stands on a glebe of 40 acres. The church is a very neat modern structure. A handsome cruciform church, in the later English style, with a square tower at the north-east angle, was erected in the demesne of Favour Royal, in 1835, at an expense of £1000, by J. C. Moutray, Esq., who has endowed it with £50 per annum, augmented with £30 per annum by the Ecclesiastical Commissioners; it is open to the public, there being no other church within three miles of Favour Royal, and is called St. Mary's, Portelare; the living is a donative, in the patronage of the founder. There is also a chapel in the eastern part of the parish. The R.C. parish is co-extensive with that of the Established Church, and contains three chapels, one at Knockconnan, built in 1820, at an expense of £700; another on the townland of Drimbriston, built in 1823, at an expense of £500; the third, built in 1787, is in the townland of Mullyoden: the two first were erected, and the last repaired, through the exertions of the Rev. C. McDermot, the parish priest. There is a national school at Moy; and there are three other public schools, of which one at Fort Singleton is supported by T. Singleton, Esq., who built the school-house, in which the curate of the parish performs divine service twice every Sunday. There are also four hedge, three Scriptural, and four Sunday schools. In that portion of the parish which is in the county of is a remarkable place called Altadawin, where it is said that St. Patrick assembled the first of his followers: it is a valley, 150 feet deep, through the centre of which a tongue of land of considerable altitude extends, and on the summit stands a large rock in the form of an altar, adjoining which is another rock, in the form of a chair. The valley is covered with trees, and a beautiful stream runs nearly through its centre. A royal residence of an independent prince of the O'Nial family is reported to have stood here formerly.

GLASSLOUGH, a post-town, in the parish of DONAGH, barony of TROUGH, county of MONAGHAN, and province of ULSTER, 5 miles (N.E.) from Monaghan, and $70^3/_4$ (N.W.) from Dublin; containing 812 inhabitants. It is situated on the road from Monaghan to Caledon, on the margin of a beautiful lake, whence the town derives its name, signifying "the green lake." It has a striking and attractive appearance, and contains excellent slated houses. It is favourably situated with regard to commerce and agriculture, but until a very late period had little or no trade. In consequence of the judicious modes which have been adopted by the present owner, Mrs. Leslie, its capabilities have been developed and it has shown decided symptoms of rapid improvement. It has now a weekly market for wheat and flax, and a fair on the third Friday in every month for cattle, sheep, pigs, and other agricultural produce. An extensive flour-mill has been lately built in the neighbourhood, for which an ample supply of wheat is obtained from Glasslough market; and mills are now being built for scutching and spinning flax, also a factory on a large scale for weaving linens by hand and power looms; the whole, when completed, will afford permanent employment to between eight and nine hundred individuals. The beautiful and extensive park and castle of Mrs. Leslie, which adjoins the town and contains upwards of 1000 acres of fine land well planted, adds much to the natural beauty of the situation. The mansion was originally of considerable grandeur, but in consequence of repeated alterations has lost all its antique features. The ancient castle was situated opposite to the town gate of the present house, and was a building of considerable strength, flanked with circular towers and defended by a moat and drawbridge, possessing also those indispensable requisites of feudal power, a keep and donjon. The site had been a place of strength long before its erection, and was granted to O'Bear McKenna by O'Nial of Ulster, on the conditions that he and his descendants should pay "Bonaghty," or tribate, and furnish white meat and oats to the Gallowglasses of O'Nial on certain days when they visited the holy well of Tubber Phadrick, near Glennan, and never to wage war with the O'Nials. This tribute was paid at stated periods in a house built of wood and osiers, at Anaghroe, or the "Red River," now the seat of William Murdoch, Esq. Near the town is the hill and rath of Drumbanagher, where, on the 13th of March, 1688, a battle was fought between a detachment of the Irish army, on its way to join the besiegers of Londonderry, and the native Protestant forces of the district, in which the latter gained a complete victory, but with the loss of their gallant colonel, Matthew Anketell, to whose memory a monument was erected in the parish church, which is still preserved. In the town is the parish church, with a tower 130 feet high: it has nothing in architectural beauty to attract notice; the interior arrangements are plain, neat, and commodious. During the erection of the tower a workman fell from the top, but escaped without suffering any material injury.

INNISKEEN, or ENNISKEEN, a parish, partly in the baronies of LOUTH and UPPER DUNDALK, county of LOUTH, and province of LEINSTER, but chiefly in the barony of FARNEY, county of MONAGHAN, and province of ULSTER, 4 miles (N.) from Louth, on the road to Castle-Blayney; containing 3698 inhabitants. According to the Ordnance survey it comprises $6192^3/_4$ statute acres, of which $86^1/_4$ are in the barony of Louth, $1116^1/_2$ in Upper Dundalk, and 4990 in Farney; 5534 acres were applotted under the tithe act. Here is a constabulary police station. The living is a rectory and vicarage, in the diocese of Clogher, and in the patronage of the Bishop the tithes amount to $£447.13.10^1/_4$. The glebe-house was erected by aid of a loan of £675 from the late Board of First Fruits, in 1821. The church is a neat plain structure with an ancient burial-ground, in which is a vault bearing the date 1672, built by Col. Mac Mahon, a descendant of the corbes of Clones: the belfry is one of the ancient round towers. In the R.C. divisions the parish is the head of a union or district, including also part of Donaghmoyne, and containing a neat chapel here and one at Drumcatton, erected on land given by F. Evans, Esq., of Mountjoy-square, Dublin, who also gave a site adjacent for a school-house. The parochial school, which is a good stone building, was erected at an expense of £200 by subscription and a grant from the Lord-Lieutenant's fund. Here are also two Sunday schools. St. Dagens is said to have founded an abbey or bishoprick here in the beginning of the sixth century, which is not mentioned later than the eleventh century, although some remains of it still exist. Here is an extensive Danish fort.

KILLANEY, a parish, partly in the barony of ARDEE, county of LOUTH, and province of LEINSTER, but chiefly in the barony of FARNEY, county of MONAGHAN, and province of ULSTER, 2 miles (E. by S.) from Carrickmacross, on the road from Carrick to Dundalk; containing 4823 inhabitants, of which number 1424 are in Louth. The rivers Glyde and Ballymackney flow through this parish; and the Earl of Essex had an interview, in 1599, at Essexford, with O'Nial, Earl of Tyrone. It comprises, according to the Ordnance survey (including $167^3/_4$ acres in the detached townland of Essexford, and $106^1/_4$ under water), $7127^1/_4$ statute acres, of which $1939^1/_4$ are in Louth, and 5188 in Monaghan; 5870 acres are applotted under the tithe act, and chiefly in tillage, and 500 acres consist of bog. The principal seats are Moynalty, the residence of T. McEvoy Gartland, Esq., and Ballymackney House, of W. Daniel, Esq. The living is a rectory and vicarage, in the diocese of Clogher, and in the patronage of the Bishop; the tithes amount to $£461.10.9^1/_4$. The church is a small ancient structure. There is a glebe-house, with a glebe of 90 acres. In the R.C. divisions this parish is partly in the union or district of Carrickmacross, and partly the head of a district, comprising also three or four townlands in the parish of Louth; it contains two chapels, one at Corcreagh, belonging to the Carrickmacross district, and the other in the village of

Killaney. About 270 children are educated in five private schools, and there is a Sunday school. Here are the ruins of an ancient church, and of a fortification on a conical hill, called Mount Killaney.

KILLEEVAN, a parish, partly in the barony of MONAGHAN, but chiefly in that of DARTRY, county of MONAGHAN, and province of ULSTER, on the river Fin, and on the road from Clones to Dublin; containing, with the post-town of Newbliss, 7273 inhabitants, of which number 87 are in the village. This parish comprises, according to the Ordnance survey, 11,571$^3/_4$ statute acres, of which 11,314$^3/_4$ are in Dartry, including a detached portion of 127$^1/_2$ acres, and 55$^3/_4$ under water; and 257 in the barony of Monaghan: of the whole, 9329 are applotted under the tithe act. The land is principally under tillage, the soil fertile, and the system of agriculture improved: there are several detached portions of bog. The principal seats are Ballinure, the residence of W. Forster, Esq.; Newbliss House, of A. Kerr, Esq.; Gortgranagh, of Mrs. Graham; Scarvey, of Major Campbell Graham; and Glinch Lodge, of J. Thompson, Esq. The living is a rectory and vicarage, in the diocese of Clogher, and in the patronage of the Bishop: the tithes amount to £518.19.2$^3/_4$. The church is a neat plain structure, for the repair of which the Ecclesiastical Commissioners have recently granted £142. The glebe house is a neat building, and the glebe comprises 64 acres. In the R.C. divisions the parish is the head of a union, comprising also the parish of Aughabog, and containing two chapels; the chapel of this parish, on the townland of Killafuddy, is a neat edifice, erected in 1817. About 680 children are taught in six public schools, of which the parochial school is chiefly supported by the incumbent; and there are four private schools, in which are about 260 children. – See NEWBLISS.

KILMORE, a parish, in the barony and county of MONAGHAN, province of ULSTER, 2$^1/_2$ miles (W. by N.) from Monaghan, on the road to Clones; containing 5095 inhabitants. According to the Ordnance survey it comprises 8689$^1/_2$ statute acres, including a detached portion of 334$^1/_4$ acres, several small lakes, and some bog. The principal seats are Ballyleck, the residence of the Hon. R. Westenra; Brandrim, of Owen Blayney Cole, Esq.; and Rosefield, of Ralph Dudgeon, Esq. The Ulster Canal will pass through the northern part of the parish. The living is a rectory and vicarage, in the diocese of Clogher, and in the patronage of the Bishop. The tithes amount to £286.3.0. There is a glebe-house, towards the erection of which the late Board of First Fruits gave £100 in 1792; the glebe comprises 43 acres. The church is a plain edifice with an elegant tower, erected in 1788, and for the repair of which £109 was lately granted by the Ecclesiastical Commissioners. In the R.C. divisions the parish forms part of the union or district of Drumsnat, and has a chapel at Corcahan. There are eight public schools, in which about 520 children are educated; and two private schools, in which are 60 children; also a Sunday school supported by the curate.

MAGHERACLOONY, a parish, in the barony of FARNEY, county of MONAGHAN, and province of ULSTER, 2$^1/_2$ miles (S.W.) from Kingscourt, on the confines of the counties of Louth, Cavan, and Meath, and on the mail coach road from Dublin to Londonderry; containing 8444 inhabitants. On the verge of this parish, at the ford of Bellahoo, a battle was fought in 1539, between the Lord Grey and O'Nial and O'Donell; at the same spot one was also fought by Gen. Ireton. The parish comprises, according to the Ordnance Survey, 12,952 statute acres (including 336$^1/_2$ under water) principally good arable and pasture land; there are a few detached bogs, and some extensive plantations, but scarcely any waste land. Of late years the land has been much improved by extensive draining and the large quantity of lime used as manure; limestone is abundant in the southern part; coal of indifferent quality is also found. A branch of the river Leggan bounds the parish for about four miles on the south-west: the principal lakes are those of Fea, Feo, Rahans, and Graghlone, besides which there are some smaller. The principal seats are Lough Fea Castle, the residence of Evelyn J. Shirley, Esq., a spacious and handsome structure in the Elizabethan style of architecture, situated in a richly planted demesne, including Lough Fea within its limits; Derry, of S. Pendleton, Esq.; and Coolderry, of G. Forster, Esq. The living is a vicarage, in the diocese of Clogher, and in the patronage of the Bishop; the rectory is impropriate in Col. Moore. The tithes amount to £1116.13.4, of which £686.13.4 is payable to the impropriator, and £430 to the vicar. The glebe-house, erected in 1816, cost £941.10.9$^1/_4$ of which £323.1.7 was a gift, and £415.7.8$^1/_2$ a loan, from the late Board of First Fruits, the residue having been supplied by the incumbent; the glebe comprises 40 acres, valued at £60 per annum. The church is a neat modern structure, built in 1835, at an expense of £738.9.2$^3/_4$ being a loan from the same Board. The R.C. parish is co-extensive with that of the Established Church, and has chapels at Rocks and Corlan; the latter, a spacious oblong structure, 90 feet by 40, was erected in 1825, and has a burial-ground attached: the site was given by E. J. Shirley, Esq., who contributed £25 towards the building. The parochial school is aided by the incumbent; the school-house is a good slated building, erected at an expense of £150, part of which was a grant from the lord-lieutenant's school fund. There are two other schools, to each of which Mr. Shirley contributes £5 per ann., and one under the National Board; also 16 private schools.

MONAGHAN, an incorporated market-town and parish, the chief town of the county, and formerly a parliamentary borough, in the barony and county of MONAGHAN, and province of ULSTER, 12$^1/_4$ miles, (W.S.W.) from Armagh, and 60 (N.N.W.) from Dublin, on the mail coach road to Londonderry; containing 11,875 inhabitants, of which number, 3848 are in the town. This place, till within a comparatively modern period, was distinguished only by a monastery, of which St. Moclodius, the son of Aedh, was

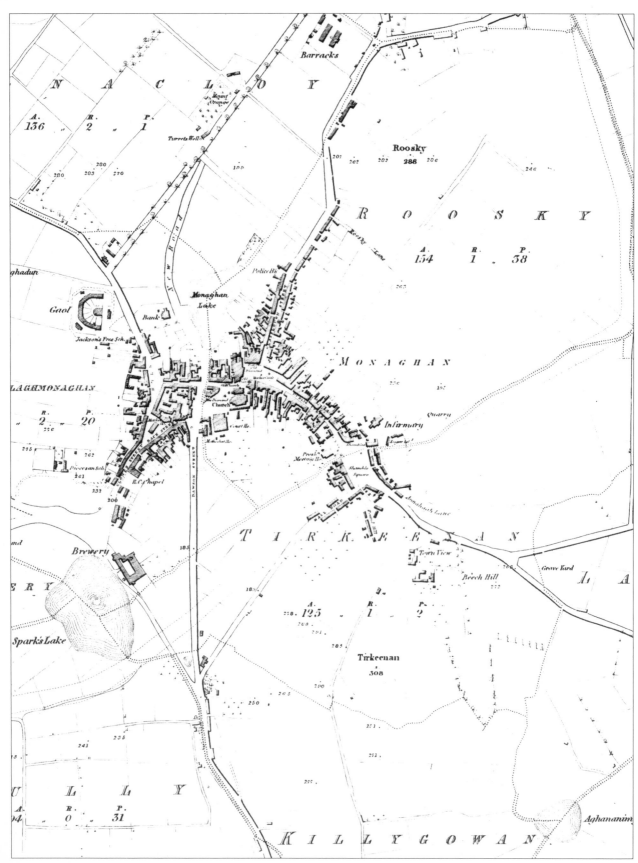

Monaghan. Part of the O.S. map of Co. Monaghan, sheet 45/46, published 1836 (reproduced at 140%).

abbot; and which, according to the Annals of the Four Masters, was plundered in 830 and again in 931. It appears from the same authority to have flourished for more than two centuries, and the names of its abbots, deans, and archdeacons (among the former of whom was Elias, the principal of all the monks of Ireland, who died in Cologne in 1042) are regularly preserved till the year 1161, after which date no further mention of it occurs. Phelim Mac Mahon, in 1462, founded on the site of the ancient abbey a monastery for Conventual Franciscans, which at the dissolution was granted to Edward Withe; but even at that time no place deserving the name of a village had arisen near the monastery, and the whole of this part of the country, under its native chiefs, the Mac Mahons, still retained the ancient customs. About the commencement of the 17th century, Sir Edward Blayney, who had been appointed seneschal of the county, erected a small fort here, which he garrisoned with one company of foot; and on the approaching settlement of Ulster, when the Lord-Deputy came to this place to make some arrangements respecting the forfeited lands, it was so destitute of requisite habitations, that he was under the necessity of pitching tents for his accommodation. On this occasion the Lord-Deputy was attended by the Lord-Chancellor and judges of assize, and by the attorney-general, the celebrated Sir John Davies, who describes the place as consisting only of a few scattered cabins, occupied chiefly by the retired soldiers of Sir Edward Blayney's garrison. Besides that fort, which was on the north side of the village, he notices another in the centre of it, which had been raised only 10 or 12 feet above the ground, and was then lying in a neglected state, although £1200 had been expended on it by the king as a means of retaining the native inhabitants of the district in subjection. The Lord-Deputy divided several neighbouring "ballibetaghs" among the soldiers residing in the town; and as the fort at this time depended on Newry for its supplies, which, from the hostility of the intervening country, were frequently precarious, he granted to Sir Edward Blayney a portion of land on which he erected the fortress of Castle Blayney. In 1611, Sir Edward obtained the grant of a market and fair; and the town, which now began to increase in population and extent, was, in 1613, made a parliamentary borough, and the inhabitants were incorporated by a charter of Jas. I, under the designation of the "Provost, Free Burgesses, and Commonalty of the Borough of Monaghan."

The town consists of one principal square in the centre, called the Diamond, in which is the linen-hall, and of another spacious opening in which is the market-house, and of three streets diverging from the principal square in a triangular direction; the total number of houses is about 580, of which many are well built, and those in the environs are neat and handsome. There are barracks for cavalry, a neat building adapted for 3 officers and 54 non-commissioned officers and privates, with stabling for 44 horses, and a small hospital. A news-room is supported by subscription; and a

savings' bank has been established, in which, in 1835, the deposits amounted to £22,016.2.5, belonging to 749 depositors. There is a large brewery in the town, but no particular manufactures are carried on; the chief trade is in agricultural produce and the sale of linen, for which this place is one of the principal marts in the county; the quantity of linen sold, in 1835, was 6641 pieces, of 25 yards each, and the average price per piece, 18s. 9d. The market days are Monday, for linen and for pigs, of which great numbers are slaughtered and sold to dealers, who send the carcasses to Belfast, where they are cured for exportation; on Tuesday for wheat, bere, barley, and rye; on Wednesday for oats; and on Saturday, for oats and potatoes: flax, yarn, butter, and provisions of all kinds are also sold here in large quantities. Fairs are held on the first Monday in every month, and are amply supplied and numerously attended. The market-house, a very commodious building, was erected by the late Gen. Conyngham, afterwards Lord Rossmore, whose arms are emblazoned over the entrance. The Ulster canal, which is now in progress, will pass through the northern part of the parish; a branch of the river Blackwater also bounds the parish on the north, running nearly parallel with the canal. These facilities of water conveyance will contribute to the benefit of the town, which is at present in a thriving state, and is progressively increasing in importance.

The corporation, by the charter of Jas. I, consists of a provost, 12 free burgesses, and an indefinite number of freemen, assisted by a recorder, two serjeants-at-mace, and other officers. The provost is annually chosen from the free burgesses on the festival of St. John the Baptist, and sworn into office on that of St. Michael; the burgesses are elected, as vacancies occur, from the freemen by a majority of their own body, by whom also freemen are admitted by favour only; the recorder and serjeants-at-mace are chosen by the corporation at large, but no recorder has been chosen since 1815, when the last, who was also the first serjeant-at-mace, died. The corporation continued to send two members to the Irish parliament till the Union, when the borough was disfranchised. The court of record, ordained by the charter to be held every Monday, with jurisdiction extending to five marks, has not been held for the last 50 years. The assizes for the county are held here, also the quarter sessions four times in the year, and petty sessions every Tuesday. There is a chief constabulary police force stationed in the town. The county court-house, situated in the centre of the town, is a handsome modern building of hewn stone, containing spacious court-rooms and all requisite offices, and in every respect well adapted to its purpose. The county gaol, completed in 1824, and situated on an eminence near the entrance to the town, is a handsome semicircular range of building, containing 75 single cells, and 11 rooms with more than one bed each, with appropriate day-rooms and airing-yards, in one of which is a tread-wheel applied to the raising of water for the supply of the prison; there are a male and female hospital, a chapel, and a school; the prison is well adapted for classification, and under very good regulations.

The parish, called also "Rackwallis," comprises, according to the Ordnance survey, 13,547½ statute acres, of which 12,758 are applotted under the tithe act, and valued at £23,013.13.2 per ann.; 26½ acres are water, and the remainder principally under tillage. The general surface is irregular and hilly, rugged towards the south, but smoother and more gently undulating towards the north. The soil is rich in the vicinity of the town, but inferior towards the south and south-west; there is but little bog in the parish, though there are large tracts in those adjoining, from which abundance of fuel is obtained. The system of agriculture is improved; limestone abounds, and there is a very fine quarry at Milltown Bridge; marl is also found, but is seldom used for manure; whinstone also forms part of the substratum. The principal seats are Rossmore Park, the residence of the Right Hon. Lord Rossmore, a handsome mansion in the Elizabethan style, situated in an extensive and beautifully diversified demesne, abounding with wild and romantic scenery and commanding some fine distant views; Castle Shane, of E. Lucas, Esq., an ancient mansion in a highly enriched and tastefully embellished demesne (within which is the site of the ancient village of Castle-Shane), with a handsome entrance lodge in the later English style of architecture, and forming an interesting object as seen from the new line of road winding through the valley; Cornacassa, of Dacre Hamilton, Esq., pleasantly situated in a highly cultivated and well-planted demesne; and Camla Vale, of Lieut.- Col. Westenra, brother of Lord Rossmore, a spacious and handsome residence, situated in grounds tastefully laid out and adjoining the demesne of Rossmore Park: there are also many handsome residences in the immediate environs.

The living is a rectory and vicarage, in the diocese of Clogher, and in the patronage of the Bishop: the tithes amount to £553.16.11. The glebe-house is a neat thatched residence, and the glebe comprises 38 statute acres, valued at £114 per annum. The church, a very handsome structure, in the later English style of architecture, with a tower and spire, was erected on the site of the former edifice in 1836, at an expense of £5330, of which £1100 was a legacy, with interest, bequeathed by the late Dowager Lady Rossmore; £1000, a bequest of Mrs. Jackson; £2000, a loan from the late Board of First Fruits, the remainder being raised by subscription. The interior contains some handsome monuments and tablets of white marble, to the late rector, the Rev. Mr. Montgomery, Mr. and Mrs. Jackson, the families of Lucas and Cole, and the lady of Col. Westenra. The R.C. parish is co-extensive with that of the Established Church; there are chapels situated respectively at Latlurken, Ardahy, and in the town. Contiguous to the chapel at Latlurken are the national school and a house and ground given by the Rossmore family for the residence of the R.C. clergyman. There are places of worship for Presbyterians in connection with the Synod of Ulster, of the second and third classes, and for those of the Seceding Synod, of the first class; also for Wesleyan and Primitive Wesleyan Methodists. The consistorial court of the diocese of Clogher is held in the town; and the presbytery of Monaghan, in connection with the Synod of Ulster, also holds its meetings here in February and October. The diocesan school for the sees of Raphoe, Kilmore, and Clogher was founded by Queen Elizabeth and is supported chiefly by the bishops and clergy of those dioceses: the school-house is a spacious and handsome edifice, towards the erection of which Lord Rossmore contributed largely, and endowed the establishment with an annuity and five acres of land. About 1400 children are taught in ten other public schools, of which the parochial school, for which a new house has been recently built, is partly supported by the rector; a free school for boys was founded by H. Jackson, Esq., who endowed it with £22.10.0 per annum, and a house rent-free; a female sewing school is also supported by the same gentleman, who endowed it with a house rent-free and a salary of £16 for the mistress; and a school at Killamarly is aided by an annual donation from W. Brook, Esq. There are also seven private schools, in which are about 300 children. The county infirmary, a good building, occupying an open and elevated site, is supported by a parliamentary grant, by the interest of a legacy of £4000 bequeathed by the late Francis Ellis, Esq., a rent-charge of £20 by the late 3. Wright, Esq., and £100 per annum from Bishop Sterne's charity; also by Grand Jury presentments and subscriptions. During the year ending Jan. 6th, 1835, it afforded relief to 286 in-patients, and medicine and attendance to 900 out-patients. There are also a mendicity society, and a penny a week society for the assistance of the poor, supported by subscription and weekly contributions from the members. An almshouse for six poor widows was founded by the late Richard Jackson, Esq., who endowed it with £25.19.0 per annum, charged on lands in the parish. A large house in the square called the Diamond is said to occupy the site of an ancient castle; and in the rear of it are some old walls, said to be the remains of the old abbey; the cemetery attached appears to have been very extensive. In levelling the ground in front of the old gaol, human bones and a skull of unusually large size were discovered. On the summit of the hill to the north of the town, and near the site of the new gaol, was a small mound of earth, marking the site of the fortress built by Sir Edward Blayney for the protection of the town, and noticed by Sir John Davies as serving both for a garrison and a gaol. Several silver coins have been found here, among which was a curious coin of one of the Henrys, and a larger coin of Jas. I, which is in good preservation; and in a meadow near the river was dug up, some years since, an ancient brass spur, similar to those in the museum of Trinity College, Dublin. On the townland of Lisard, about two miles to the south-west of the town, is a perfect fort, with a rampart and fosse; it is situated on an eminence commanding the surrounding country.

MUCKNOE, a parish, in the barony of CREMORNE, county of MONAGHAN and province of ULSTER, on the road from Carrickmacross to Armagh; containing, with the post-town of Castle-Blayney (which is separately described), 9717 inhabitants. This parish comprises 17,194 statute acres, according to the Ordnance survey, of which 14,155 are applotted under the tithe act, 377¾ are in Mucknoe lake, and 163 in smaller lakes; the land consists chiefly of arable and pasture, but there are large detached tracts of bog, and a considerable portion is mountain, of which Mullyash rises 1034 feet above the level of the sea. The principal crops are oats, flax, and potatoes: stone quarries are worked for building; and there are two cornmills. Monthly fairs are held at Castle-Blayney. Castle-Blayney, the seat of Lord Blayney, is noticed under the head of that town. The living is a rectory and vicarage, in the diocese of Clogher, and in the patronage of the Bishop; the tithes amount to £436. 3. 1. The glebe-house was erected in 1828, at an expense of £1027, of which £184 was a gift and £553 a loan from the late Board of First Fruits; the glebe comprises 20 acres, valued at £39 per annum. The church stands in Castle-Blayney: it was erected in 1810 by a loan of £1000 from the same Board, and gifts of £200 from the late Lord Blayney, £100 from Lord Templeton, and £50 from Lady Eliz. Alexander. In the R.C. divisions the parish is partly in the union of Clontibret, and partly a benefice in itself; it has two chapels, one at Oram, and the other in Castle-Blayney, which is a neat building. There are four places of worship for Presbyterians; one in connection with the Synod of Ulster, of the second class; two at Frankfort and Garmoney Grove, in connection with the Seceding Synod, the latter of the second class; and one belonging to the Scotch Covenanters. There is also a meeting-house for Wesleyan Methodists. About 700 children are educated in 11 public schools, of which the parochial school is aided by the incumbent; and a female school is supported by Lady Blayney; and in 11 private schools are about 540 children.

NEWBLISS, a market and post-town, in the parish of KILLEEVAN, barony of DARTRY, county of MONAGHAN, and province of ULSTER, 4 miles (E.S.E.) from Clones, and 66 (N.W.) from Dublin, on the road from Clones to Dublin; containing 497 inhabitants. It is situated on the estate, and contiguous to the fine demesne and plantations, of Andrew Ker, Esq., M.D.; and consists of one wide street, containing 95 houses, mostly of respectable appearance. It is a station of the constabulary police, and has a sub-post-office to Clones and Cootehill. The market, which is on Saturday, is principally for pigs and flax; and fairs are held on the last Saturday in each month, chiefly for cattle and pigs: the market-house and shambles are neat buildings, and there is a good inn. Here are a neat meeting-house for Presbyterians, erected in 1816; a school under the London Hibernian Society; and a dispensary.

ROCKCORRY, a village, in the parish of EMATRIS, barony of DARTRY, county of MONAGHAN, and province

of ULSTER, 4 miles (N.E.) from Cootehill, on the old road to Monaghan; the population is returned with the parish. The place derives its name from the family of Corry, on whose estate it is situated, and whose residence is contiguous to the village. It consists of one wide street, of which many of the houses are of respectable appearance, and it has a neat market-house. The market is on Wednesday, and there is a fair on the last Wednesday in each month. Here is a station of the constabulary police, and petty sessions are held on alternate Wednesdays. In the village are meeting-houses for Presbyterians of the Seceding Synod, and for Wesleyan Methodists; the former is of recent erection, and both are neat buildings. An infants' school, chiefly supported by Mrs. Devereux, is held in the market-house, to which a sewing-school is attached; and there is a dispensary.

SCOTSHOUSE, a village, in the parish of CURRIN, barony of DARTRY, county of MONAGHAN, and province of ULSTER, 5½ miles (N.W.) from Cootehill, on the road from Clones to Stradone: the population is returned with the parish. It is a station of the constabulary police, and contains the parochial church and R.C. chapel. Near the village is Hilton, the handsome seat of Col. Madden.

SMITHSBOROUGH, a village, in the parish of CLONES, barony and county of MONAGHAN, and province of ULSTER, 5 miles (W.S.W.) from Monaghan (to which it has a penny post), on the road to Clones; containing 244 inhabitants. This place is called after a gentleman named Smith, who here established monthly fairs, in the latter part of the last century, only one of which, that held on Whit-Monday for black cattle, is now kept up. The village consists of 58 houses, and contains a meeting-house for Presbyterians in connection with the Seceding Synod, a modern structure; and a dispensary. It is a constabulary police station; and there is a school of about 60 children.

TULLYCORBET, a parish, partly in the barony of CREMORNE, but chiefly in that of MONAGHAN, county of MONAGHAN, and province of ULSTER, 3 miles (N. by E.) from Ballibay, on the road to Monaghan; containing 4833 inhabitants. It comprises 7913½ statute acres, according to the Ordnance survey, of land of good quality, which is generally well cultivated: there are several lakes within its limits, the two largest of which, Cordoo and Corfin, are near one another: there is a considerable extent of bog. Besides the usual crops of wheat, oats, barley and potatoes, rye and flax are grown; and a considerable quantity of linen is manufactured in the houses of the farmers. The mail coach road from Dublin to Derry skirts the parish on the east. The living is a rectory and vicarage, in the diocese of Clogher, forming the corps of the prebend of Tullycorbet in the cathedral of Clogher, and in the patronage of the Bishop: the tithes amount to £400. The glebe-house, which is in a dilapidated state, was built in 1773 by the then incumbent, at an expense of £634.10.0: the glebe, comprising 42 acres, is valued at £63 per annum. The church is a small and plain

Gola House. Engraved by A. Butler and published by Stannard & Dixon. Not dated, probably 1855.

but neat edifice, situated on an eminence and erected at an expense of £850, by a loan from the late Board of First Fruits in 1831. In the R.C. divisions the parish is the head of a union or district, comprising also that of Ballibay; in each parish there is a chapel. There are three places of worship for Presbyterians; two situated respectively at Bradox and Cahans, belonging to the Seceding Synod, the latter being of the first class; and one for Covenanters, connected with that in the parish of Muckno. The parochial school is aided by the incumbent; there is a school at Creagh; in hoth these there are about 170 boys and 150 girls. There are also five private schools, in which are about 250 boys and 90 girls.

TYDAVNET, a parish, in the barony and county of MONAGHAN, and province of ULSTER, 3½ miles (N. N. W). from Monaghan, on the road by Brookborough to Enniskillen; containing 11,352 inhabitants. This parish, which is intersected by a rapid stream descending from the Slievebaugh mountains, comprises, according to the Ordnance survey, 26,502 statute acres, of which 163 are water, and 20,253 are applotted under the tithe act and valued at £14,400 per annum. There is an extensive tract of mountain and bog, the former of which, though rough, is capable of being reclaimed; and there are nineteen lakes within the parish, of which only one near Mount Louise and one near Slack's Grove are considerable. The Slievebaugh mountains entirely enclose the parish on the north and west; on the former side is their highest point called Cairnmore, commanding a most extensive and interesting prospect. Immediately around this point is the only part of these mountains susceptible of improvement or embellishment, and here a picturesque glen opens towards the low country. On the north-east border of the parish is a very large tract of bog; and there are numerous smaller bogs, supplying an abundance of fuel. The lands under cultivation vary very much in quality; the principal crops are wheat, oats, barley and flax, of the last of which much is grown, and there is at Lemacallagh a mill for scutching it, which is of great benefit to the neighbourhood: there is but a small proportion of grass land, except what is in demesne, though portions of the mountains afford rough pasture. Near Cairnmore is a limestone quarry, and on the summit of the mountain is an extensive quarry for millstones; the stone on the northern side is a soft whitish freestone, and on the southern, a hard reddish grit interspersed with flint. At Scotstown is a depot for these stones, which, after being worked to their proper form in the quarry, are suffered to roll down the mountain; on the north side, just below the rock, is a large, deep, and stormy lake. On the townland of Knockotally good freestone for building is quarried for the supply of the neighbourhood; and the hills also abound with potters' clay. The principal seats are Tullaghan, the property of the Rev. Sir Thos Forster, Bart., whose family formerly resided here; Gola, of J. Woodright, Esq.; Poplar Vale, of Major E, Richardson; Raconnel, of Col. R. Lucas;

Mount Louise, of R. Evatt, Esq.; Clenamully, of E. Fiddes, Esq.; Slack's Grove, of R. Jackson, Esq.; Newgrove, of M. Hawkshaw, Esq.; Mullaghmore, of J. Rose, Esq., greatly improved and extensively planted by the proprietor; and Carrachor, of J. Wright Esq. Fairs are held at Scotstown on the 17th of every month, and also in the village of Tydavnet on Jan, 19th, March 2nd and 31st, June 24th and Sept. 28th, and there is a constabulary police force at each of those places.

The living is a rectory and vicarage, in the diocese of Clogher, and in the patronage of the Bishop; the tithes amount to £664.12.3³/₄. The glebe-house was built in 1824, at an expense of £1581 British, of which £900 was a loan from the late Board of First Fruits, and the remainder was defrayed by the then incumbent; the glebe comprises 40 acres, valued at £80 per annum. The church is a neat modern edifice, situated in the village of Ballinode; it was enlarged in 1830, at an expense of £471, defrayed by the parish, and the Ecclesiastical Commissioners have lately granted £116 for its further improvement. The R.C. parish is co-extensive with that of the Established Church; there are two chapels, one of which is near Scotstown. On the eastern verge of the parish is a place of worship for Presbyterians in connection with the Seceding Synod, of the first class, to which a school is attached, and there is another for Wesleyan Methodists. About 1100 children are taught in ten public schools, of which four are partly supported by the rector, and one on his own estate by Capt. Woodright; and there are four private schools, in which are about 250 children, and a dispensary. A portion of this parish is about to be attached to a perpetual curacy in the parish of Aghalurcher, where a church is now being built from a grant by the late Board of First Fruits, and which will be formed into a district parish.

TYHALLON, or TEHOLLAND, a parish, partly in the barony of CREMORNE, but chiefly in that of MONAGHAN, county of MONAGHAN, and province of ULSTER, 2 miles (E.N.E.) from Monaghan, on the turnpike road to Armagh and on a branch of the river Blackwater; containing 4846 inhabitants. It comprises, according to the Ordnance survey, 5949¹/₂ statute acres of excellent land, (823¹/₄ being within the barony of Cremorne, and 5126¹/₄ within that of Monaghan,) which is nearly all under tillage. there being very little wasteland, but to the east there is a tract of bog. The line of the Ulster canal passes through the parish from east to west. There are some limestone quarries, which are used for building and other purposes. The linen manufacture is carried on in private dwellings. Here is a constabulary police station, The gentlemen's seats are Bessmount Park, the residence of A. Nixon Montgomery, Esq.; Dromore, of C. Hawshaw, Esq.; Liscarney, of Major Ross; Coolmain, of J. Goudy, Esq.; and Sallymount, of T. Robinson, Esq. The living is a rectory and vicarage, in the diocese of Clogher, being the corps of the prebend thereof in the cathedral of Clogher, and in the patronage of the Bishop; the tithes amount to £350. The glebe comprises 40 acres, valued at £80 per ann.: the glebe-house, which is near the church, was improved by the incumbent, in 1820, at an expense of £370, The church is a plain modern structure, built in 1788 at an expense of £277, defrayed by parochial assessment. The R.C. parish is co-extensive with that of the Established Church; the chapel is a spacious edifice, built in 1827 at an expense of £1000. The parish school is aided by the incumbent and a legacy of £500 by the late Dr. Maxwell, of Falkland, £150 of which was to build a school-house and the interest of the remainder for the master, &c.: there are three other schools; in all which about 340 children are taught. There is also a private school, in which are about 20 children. The late-Richardson, Esq., bequeathed £100, the interest of which continues to be divided among the poor.

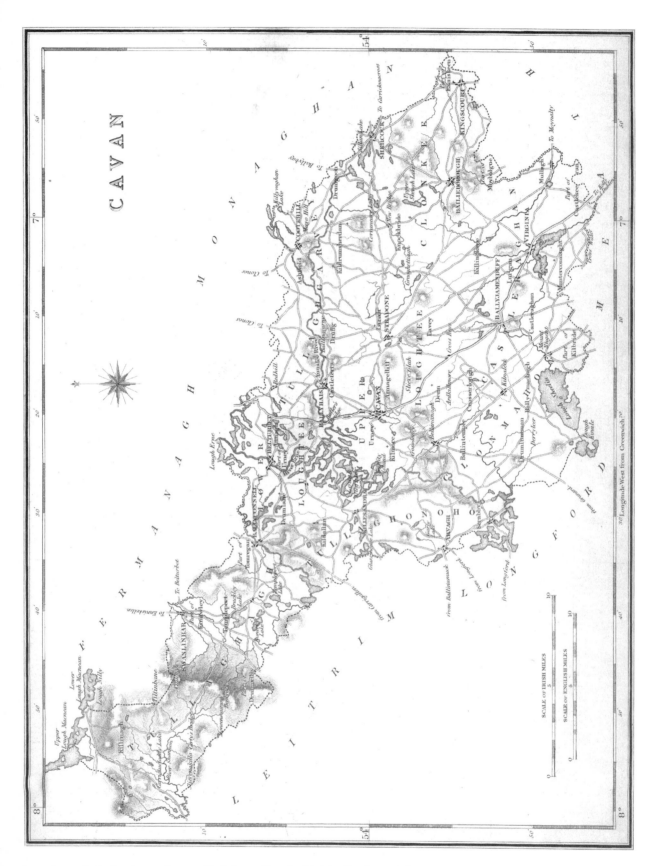

Cavan. Drawn by R. Creighton and engraved by I. Dower. From Lewis's Atlas (London, 1837).

76

COUNTY CAVAN

A

TOPOGRAPHICAL DICTIONARY

CAVAN (County of), an inland county of the province of ULSTER, bounded on the north by the county of Fermanagh; on the west, by that of Leitrim; on the south, by those of Longford, Westmeath, and Meath; and on the east and north-east, by that of Monaghan. It extends from 53° 43' to 54° 7' (N. Lat.); and from 6° 45' to 7° 47' (W. Lon.); and comprises, according to the Ordnance Survey, 477,360 statute acres, of which 421,462 are cultivated land, 30,000 unimproved mountain and bog, and 22,141 are under water. The population, in 1821, was 195,076; and in 1831, 228,050.

According to Ptolemy, this tract, with the districts included in the adjacent counties of Leitrim and Fermanagh, was occupied by the Erdini, designated in the Irish language Ernaigh, traces of which name are yet preserved in that of Lough Erne and the river Erne, upon which and their tributaries these districts border. This district, exclusively of the greater part of the present county of Fermanagh, formed also the ancient principality of Breghne, Brefine, Brefne, Breffny, or Brenny, as it has been variously spelt, which had recognised limits from time immemorial, and was divided into the two principalities of Upper or East Breifne and Lower or West Breifne, the former composed almost entirely of the present county of Cavan, and the latter of that of Leitrim. East Breifne was often called Breifne O'Reilly, from its princes or chiefs having from remote ages borne that name: they were tributary to the O'Nial of Tiroen long before the arrival of the English, although Camden says that in his time they represented themselves as descended from the English family of Ridley, but were entirely Irish in manners. The county is celebrated in the history of the wars in Ireland for the fastnesses formed by its woods, lakes, and bogs, which long secured the independence of its native possessors. Cavan was one of the counties formed in Ulster, in 1584, by Sir John Perrott, lord-deputy of Ireland, and derived its name from the principal seat of its ancient rulers, which is still the provincial capital: in the following year it was represented in a parliament held in Dublin by two loyal members of the family of O'Reilly. Both Breffnys anciently formed part of Connaught, but the new county was incorporated with Ulster. The O'Reillys were at this time a warlike sept, particularly distinguished for their cavalry, and not living in towns, but in small castles scattered over the country. In order to lessen their influence by partitioning it among different leaders, and thus reduce them to the English law, it was resolved to divide the country into baronies and settle the proprietorship of each exclusively on a separate branch of the families of the former proprietors. Sir John O'Reilly, then chief lord of the country, had covenanted to surrender the whole to Queen Elizabeth, and on the other part Sir John Perrott had covenanted that letters patent should be granted to him of the whole; but this mutual agreement led to no result, and commissioners were sent down to carry the division into effect. By them the whole territory was partitioned into seven baronies, of which, two were assigned to Sir John O'Reilly free of all contributions; a third was allotted to his brother, Philip O'Reilly; a fourth to his uncle Edmond; and a fifth to the sons of Hugh O'Reilly, surnamed the Prior. The other two baronies, possessed by the septs of Mac Kernon and Mac Gauran, and remotely situated in the mountains and on the border of O'Rorke's country, were left to their ancient tenures and the Irish exactions of their chief lord, Sir John, whose chief-rent out of the other three baronies not immediately possessed by bim was fixed at 10s. per annum for every pole, a subdivision of land peculiar to the county and containing about 25 acres: the entire county was supposed to contain 1620 of these poles.

But these measures did not lead to the settlement of the country; the tenures remained undetermined by any written title; and Sir John, his brother, and his uncle, as successive tanists, according to the ancient custom of the country, were all slain while in rebellion. After the death of the last, no successor was elected under the distinguishing title of O'Reilly, the country being broken by defeat, although wholly unamenable to the English law. Early in the reign of

James I, the lord-deputy came to Cavan, and issued a commission of inquiry to the judges then holding the assize there concerning all lands escheated to the Crown by attainder, outlawry, or actual death in rebellion; and a jury of the best knights and gentlemen that were present, and of whom some were chiefs of Irish septs, found an inquisition, first, concerning the possessions of various freeholders slain in the late rebellion under the Earl of Tyrone, and secondly, concerning those of the late chiefs of the Country who had shared the same fate; though the latter finding was obtained with some difficulty, the jurors fearing that their own tenures might be invalidated in consequence. Nor was this apprehension without foundation; for, by that inquisition, the greater part, if not the whole, of the county was deemed to be vested in the Crown, and the exact state of its property was thereupon carefully investigated. This being completed, the king resolved on the new plantation of Ulster, in which the plan for the division of this county was as follows: the termon, or church lands, in the ancient division, were 140 poles,or about 3500 acres, which the king reserved for the bishop of Kilmore; for the glebes of the incumbents of the parishes to be erected were allotted 100 poles, or 2500 acres; and the monastery land was found to consist of 20 poles, or 500 acres. There then remained to be distributed to undertakers 1360 poles, or 34,000 acres, which were divided into 26 proportions, 17 of 1000 acres each, 5 of 1500, and 4 of 2000, each of which was to be a parish, to have a church erected upon it, with a glebe of 60 acres for the minister in the smallest proportions, of 90 in the next, and of 120 in the largest. To British planters were to be granted six proportions, viz., three of the least, two of the next, and one of the largest, and in these were to be allowed only English and Scottish tenants; to servitors were to be given six other proportions, three of the least, two of the middle, and one of the largest, to be allowed to have English or Irish tenants at choice; and to natives, the remaining fourteen, being eleven of the least, one of the middle, and two of the greatest size. There then remained 60 poles or 1500 acres, of which 30 poles, or 750 acres, were to be allotted to three corporate towns or boroughs, which the king ordered should be endowed with reasonable liberties, and send burgesses to parliament, and each to receive a third of this quantity; 10 other poles, or 250 acres, were to be appendant to the castle of Cavan; 6 to that of Cloughoughter; and the remaining 14 poles, or 346 acres, to be for the maintenance of a free school to be erected in Cavan.

Two of the boroughs that were created and received these grants were Cavan and Belturbet, and the other 250 acres were to be given to a third town, to be erected about midway between Kells and Cavan, on a site to be chosen by the commissioners appointed to settle the plantation; this place was Virginia, which, however, never was incorporated. The native inhabitants were awed into acquiescence in these arrangements, and such as were not freeholders under the above grants, were to be settled within the county, or removed by order of the commissioners. The lands thus divided were the then profitable portions, and to each division a sufficient quantity of bog and wood was super-added. A considerable deviation from this project took place in regard to tithes, glebes, and parish churches. A curious record of the progress made by the undertakers in erecting fortified houses, &c., up to the year 1618–19, is preserved in Pynnar's Survey; the number of acres enumerated in this document amounts to 52,324, English measure, and the number of British families planted on them was 386, who could muster 711 armed men. Such was the foundation of the rights of property and of civil society in the county of Cavan, as existing at the present day, though not without subsequent disturbance; for both O'Reilly, representative of the county in parliament, and the sheriff his brother, were deeply engaged in the rebellion of 1641. The latter summoned the R.C. inhabitants to arms; they marched under his command with the appearance of discipline; forts, towns, and castles were surrendered to them; and Bedel, Bishop of Kilmore, was compelled to draw up their remonstrance of grievances, to be presented to the chief governors and council.

Cavan is partly in the diocese of Meath, and partly in that of Ardagh, but chiefly in that of Kilmore, and wholly in the ecclesiastical province of Armagh. For civil purposes it is divided into the eight baronies of Castleraghan, Clonmahon, Clonkee, Upper Loughtee, Lower Loughtee, Tullaghgarvey or Tullygarvey, Tullaghonoho, or Tullyhunco, and Tullaghagh or Tullyhaw. It contains the disfranchised borough and market-towns of Cavan and Belturbet; the market and post-towns of Arvagh, Bailieborough, Ballyconnell, Ballyhaise, Ballyjamesduff, Cootehill, Killesandra, Kingscourt, Stradone, and Virginia; the market-towns of Ballinagh and Shercock; the post-towns of Crossdoney, Mount-Nugent, and Scrabby; the modern and flourishing town of Mullagh; and the villages of Butlersbridge and Swanlinbar, each of which has a penny post. Prior to the Union it sent six members to the Irish parliament, two for the county at large, and two for each of the boroughs of Cavan and Belturbet; but since that period its only representatives have been the county members returned to the Imperial parliament and elected at Cavan. The constituency, as registered under the act of the 2nd and 3rd of Wm. IV, cap. 89, amounted, on the 1st of February, 1836, to 2434 electors, of whom 317 were £50, 236 £20, and 1652 £10 freeholders; 17 were £20 rent-chargers; 6 were clergymen registering out of benefices of £50; and 27 were £20, and 179 £10 leaseholders. It is in the north-west circuit: the assizes are held at Cavan, in which are the county court-house and gaol. Quarter sessions are held in rotation at Cavan, Bailieborough, Ballyconnell, and Cootehill; and there are a sessions-house and bridewell at each of the three last-named towns. The number of persons charged with criminal offences and committed to prison, in 1835, was 478, of whom 62 were females; and of civil bill commitments, 112. The local government is vested in a lieutenant, 10 deputy-lieutenants, and 85 other magistrates, including the provost of Belturbet, who is a magistrate of the county ex officio. There are 23 constabulary police stations, having in the whole a force of 8 chief and 22 sub-constables, and 151 men, with 8 horses, maintained equally by Grand Jury presentments and by Government. The county infirmary and fever hospital are situated at Cavan; and there are 18 dispensaries, situated respectively at Arvagh, Bailieborough, Ballyjamesduff, Ballyconnell, Belturbet, Ballymacue, Ballinagh, Ballyhaise, Cootehill, Crossdoney, Cavan, Killesandra, Kingscourt, Mullagh, Shercock, Swanhinbar, Stradone, and Virginia; all of which are maintained partly by Grand Jury presentments and partly by voluntary contributions in equal portions. The amount of Grand Jury presentments for 1835, was £22,525.4.9, of which £1860.8.9 was for the public roads of the county at large; £7287.19.8 for the public roads, being the baronial charge; £6792.15.9 for public buildings and charities, officers' salaries, &c.; £4033.5.0 for police; and £2550.15.7 in repayment of a loan advanced by Government. Cavan, in military arrangements, is included in the northern district, and contains the stations of Belturbet and Cavan, the former for cavalry and the latter for infantry, which afford unitedly accommodation for 13 officers, 286 men, and 101 horses.

The county lies about midway in the island between the Atlantic Ocean and the Irish sea, its two extreme points being about 20 miles distant from each. The surface is very irregular, being every where varied with undulations of hill and dale, occasionally rocky, with scarcely a level spot intervening; but the only mountainous elevations are situated in its northern extremity. To the north-west the prospect is bleak, dreary, and much exposed; but in other parts it is not only well sheltered and woody, but the scenery is highly picturesque and attractive; numerous lakes of great extent and beauty adorn the interior; and, generally, the fea hires of the country are strikingly disposed for landscape decoration. Yet these natural advantages are but partially improved, though in no part of Ireland are there demesnes of more magnificence and beauty. The scenery of the lakes is varied by numerous beautiful islands, and lofty woods overhang tlre river Erne, which flows into the celebrated lake of that name in the neighbouring county of Fermanagh. Bruce hill forms a striking object in the southern extremity of the county; the Leitrim mountains overlook its western confines; while towards the north-west rises the bleak, barren, and lofty range of the Slieve Russell mountains. But the chief mountains are those which separate this county and province from Connaught, encircling Glangavlin, namely, the Lurganculliagh, the Cuilagh, Slieveriakilla, and the Mullahuna, the highest of which is 2185 feet above the level of the sea Some of the lakes cover ninny hundred acres, several of the smaller are nearly dry in summer, and might be effectually drained; all abound with fish, and their waters are remarkably clear. The streams issuing from some of them flow through the vales with much rapidity; their final destination is Lough Erne or Lough Ramor. A ridge of hills

crosses the county nearly from north to south, dividing it into two unequal portions: on the summit, near Lavy chapel, is a spring, a stream descending from which takes an easterly course towards Lough Ramor and into the Boyne, which empties itself into the Irish sea in Drogheda harbour; another stream flows westward through Lough Erne into the Atlantic, on the coast of Donegal. From the elevation and exposure of the surface, the climate is chilly, though at the same time salubrious; the exhalations from its numerous lakes being dispelled by the force of the gales. The soil in its primitive state is not fertile, being cold, in many places spongy, and inclined to produce rushes and a spiry aquatic grass: it commonly consists of a thick stratum of stiff brown clay over an argillaceous substratum; but when improved by draining and the application of gravel or lime, it affords a grateful return of produce. In the vales is found a deep brown clay, forming excellent land for the dairy.

Agriculture is very little improved: the chief crops are oats and potatoes; in some districts a considerable quantity of flax is cultivated, and wheat, within the last two or three years, has become a more common crop. Green crops are seldom or ever grown, except by some of the nobility and gentry. Lord Farnham has in cultivation a large and excellent farm, and around Virginia are evidences of a superior system of husbandry. The chief proprietors afford by example and encouragement every inducement to agricultural improvement, but with little success, except in the introduction of the iron plough, which has been generally substituted for spade labour, by which the land was formerly almost exclusively cultivated. Into the mountain districts, however, neither the plough nor wheel car has yet found its way; the spade, sickle, and flail are there the chief agricultural implements, cattle and pigs the common farm stock, and oats and potatoes the prevailing crops. The sides of the mountains are generally cultivated for oats to a considerable height, and their summits are grazed by herds of small young cattle. This practice more especially prevails in the barony of Tullaghagh, in the mountain district between the counties of Fermanagh and Leitrim, generally known as "the kingdom of Glan," but more properly called Glangavlin, or the country of the Mac Gaurans. To this isolated district there is no public road, and only one difficult pass; in some places a trackway is seen by which the cattle are driven out to the fairs of the adjacent country. It is about 16 miles in length by 7 in breadth, and is densely inhabited by a primitive race of Mac Gaurans and Dolans, who intermarry and observe some peculiar customs; they elect their own king and queen from the ancient race of the Mae Gaurans, to whom they pay implicit obedience. Tilling the land and attending the cattle constitute their sole occupation; potatoes and milk, with, sometimes, oaten bread, their chief food; and the want of a road by which the produce of the district might be taken to the neighbouring markets operates as a discouragement to industry and an incentive to the illicit application of their surplus corn. Wheat might be advantageously cultivated in most of the southern parts of the county, by draining and properly ploughing the land; a great defect consists in not ploughing sufficiently deep, from which cause the grain receives but little nourishment, and the land soon becomes exhausted, and is allowed to recover its productiveness by natural means. Hay seeds are scarcely ever sown. The farms are mostly small; and in many parts the farmer has looms in his house for weaving linen, on which he mainly depends for support, and hence neglects his land. Weaving, however, has of late somewhat declined, but tillage has not improved in proportion. Barley is sometimes sown, and the crop is generally good. In consequence of the system here. practised of shallow ploughing and the unchecked growth of weeds, flax does not flourish in this so well as in some of the other northern counties, but it is still an amply remunerative crop. The fences in most parts are bad, consisting chiefly of a slight ridge of earth loosely thrown up. Draining and irrigation are wholly unpractised, although the country offers great facility for both; the gentle elevations are generally dry, and afford, beneath the surface, stones for draining; and the low grounds abound with springs, whose waters might be applied to the beneficial purposes of irrigation. Large allotments in the occupation of one individual are found only in the mountainous districts, and are applied to the grazing of young cattle during the summer months.

In the demesnes of the gentry some sheep are fattened; but there are no good sheepwalks of any extent, except in the neighbourhood of Cavan, which district, indeed, is so superior to any other part of the county for fattening, that oxen are fed to as great size as in any part of Ireland. Dairy farms are by no means numerous, although the butter of Cavan is equal to that of any other part of the kingdom. The breed of cattle varies in almost every barony: that best adapted to the soil is a cross between the Durham and the Kerry, but the long-horned attains the greatest size. In the mountain districts the Kerry cow is the favourite; and in the lower or central parts, around Cavan, are some very fine Durham cattle and good crosses with the Dutch. The sheep are mostly a cross between the New Leicester and the old sheep of the country; the fleece, though mostly light, is good, and the mutton of excellent flavour. The horses are a light, hardy, active breed, well adapted to the country. The breed of pigs has been much improved, and although they do not attain a large size, they are profitable and readily fatten. Lime is the general manure, although in some parts the farmer has to draw it many miles; and calcareous sand and gravel, procured from the escars in the baronies of Tullaghonoho and Loughtee, are conveyed for that use to every part of the county where the roads permit, and sometimes even into the hilly districts, by means of two boxes, called "bardocs," slung across the back of a horse, which is the only means of conveyance the inhabitants of those parts possess. The woods were formerly very considerable, and the timber of uncommon size, as is evinced by the immense trees found in the bogs; but

demesne grounds only are now distinguished by this valuable ornament. There are, however, numerous and extensive plantations in several parts, which in a few years will greatly enrich the scenery, particulary around the lakes of Ramor and Shellin, also near Stradone, Ballyhaise, Ballymacue, Fort Frederic, Farnham, Killesandra, and other places. The county contains bogs of sufficient extent for supplying its own fuel, and of a depth every where varying, but generally extremely great: they commonly lie favourably for draining, and the peat yields the strong red ashes which form an excellent manure. There is likewise a small proportion of moor, having a boggy surface, and resting on partial argillaceous strata: in these a marl, highly calcareous and easily raised, most commonly abounds. The fuel in universal use is peat.

The minerals are iron, lead, silver, coal, ochres, marl, fullers' earth, potters' clay, brick clay, manganese, sulphur, and a species of jasper. Limestone and various kinds of good building stone are also procured, especially in the north-western extremity of the county, which comprises the eastern part of the great Connaught coal field. A very valuable white freestone, soft to work but exceedingly durable, is found near Ballyconnell and at Lart, one mile from Cavan. The substratum around the former place is mostly mountain limestone, which dips rapidly to the west, and appears to pass under the Slieve Russell range of mountains, which are composed of the new red sandstone formation, with some curious amalgamations of greenstone. To the west of Swanlinbar rises the Bealbally mountains, through which is the Gap of Beal, the only entrance to Glangavlin; and beyond, at the furthest extremity of the county, is Lurganculliagh, forming the boundary between Ulster and Connaught. The base of this mountain range is clay-slate; the upper part consists entirely of sandstone, and iiear the summit is a stratum of mountain coal, ten feet thick, in the centre of which is a vein of remarkably good coal, but only about eight inches in thickness. The coal is visible on the eastern face of the mountain, at Meneack, in this county, where some trifling workings have been made, to which there is not even a practicable road; its superficial extent is supposed to be about 600 acres. The sandstone of these mountains, in many parts, forms perpendicular cliffs of great height; and the summit of Cuilagh, which is entirely composed of it, resembles an immense pavement, traversed in every direction by great fissures. Frequently, at the distance of from 80 to 100 yards from the edge of the precipice, are huge chasms, from twelve to twenty feet wide, extending from the surface of the mountain to the bottom of the sandstone. Some of the calcareous hills to the west of the valley of Swanlinbar rise to a height of 1500 feet, and are overspread with large rolled masses of sandstone, so as to make the entire elevation appear at first sight as if composed of the same. Iron ore abounds among the mountains of this part of the county, and was formerly worked. A lead mine was worked some years ago near Cootehill, and lead and silver ore are found in the stream descending from the mountain of Ortnacullagh, near Ballyconnell, In the district of Glan is found pure native sulphur in great quantities, particularly near Legnagrove and Dowra; and fullers' earth and pipe clay of superior quality exist in many parts. Proceeding towards the Fermanagh mountains, beautiful white and red transparent spars are found within a spade's depth of the surface; and here are two quarries of rough slate. Potters' clay, in this part of the county, occurs in every townland, and some of it is of the best and purest kind; patches of brick clay of the most durable quality are also common.

The chief manufacture is that of linen, upon which the prosperity of the inhabitants entirely depends, as it is carried on in almost every family. The average quantity of linen annually manufactured, and sold in the county, was estimated, at the commencement of the present century, to amount in value to £70,000; and pieces to the value of above £20,000 more are carried to markets beyond its limits. The number of bleaching establishments at the same period was twelve, in which about 91,000 pieces were annually finished. The quantity made at present is much greater, but the article is considerably reduced in price. Some of the bleach-greens are out of work, but, from the improvement of the process, a far greater number of webs is now bleached than was formerly; in 1835, nearly 150,000 pieces were finished, mostly for the English market. These establishments, around which improvements are being made every year, and which diffuse employment and comfort among a numerous population, are principally in the neighbourhoods of Cootehill, Tacken, Cloggy, Bailieborough, Scrabby, and Killiwilly. Frieze is made for home use, especially in the thinly peopled barony of Tullaghagh. The commerce of the county is limited and of little variety: its markets are remarkable only for the sale of yarn, flax, and brown linen; the principal are those of Cootehill and Killesandra.

The chief river is the Erne, which has its source in Lough Granny, near the foot of Bruce hill, on the south-western confines of the county, whence it pursues a northern course into Lough Oughter, and hence winds in the same direction by Belturbet into Lough Erne, which, at its head, forms the northern limit of the county. In most other parts the waters consisting of numerous lakes and their connecting streams, are with few exceptions tributary to the Erne. The Shannon has its source in a very copious spring, called the Shannon Pot, at the foot of the Cuilagh mountain in Glangavlin, in the townland of Derrylaghan, four miles south of the mountain road leading from Enniskillen to Manor-Hamilton, and nine miles north of Lough Allen: from this place to Kerry Head, where it falls into the sea, it pursues a course of 243 miles, of which it is navigable 234 miles, and during that distance has a fall of not. more than 148 feet. The Blackwater has its source in a lake at Bailieborough Castle, and flows on by Virginia into Lough Ramor, whence it enters the county of Meath, and becomes a tributary to the Boyne. A line of artificial navigation has been proposed from Belturbet by Cootehill into the county of Monaghan. The old lines of roads are injudiciously formed, so as to encounter the most formidable hills. Although the new lines are made to wind through the valleys, yet, with the exception of those very recently made, they are of inferior construction. The material formerly used was clay-slate, which pulverised in a short time; but, since the recent grand jury act came into operation, the newest lines have been well laid out, and the only material now used is limestone or greenstone. Several new and important lines have been formed, and others are in progress or contemplated: among the roads which promise to be of the greatest advantage are those through the wild district of Glangavlin; they are all made and kept in repair by grand jury presentments.

The remains of antiquity are comparatively few and uninteresting. The most common are cairns and raths, of which the latter are particularly numerous in the north-eastern part of the county, and near Kingscourt: in one at Rathkenny, near Cootehill, was found a considerable treasure, together with a gold fibula. There are remains of a round tower of inferior size at Druinlaiie. The number of abbeys and priories was eight, the remains of none of which, except that of the Holy Trinity, now exist, so that their sites can only be conjectured. Few also of the numerous castles remain, and all, except that of Cloughoughter, are very small. Though there are many good residences surrounded with ornamented demesnes, the seats of the nobility and gentry are not distinguished by any character of magnificence; they are noticed under the heads of the parishes in which they are respectively situated. The more substantial farmers have good family houses; but the dwellings of the peasantry are extremely poor, and their food consists almost entirely of oatmeal, milk, and potatoes. The English language is generally spoken, except in the mountain districts towards the north and west, and even there it is spoken by the younger part of the population, but the aged people all speak Irish, particularly in the district of Glan. With regard to fish, the lakes afford an abundance of pike, eels, and trout; and cod, salmon, and herrings, are brought in abundance by hawkers. The chief natural curiosities are the mineral springs, of which the most remarkable are those at Swanlinbar and Derrylyster, the waters of which are alterative and diaphoretic; those at Legnagrove and Dowra, containing sulphur and purging salt, and used in nervous diseases; the well at Owen Breun, which has similar medicinal properties; and the purgative and diuretic waters of Carrickmore, which are impregnated with fixed air and fossil alkali. The mineral properties of a pool in the mountains of Loughlinlea, between Bailieborough and Kingscourt, are also very remarkable. In 1617, Sir Oliver Lambart was created baron of Cavan, and this title was raised to an earldom in favour of his son Charles, by whose lineal descendants it is still enjoyed.

ANNAGELIFFE, a parish, in the barony of UPPER LOUGHTEE, county of CAVAN, and province of ULSTER, 1 mile (N.E. by E.) from Cavan, on the road from that place to Virginia; containing 4341 inhabitants. It comprises, according to the Ordnance survey, $8260\frac{1}{4}$ statute acres, of which 5096 are applotted under the tithe act. The living is a vicarage, in the diocese of Kilmore, forming, with that of Urney, the union of Urney and Annageliffe, in the patronage of the Bishop; the rectory is impropriate in the Representatives of Richard, Earl of Westmeath. The tithes amount to £217.16.11$\frac{1}{2}$, of which £62.2.2$\frac{1}{2}$ is payable to the impropriator, and £155.14.9 to the vicar. In the R.C. divisions this parish forms part of the union or district of Urney, or, as it is more commonly called, Cavan: the chapel is a large building, situated at Stragolla. There are a parochial school, and a school on the townland of Curlurgan; also four hedge schools.

ANNAGH, or BELTURBET, a parish, partly in the barony of LOWER LOUGHTEE, but chiefly in that of TULLAGHGARVEY, county of CAVAN, and province of ULSTER, on the road from Ballyconnell to Cavan; containing, with the greater part of the market and post-town of Belturbet, 12,269 inhabitants. It comprises, according to the Ordnance survey, 19,145$\frac{1}{4}$ statute acres, of which 12,340 are in Tullaghgarvey; about 16,000 are arable and pasture, 2000 are bog and waste, 300 are woodland, and 200 are common: of its entire area, 14,936 acres are applotted under the tithe act. The principal seats are Castle Saunderson, the residence of A. Saunderson, Esq.; Erne Hill, of G. M. Knipe, Esq.; Clover Hill, of J. Saunderson, Esq.; and Red Hill, of – White, Esq. The living is a rectory and vicarage, in the diocese of Kilmore, and in the patronage of Lord Farnham: the tithes amount to £384.4.7$\frac{1}{2}$. The church is a handsome edifice, for the repairs and enlargement of which the late Board of First Fruits granted £2600, in 1812 and 1814; and the Ecclesiastical Commissioners have recently granted £112 for its further repair. The glebe-house was purchased by aid of a loan of £844, in 1810, from the same Board; the glebe comprises 400 acres. In 1813, forty-seven townlands of the parish were disunited, to form the perpetual cure of Killoughter. This parish is divided into the two R.C. districts of Annagh West and Annagh East, or Killoughter, the former containing a chapel at Drumalee, and the latter at Red Hill. There are two places of worship for Wesleyan Methodists, one of which belongs to the Primitive class. A school is supported by the Trustees of Erasmus Smith's charity; and there are schools at Drumlaney, Killoughter, and Drumloor; also an infants' and two other schools, besides six private pay schools. The ruins of the old church yet exist. – See BELTURBET.

ARVAGH, a market and post-town, and a parish, in the barony of TULLOGHONOHO, county of CAVAN, and province of ULSTER, 10$\frac{3}{4}$ miles (S.W.) from Cavan, and, by way of that town, 66 miles (N.W. by W.) from Dublin; containing 4580 inhabitants, of which number, 422 are in the town. This parish is situated on the road from Killesandra to Scrabby, near the point of junction of the three counties of Cavan, Leitrim, and Longford, and was

formed by the disunion of thirty townlands from the parish of Killesandra. Near the town is the lake of Scraba, one of the sources of the river Erne, which, with the lakes through which it runs, is commonly called in its entire extent Lough Erne. The market is on Friday, and is well supplied with provisions: the market-house, situated in the centre of the town, was built by the Earl of Gosford, to whom the town belongs. Fairs are held on Jan. 28th, March 25th, April 1st, May 2nd, June 8th, Aug. 8th Sept. 23rd, Nov. 1st, and Dec. 23rd. Here is a station of the constabulary police. The living is a perpetual cure, in the diocese of Kilmore, and in the patronage of the Vicar of Killesandra: the perpetual curate has a fixed income of £75 per annum late currency, of which £50 is paid by the incumbent of Killesandra, and £25 from the funds of the Ecclesiastical Commissioners. The church was built by aid of a gift of £900 and a loan of £100, in 1819, from the late Board of First Fruits. The glebe-house is small but conveniently built; and the glebe comprises 21 acres. In the R.C. divisions this parish remains included in the union or district of Killesandra, and has a chapel, situated at Corronee. There is a place of worship for Wesleyan methodists. There are two public schools, one in the town and the other at Corronary, and other private and Sunday schools in the parish.

ASHFIELD, a parish, in the barony of TULLAGHGARVEY, county of CAVAN, and province of ULSTER $\frac{1}{2}$ a mile (S.W.) from Cootehill, on the road to Belturbet; containing 3013 inhabitants. It formerly constituted part of the parish of Killersherdiny, from which it was separated in 1799; and comprises 4426 acres, as applotted under the tithe act, and valued at. about £4006 per annum. The land is in general good, and there is very little waste; the system of agriculture is slowly improving. The manufacture of linen for broad sheeting is carried on to a considerable extent. Ashfield Lodge, the seat of Col. Clements, is beautifully situated on an eminence within view of the church, beneath which swiftly flows the Cootehill river, a tributary to Lough Erne, and is surrounded with extensive plantations. Fort Henry, formerly a seat of the Clements family, is now that of the Rev. J. Thompson. The living is a perpetual curacy, in the diocese of Kilmore, and in the patronage of the Vicar of Killersherdiny, with which parish the tithes are included and are payable to the vicar the perpetual curate has a fixed annual income of £100, of which £50 is payable by the Ecclesiastical Commissioners. The church is a handsome edifice, with a lofty spire, occupying a very elevated site; it was built by aid of a gift of £500 from the late Board of First Fruits, in 1795, and, in 1818, the Board also granted £500, of which one half was a gift and the other a loan. The glebe-house was built by a gift of £450 and a loan of £50 from the same Board, in 1812; the glebe comprises 20 acres. In the R.C. divisions this parish forms part of the union or district of Killersherdiny: the chapel is situated at Drummurry. Besides the parochial school, there is one at Doohurrick under the patronage of Mrs. Glements; also three private pay schools.

BAILIEBOROUGH, or MOYBOLOGUE, a market and post-town, and a parish, partly in the barony of LOWER KELLS, county of MEATH, and province of LEINSTER, and partly in that of CASTLERAHAN, but chiefly in that of CLONKEE, county of CAVAN, and province of ULSTER, $11\frac{1}{2}$ miles (N.W. by N.) from Kells, and $42\frac{1}{4}$ miles (N.W.) from Dublin; containing 10,480 inhabitants, of which number, 1085 are in the town. This town is situated on the road from Cootehill to Kells, and consists of only one street, containing 165 houses. The market is the largest in the county, and is on Monday. Fairs are held on Feb. 17th, May 17th, June 15th, Aug. 14th, Oct. 14th, and Nov. 17th. The Hilary and Midsummer general quarter sessions are held here: the court-house was enlarged and improved in 1834. The bridewell was built in that year, and contains five cells and two yards, with separate day-rooms and yards for female prisoners. A manorial court is held yearly; and here is a station of the constabulary police.

In the incumbent's title this parish is denominated Moybologue, otherwise Bailieborough: it was formed by act of council in 1778, by separating from the parish of Killan, now called Shercock, 29 townlands, including the town of Bailieborough, and uniting them to the parish of Moybologue. It comprises 17,152 statute acres, as applotted under the tithe act. The land is generally of good quality: that part of the parish which is in the county of Meath is cultivated for all kinds of grain. Several small bogs are scattered over its surface, which are diminishing in extent either by draining or digging for fuel. There are some quarries of an inferior kind of stone, chiefly used for building, and about a mile from the town is an extensive bleach-green, with a comfortable house and small demesne, the residence of W. Spear, Esq. Bailieborough Castle, the seat of Sir Wm. Young, Bart., is situated in a fine demesne, and occupies the site of an ancient fortress described in Pynnar's Survey, under the head of Tonregie, as a vaulted castle, with a bawn 90 feet square, and two flanking towers, attached to which were 1000 acres of land: this ancient castle remained standing till within a few years, when it was pulled down to make room for additions and improvements in the present house. Near the town also are Bexcourt, the seat of the Rev. E. Mahafty; and the glebe-house, the residence of the Rev. J. Gumley. The living is a united rectory and vicarage, in the diocese of Kilmore, and in the patronage of the Bishop. The tithes amount to £553.1.0, of which £314.1.0 is payable by the Moybologue portion of the parish, and £239 by the townlands added to it. The old church being a dilapidated building, a new one is in course of erection. The glebe-house was built by a gift of £100 and a loan of £900, in 1811, from the late Board of First Fruits; the glebe consists of two farms near the church, comprising 117 acres, and 43 acres of bog. In the R.C. divisions the parish is partly in the union or district of Killan or Shercock, and partly in that of Kilmainham and Tivorcher: the chapel of the former is situated in the town of Bailieborough; and that of the latter, which is in the county and diocese of Meath, at Tivorcher.

There are two meeting-houses for Presbyterians; one in connection with the Synod of Ulster, of the third class; and the other in connection with the Seceding Synod, of the first class. The Wesleyan Methodists have also a place of worship, in which divine service is performed every alternate Sunday. The parochial school, at Lisnalea, is supported by the incumbent; and there are three other public schools, in which 180 boys and 110 girls are taught, and a school is in progress at Kellan. There are 13 private schools, in which are about 500 boys and 250 girls. A dispensary was established in 1822.

BALLINAGH, a market-town, partly in the parish of BALLINTEMPLE, but chiefly in that of KILMORE, barony of CLONMAHON, county of CAVAN, and province of ULSTER, 4 miles (S.W.) from Cavan, on the road to Granard; containing 702 inhabitants. This town was entirely destroyed by fire in a disturbance which took place in 1794; it consists at present of two streets crossing each other at right angles, and in 1831 contained 135 houses, the greater part of which are thatched, and of which three only are in the parish of Ballintemple. The market is on Saturday, and is held in a neat plain market-house. Fairs are held on March 31st, June 6th, August 5th, Oct. 3rd, and Dec. 21st. This is a station of the constabulary police; and petty sessions are held every alternate Wednesday. There is a R.C. chapel; also a good slated school-house, containing on the ground floor a school-room for boys, and on the upper story, one for girls. – See KILMORE.

BALLINTEMPLE, a parish, in the barony of CLONMAHON, county of CAVAN, and province of ULSTER, $6\frac{3}{4}$ miles (S. by W.) from Cavan, containing, with part of the town of Ballinagh, 4982 inhabitants. This parish is situated on the road from Virginia to Killyshandra, and comprises, according to the Ordnance survey, including $54\frac{1}{4}$ under water, $10,657\frac{3}{4}$ statute acres, of which 8074 are applotted under the tithe act. It is a vicarage, in the diocese of Kilmore, and forms part of the union and corps of the deanery of Kilmore; the rectory is impropriate in the representatives of Richard, Earl of Westmeath. The tithes amount to £259, of which £104 is payable to the impropriators, and the remainder to the vicar. The church was erected in 1821 by aid of a loan of £1200 from the late Board of First Fruits. The glebe comprises 103a. 1r. 29p. of profitable land, valued at £87.13.10 per annum. The R.C. parish is co-extensive with that of the Established Church; there are three chapels, called respectively the upper and lower chapels and the chapel of ease. The parochial school and two others afford instruction to about 180 boys and 60 girls; and there are also three private pay schools, in which are about 170 boys and 50 girls. – See BALLINAGH.

BALLYCONNELL, a market and post-town, in the parish of TOMREGAN, barony of TULLAGHAGH, county of CAVAN, and province of ULSTER, $12\frac{1}{2}$ miles (N.W. by W.) from Cavan, and 68 miles (N.W. by W.) from Dublin; containing 453 inhabitants. This place had its origin in the English settlement in the time of Jas. I, when Capt. Culme and Walter Talbot received 1500 acres, on which, at the time of Pynnar's survey in 1619, was a strong bawn 100 feet square and 12 feet high, with two flanking towers and a strong castle, three stories high, the whole occupying a site well adapted for the defence of the surrounding country. The town is situated on the road from Belturbet to Swanlinbar, and consists of two streets, together containing about 80 houses. The market is on Friday, and is well supplied with corn and provisions; and fairs are held on Jan. 3rd, Feb. 13th, March 17th, April 18th, May 16th, June 24th, July 29th, Aug. 29th, Sept. 26th, Oct. 25th, and Dec. 3rd, chiefly for cattle, pigs, and corn. It is a constabulary police station; the Easter and October sessions for the county are held here, and petty sessions every alternate Monday. The court-house is a handsome stone building; and attached to it is a bridewell containing three cells, with separate day-rooms and airing-yards for male and female prisoners. Here is the parish church, which has been lately repaired by a grant of £106 from the Ecclesiastical Commissioners. A schoolhouse has been built at an expense of £227, defrayed partly by the incumbent, partly by the proprietor of the Ballyconnell estate, and partly by Government. Ballyconnell house, the residence of J. Enery, Esq., is beautifully situated in a fine demesne on the Woodford river, which winds through the extensive and well-wooded grounds in its course to Lake Annagh and Lough Erne the house was erected in 1764, by the late G. Montgomery, Esq., on the site of the castle of Ballyconnell, which was entirely destroyed by an accidental fire. There is a chalybeate spring in the demesne.

BALLYHAISE a market and post-town, in the parish of CASTLETERRA, barony of UPPER LOUGHTEE, county of CAVAN, and province of ULSTER, 3½ miles (N.W.) from Cavan, and 59 miles (N.W.) from Dublin, on the road from Cavan to Cootehill; containing 142 houses and 761 inhabitants. Ballyhaise House, the seat of W. Humphreys, Esq., is a spacious mansion, with an elevated front curiously ornamented with arches. The linen trade was formerly carried on here to a very considerable extent, but is now extinct. There is a tanyard, employing 7 or 8 persons; and near the town are some extensive flour and oatmeal-mills. The market is on Saturday; and fairs are held on the 1st of March, April 11th, May 18th, June 20th July 3th, Aug. 30th, Oct. 3rd, Nov. 6th, and Dec. 13th, chiefly for horses, cattle, and pigs. The market-house is an arched edifice built of brick, and of singular appearance. Here is a station of the constabulary police. The parochial church, a remarkably neat edifice in excellent repair, is situated just without the town; and there is also a R.C. chapel.

BALLYJAMESDUFF, a market and post-town, and a district parish, in the barony of CASTLERAHAN, county of CAVAN, and province of ULSTER, 8½ miles (S.E.) from Cavan, and 44¾ miles (N.W. by W.) from Dublin; containing 3227 inhabitants, of which number, 863 are in the town. The town is situated on the old mail coach road from Virginia to Cavan, and consists of five streets,

containing together 150 houses. The market is on Tuesday, and is amply supplied; and fairs are held on Feb. 4th, March 8th, April 16th, May 7th, June 10th, July 17th, Aug. 15th, Sept. 2nd, Oct. 26th, Nov. 29th, and Dec. 23rd. Here is a constabulary police station, and petty sessions are held. The parish was created in 1831, by disuniting nine townlands from the parish of Castleraghan five from that of Denn, two from Lurgan, and four from the parish of Kildrumferton. The living is a perpetual curacy, in the diocese of Kilmore, and in the patronage of the several Incumbents of the above parishes, who present in rotation: the stipend of the perpetual curate is £80 per annum, towards which £30 is contributed by the incumbent of Castleraghan, £20 by the incumbent of Kildrumferton, and £15 each by the incumbents of Denn and Lurgan. The church is a plain edifice, erected in 1834 by aid of a grant of £900 from the Ecclesiastical Commissioners, and subscriptions amounting to £200. In the R.C. divisions the parish forms part of the union or district of Castleraghan and Munterconnaught; the chapel is a spacious building. There is a place of worship for Presbyterians in connection with the Synod of Ulster, and of the third class; also two for Wesleyan Methodists. A school at Remonan is supported by Lord Farnham, and another at Ballyjamesduff is aided by private subscriptions: about 140 boys and 150 girls are instructed in these schools; and there are three pay schools, situated respectively at Rawson, Lackenmore, and Lackenduff, in which are about 180 boys and 90 girls.

BALLYMACHUGH, a parish, in the barony of CLONMAHON, county of CAVAN, and province of ULSTER, 6¼ miles (E.N.E.) from Granard; containing 3428 inhabitants. This parish is situated on the borders of Lough Sheelan, on the confines of the counties of Longford and Meath, and comprises, according to the Ordnance survey, 7728½ statute acres, of which 1827¾ are water. The system of agriculture is improving; oats and potatoes are the principal crops. The gentlemen's seats are Arley Cottage, that of Lord Farnham, and Fortland, of W. Gosling, Esq. Petty sessions for the district are held in the school-house every third Saturday. It is a vicarage, in the diocese of Ardagh, and is part of the union of Granard; the rectory is impropriate in the Misses Blundell the tithes amount to £265.16.11, of which £118.3.1 is payable to the impropriators, and £147.13.10 to the vicar. The church, a plain building, has been recently enlarged at an expense of £800. The glebe comprises 11 acres, valued at £1.16.0 per acre. The R.C. parish is co-extensive with that of the Established Church; the chapel is a large plain building recently erected. The parochial school for boys and girls is aided by donations from Lord Farnham and the incumbent; at Ballynany there is a school, and one at Orley is supported by Lord Farnham, by whom the school-house was built; in these schools are about 280 boys and 230 girls. There is also a Sunday school at Orley. A dispensary is also supported in the customary manner. On an island in the lake are the ruins of Crover castle, and on another, those of an old church covered with ivy.

BALLYMAGAURAN, a village, in the parish of TEMPLEPORT, barony of TALLAGHAGH, county of CAVAN, and province of ULSTER, 4 miles (N.E.) from Ballinamore, on the road to Killesandra; containing 20 houses and 89 inhabitants. Fairs are held on May 23rd, Aug. 12th, and Nov. 23rd, of which the last is a good fair for cattle. Some remains of the old castle, which was destroyed by Cromwell, yet exist. – See TEMPLEPORT.

BELTURBET, an incorporated market and post-town, partly in the parish of DRUMLANE, but chiefly in that of ANNAGH, barony of LOWER LOUGHTEE, county of CAVAN, and province of ULSTER, 12 miles (N.N.W.) from Cavan, and 67 (N.W.) from Dublin; containing 2026 inhabitants. It is pleasantly situated on the river Erne, on the road from Cavan to Ballyconnell, and owes its origin to the Lanesborough family, whose patronage has also contributed materially to its prosperity. In 1610, certain conditions were proposed by the lords of the council in England to Sir Stephen Butler, of Bealetirbirt, Knt., for establishing a market here and erecting a corporation; and in 1613 it received its first charter, whereby the king, on petition of the inhabitants, and for the purpose of furthering the plantation of Ulster, incorporated the village and its precincts into a borough. By an indenture in 1618 Sir Stephen Butler, in fulfilment of the conditions of the lords of the council, granted and confirmed to the corporation certain parcels of land amounting altogether to 284 acres, also a weekly market and two annual fairs, and a weekly court of record, the whole to be held of him or his successors in the fee, in fee-farm for ever, at the rent of 30s. yearly. This indenture contains a covenant on the part of the corporation that all the inhabitants should be ready at all times to be mustered and trained to arms whenever required by Sir Stephen, or his heirs or assigns, or by the Muster-master General of Ulster, or any of the king's officers duly authorised; and that they should grind their corn at Sir Stephen's mill. By Pynnar's survey, made in 1619, it appears that the newly erected houses were built of cage work, and all inhabited by English tradesmen, who had each a garden, four acres of land, and commonage for a certain number of cows and horses. In 1690, the town, being garrisoned by a body of the forces of Jas. II, was taken by surprise by the Enniskilleners, who fortified it for their own party. It contains several neat houses, but the greater number are indifferently built and thatched. The wide expanse of Lough Erne to the north, and the varied character of the surrounding scenery, impart to the environs an interesting and highly picturesque appearance. A handsome bridge of three arches is in course of erection over the Erne, for which the Board of Works has consented to grant a loan of £1700, and has already advanced £500 on account. There is a cavalry barrack for 7 officers, 156 non-commissioned officers and men, and 101 horses. A very extensive distillery belonging to Messrs. Dickson, Dunlop, and Co., was erected in 1825 at an expense of £21,000, and enlarged and improved in 1830, at an additional cost of £6000: it is wrought by never-failing water power, and the quantity of whiskey made annually is from 90,000 to 100,000 gallons; about 100 persons are usually employed. There are also some malting establishments. The river Erne opens a communication through Lough Fine to within three miles of Ballyshannon; but in dry weather the navigation is interrupted by shoals, which might be removed, to the great improvement of the trade of the town. The market is on Thursday, and is principally for butter, oatmeal, potatoes, and yarn, of which last there is a good supply. Fairs are held on Ash-Wednesday, Sept. 4th, and the first Thursday in every other month. Here is a station of the constabulary police.

The charter of Jas. I, granted in 1613, after incorporating the inhabitants, empowered them to return two representatives to the Irish parliament and to hold a court of record every Tuesday, before the provost, with jurisdiction to the extent of five marks, besides conferring other privileges, which were confirmed by the indenture made between Sir Stephen Butler and the corporation, by which the jurisdiction of the court of record in all actions, personal or mixed, was extended to £6.13.4, and it was ordered to be held before the bailiff and stewards of the corporation every Saturday. The corporation is styled "the Provost, Burgesses, Freemen, and Inhabitants of the borough of Belturbet," which in some degree differs from the style prescribed by the charter of Jas. I and the indenture. The officers named in the charter are a provost, twelve free burgesses, and two serjeants-at-mace; the other officers are a treasurer, town-clerk, herd, marshal-keeper or corporation gaoler, pound-keeper, foreman of the market jury, and weigh-master. The provost is by the charter to be elected by the provost and free burgesses from among the latter annually on the 24th of June, and sworn in upon Sept. 29th. The burgesses are chosen from among the inhabitants by the provost and free burgesses, and by the usage of the corporation must be freemen prior to their election; there are at present only nine or ten, all non-resident, and they were formerly entitled to certain privileges and emoluments now lost. No recognised right to the freedom at present exists, nor does it appear that any freemen have been admitted by the provost and burgesses for many years, except for the purpose of qualifying persons immediately after elected burgesses. The town-clerk and other officers of the corporation, whose offices have not fallen into desuetude, are appointed by the provost. The municipal affairs are regulated by the inhabitants assembled by the provost at what are termed "Town Courts," which are held before the provost generally eight or ten times in the year, and in which are made by-laws for the government of the town, the corporation property is regulated, and complaints of trespass respecting commonage and upon the private lands within the district are referred for investigation and adjustment to the market jury. This jury consists of not less than twelve members appointed from the inhabitants by the provost, and sworn in at the town court; its duties are not only to inspect the meat brought to market, of which the foreman is appointed

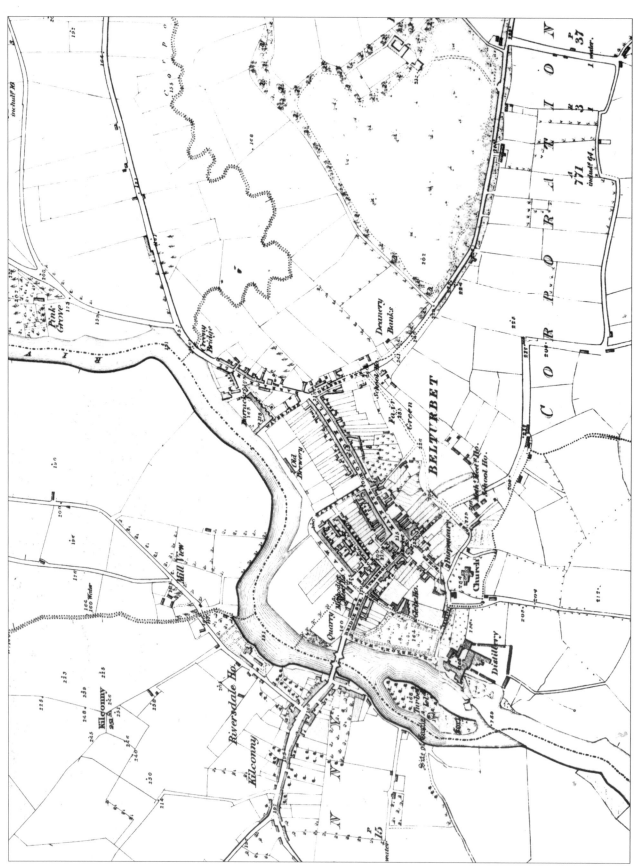

Belturbet. Part of the O.S. map of Co. Monaghan, sheet 15, published 1837 (reproduced at 140%).

clerk by the provost, but to superintend the property of the corporation generally, forming, in fact, a court of arbitration, and exercising a jurisdiction highly beneficial to the inhabitants.

The borough returned two members to the Irish parliament until the Union, when the £15,000 awarded as compensation for the abolition of its franchise was paid to Armar, Earl of Belmore, who had a short time previously purchased the borough for that amount from the Earl of Lanesborough. It comprises the town and precincts, forming a district termed "the corporation," the boundaries of which are clearly defined. The provost is chief magistrate, and is by usage the first magistrate named upon the commission in the county, and next in rank to the lieutenant; he formerly sat with the judges at the county assizes, but has not for many years exercised this privilege. The court of record, in which he presided, has fallen into disuse for nearly 30 years. Petty sessions are held by the county magistrates every Saturday in the market-house, of which the upper part is appropriated to that use and the lower to the purpose of the market. Beneath this building was the corporation gaol, a damp and unhealthy prison, which was prohibited to be used as a place of confinement after the passing of the act of the 7th of Geo. IV, c. 74. The commons in possession of the corporation comprise about 120 acres; the right of commonage enjoyed by the inhabitants is regulated by the possession of the whole or a portion of a homestead, to which also a proportionate quantity of bog is annexed: these homesteads include certain portions of the front of streets, defined and granted to individuals on the original foundation of the town, and subsequently divided among different tenants, and the right to commonage was by usage similarly apportioned. The lands allotted for the private occupation of the burgesses are said to have been granted to them and their heirs, instead of their successors, and, tinder the name of "burgess acres," are divided and separately enclosed as private properties. The only revenue which the corporation now possesses is derivable from some nominal reservations on fee-farm grants made, within the last few years, of small portions of the commons, the fines on which, amounting to £175, were applied to the repairs of the market-house.

The parish church of Annagh, a neat edifice with a tower surmounted by a spire, is situated in the town it was rebuilt by a loan of £923 from the late Board of First Fruits in 1828, and of £800 in 1829. It is in contemplation to erect a handsome R.C. chapel. The parochial school for boys is on the foundation of Erasmus Smith, and was built on an acre of ground granted by the corporation, who also gave a site for the erection of a school for girls on the same establishment, which is supported by subscription; and there is an infants' school, also a dispensary. Six almshouses for poor widows were built on a site granted by the corporation in 1733, the inmates of which are supported by a legacy bequeathed by a Mr. Maunsell, of Dublin, and distributed by the rector. He also distributes the interest of

£100 paid by the Earl of Lanesborough's agent, £3 per ann. derived from a charity called Fellor's List, and £6 per ann. accruing from another charity; and there is a house in the town bequeathed by Benjamin Johnson for the benefit of the poor, and let for £1.16.11 per annum. In the churchyard are vestiges of a strong fortification enclosing an extensive area, with bastions and salient angles of great strength; about two miles distant are some venerable ecclesiastical ruins, with others at Clinosy; and in the vicinity are the remains of an ancient castle. – See ANNAGH and DRUMLANE.

BUTLERSBRIDGE, a village, in the parish of CASTLETERRA, barony of UPPER LOUGHTEE, county of CAVAN, and province of ULSTER, 3 miles (N.N.W.) from Cavan; containing about 40 houses and 211 inhabitants. It is pleasantly situated on the river Ballyhaise, and on the road from Cavan to Enniskillen, and has a fair on the second Monday in every month throughout the year. Here is a R.C. chapel of ease to those of Castleterra and Ballyhaise; and a daily penny post to Cavan and Belturbet has been established.

CASTLERAHAN, a parish, in the barony of CASTLERAHAN, county of CAVAN, and province of ULSTER; containing, with the post-town of Ballyjamesduff, 6960 inhabitants, This parish is situated on the road from Virginia to Mount-Nugent, and comprises, according to the Ordnance survey, 10,315 statute acres (including $102\frac{1}{2}$ in Lough Ramor), of which 9722 are applotted under the tithe act. Contiguous to the town is a small lake, near which a shaft was sunk some few years since, and indications of coal were discovered. The gentlemen's seats are Fort Frederick, the residence of R. Scott, Esq., and Mount Prospect, of T. Nugent, Esq. Since the census of 1831, nine townlands have been separated from this parish to form, with portions of other parishes, the district parish of Ballyjamesduff, which see. The living is a rectory and vicarage, in the diocese of Kilmore, and in the patronage of the Bishop: the tithes amount to £304.1.10$\frac{1}{2}$. The church, a small ancient building, is in very indifferent repair. The glebe-house, a handsome residence, was rebuilt in 1818, by aid of a gift of £100 and a loan of £1500 from the late Board of First Fruits: the glebe comprises 350 acres. In the R.C. divisions this parish is the head of a union or district, comprising also the parishes of Munterconnaught and Ballyjamesduff. The chapel, a large handsome edifice, erected in 1834, at an expense of £2000, is situated in the townland of Cormeen. There is a place of worship for Presbyterians in connection with the Synod of Ulster, of the third class. The parochial school is supported by subscription aided by an annual donation of £10 from the rector; a school at Clonkuffe has an endowment of two acres of land by the Bishop. and is aided by subscription; and there is a school at Ennagh, supported by Miss Sankee. In these schools about 160 boys and 60 girls are instructed; and there are four pay schools, in which are about 220 boys and 100 girls. Near Ballyjamesduff (which see) are two Danish raths.

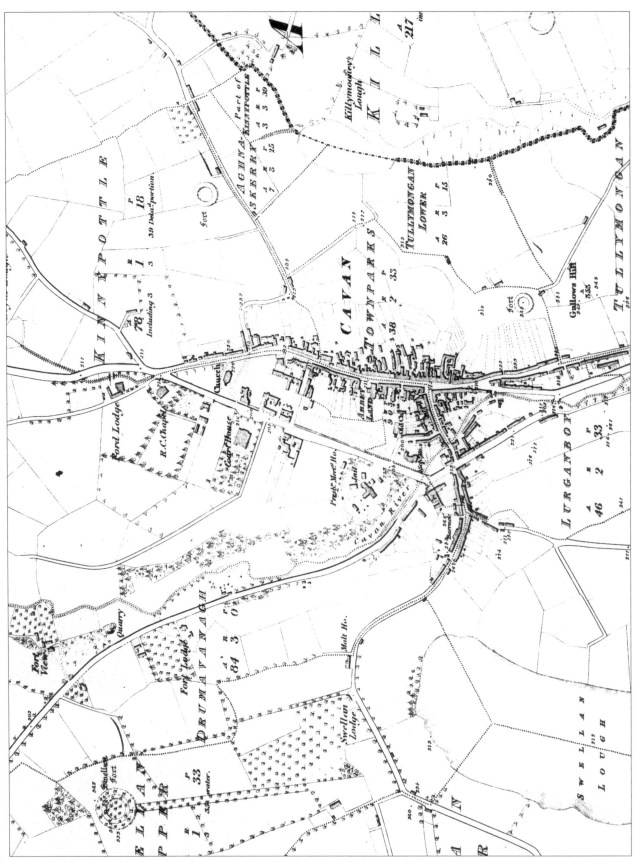

Cavan. Part of the O.S. map of Co. Monaghan, sheet 20, published 1837 (reproduced at 140%).

CASTLETERRA, a parish, in the barony of UPPER LOUGHTEE, county of CAVAN, and province of ULSTER; containing, with the post-town of Ballyhaise, 6502 inhabitants. This parish is situated on the road from Cavan to Cootehill, and comprises, according to the Ordnance survey, $9980^3/_4$ statute acres (including $151^1/_2$ under water), of which 9526 are applotted under the tithe act; about 900 acres are woodland, mountain, or bog, and the remainder is arable or pasture. There is an iron mine, which has never been worked; and a new road is being made through the parish from Ballyhaise to Cavan. The principal seats are Ballyhaise House, the residence of W. Humphreys, Esq.: Lisnagowan, of Mrs. Humphreys; and the glebe-house, of the Rev. G. Knox. The living is a rectory and vicarage, in the diocese of Kilmore, and in the patronage of the Bishop: the tithes amount to £288.10.0. The church is a handsome building, repaired in 1819 by aid of a loan of £1200 from the late Board of First Fruits. There is a glebe-house, with a glebe of 195 acres. The R.C. parish is co-extensive with that of the Established Church, and has chapels at Ballyhaise, Castleterra, and Butler's-bridge, of which Ballyhaise chapel, built in 1810, cost £400; and Castleterra, built in 1829 cost £650. The parochial school-house is built of stone, and cost £270, one-half of which was paid out of the lord-lieutenant's school fund, the other half by subscriptions. It is under the patronage of W. Humphreys, Esq., and is aided by an annual donation from the incumbent, who also partially maintains three other schools: there are national schools at Ballyhaise and Butlerstown. About 260 boys and 240 girls are educated in these schools; and about 60 boys and 100 girls are educated in private schools. In 1777, Brockhill Newburgh, Esq., bequeathed £10 annually, charged on his estate at Ballyhaise, for the repair of the church; also £10 annually out of the Redhills estate, for bread to be distributed weekly among the poor of the parish. About two miles from Ballyhaise there is a chalybeate spring. – See BALLYHAISE.

CAVAN, an incorporated market and post-town, (formerly a parliamentary borough) in the parish of URNEY, barony of UPPER LOUGHTEE, county of CAVAN (of which it is the chief town), and province of ULSTER, $25^1/_2$ miles (S.E. by S.) from Enniskillen, and 55 (N.W. by W.) from Dublin; containing 2931 inhabitants. This town was, from a period of remote antiquity, the seat of the O'Reillys, tanists of the district now forming the county to which it gives name, and who had a castle here, of which there are no other remains than some vaults and part of the foundation. A monastery for friars of the order of St. Dominick was founded here in 1300, and dedicated to the Blessed Virgin, by Giolla-Jisoa-Ruadh O'Reilly, dynast of Breffny; but about the year 1393, the monks were expelled by the same sept, and others of the Franciscan order substituted in their place. In 1468 the monastery, and Bally-Reilly, the castle above noticed, were burnt by the English under the Lord-Deputy Tiptoft, Earl of Worcester; but the former appears to have been restored previously to the year

1499, and to have been occupied by friars of the order of the Strict Observance. It was again reformed by John, son of Cahal O'Reilly, in 1502, and provincial chapters of the order were held in it in 1521, 1539, and 1556. Owen O'Nial, the celebrated general of the Irish army, who died by poison, as is supposed, at Cloughoughter, was buried in this abbey, in 1649. There are no remains of the establishment, which was commonly called Keadue; the tithes now belong to the Dean of Kilmore, and in his title are described as "the rectory of Keadue."

In the early part of the reign of Jas. I, the lord-deputy pitched his tent to the south of the town, which is described as being a very unimportant place, for the purpose of reducing this part of the country to the observance of English laws and customs. Under the partition of lands made pursuant to an inquisition as stated in the article on the county, ten poles were allotted to the town of Cavan, which the king proposed to incorporate; ten poles to the castle, and 14 to the maintenance of a free school to be erected in the town. In 1610, Jas. I granted the inhabitants a charter of incorporation, in the preamble of which it is stated that the town was the only place of trade in the county, and the only town where the justices could conveniently meet for their assize and gaol delivery, and that the inhabitants during the late insurrection, had supplied the garrison and performed good and acceptable service to Queen Elizabeth, from time to time, according to their best abilities. The commissioners for the plantation of Ulster reserved and set out eight poles of land, adjoining the town, to be granted to the new corporation; and the charter constituted the town and all lands within the compass of one mile from the stone house or castle in which Walter Bradie then dwelt, with the exception of the castle of "the Cavan," or O'Reilly's castle, and the two poles of land called Rosgolyan, the Borough of Cavan. This place was the scene of some skirmishing in the time of Cromwell, and till very lately a house was standing in the principal street, in which he is said to have resided for several weeks. In 1690, some of the forces of Jas. II, having assembled here for the purpose of attacking Belturbet, the Enniskilleners, under their victorious leader Wolsey, marched hither with a view to take them by surprise; but the Duke of Berwick having arrived with a considerable reinforcement, they had, with a force of only 1000 men, to contend with 4000 of the enemy. Wolsey, however, attacking them with spirit, the native forces of James fled at the first onset, when the Enniskilleners burst into the town and began to plunder it; those who had fled to the fort now sallied out to renew the engagement. Wolsey, as the only means of recalling his men, set fire to the town, and having rallied his forces, completed the victory with great slaughter. Human bones have been found in great numbers on the side of the hill overhanging the town, where the battle took place.

The town is situated on the road from Dublin to Enniskillen, and consists of several streets, of which the principal contains some well-built houses; there are infantry barracks capable of accommodating six officers and 130 non-commissioned officers and privates. A large gardens handsomely laid out in walks and planted, was left by the will of the late Lady Farnham, under certain restrictions, as a promenade for the inhabitants. Though in the midst of a manufacturing district, there is little trade carried on. The market, originally granted in the 1st of Jas. I to John Binglie, gent., and subsequently by the charter of the 8th of Jas. I to the corporation, is on Tuesday, but is chiefly for potatoes and meal; a very small quantity of yarn is brought for sale. Fairs, chiefly for young cattle and horses, are held on Feb. 1st, April 4th, May 14th, June 30th, Aug. 14th, Sept. 25th, and Nov. 12th, and a chief constabulary police force has been established here. Farnham, the seat of Lord Farnham, is one of the noblest ornaments of the county, for though the house does not possess much exterior magnificence, it is surrounded by a demesne of nearly 3000 acres, comprising the richest pastures and the greatest variety of scenery, adorned with wood and water, and everywhere improved by art. Lough Oughter, on one side of it, spreads out from under the woods of Killy, and encircles many beautiful islands crowned with the finest timber. One of these, named Cloughoughter, was the place of confinement of the venerable Bishop Bedell, when in the hands of the insurgents, in the war of 1641: the tower in which he was imprisoned is now a fine ruin. Nearly adjoining the demesne is Castle Saunderson, the seat of A. Saunderson, Esq., surrounded by a luxuriant demesne commanding the most beautiful views of Lough Erne. Clover Hill, an excellent mansion, the seat of J. Sanderson, Esq., has also a very beautiful demesne, richly adorned, and bordered by a spacious lake. Under the charter of Jas. I, the corporation consists of a sovereign, two portreeves, twelve burgesses, and an indefinite number of freemen, assisted by a recorder, town-clerk, and other officers. But the regular appointment of these officers has been discontinued for several years; the sovereign and deputy are stationary in office, and are now the only representatives of the corporation. The town and the lands enumerated in the charter are held at a fee-farm rent of £1 English currency per annum. The same charter conferred the privilege of returning two members to the Irish parliament, which was exercised till the period of the Union, when £15,000 awarded as compensation for the abolition of the franchise was paid in moieties to Theophilus Clements and T. Nesbitt, Esqrs. The charter granted to the corporation a borough court of record, to be held before the sovereign and two or more burgesses, every three weeks; but this court has not been held since 1796. The assizes, and the Hilary and Midsummer quarter sessions, are held here; petty sessions are also held every week. The county court-house is a fine spacious building, with a portico in front. The county gaol is a very spacious building, to which additions have been recently made on the radiating principle; it contains in the whole 68 cells, 8 day-rooms, and 10 airing-yards, in one of which is a tread-mill, and is well adapted for the classification of prisoners;

a good school has been established in it. The average number of prisoners is 120; and the whole expense of the gaol, for 1835, was £1190.3.5½.

The parish church of Urney is situated in the town. The R.C. chapel, erected in 1824, at an expense of £1000, is a neat building; over the altar is a painting of the Descent from the Cross. On the confines of the town is a classical school of royal foundation, under the charter of the 2nd of Chas. I, which vested several townlands in the counties of Armagh, Cavan, Fermanagh, Donegal, and Tyrone, in the primate and his successors in trust for the endowment of schools in each of those counties. By a late act of parliament the management has been transferred to a Board of Commissioners of Education: the nomination of master rests with the lord-lieutenant. The school-house, erected in 1819, at an expense of £800, is a spacious building, calculated for the reception of 100 pupils, and beautifully situated on a lawn bounded by a branch of the Erne, and surrounded with an amphitheatre of hills. The income arising from the endowment is £641.13.5 per annum, out of which the master receives a salary of £400, and the remainder is appropriated to the repayment of a loan from Government for the buildings. Several parochial and Sunday schools are supported by subscriptions; and a handsome school-house has been erected in the town, in which a school is supported by Lord Farnham. The county infirmary is a plain building capable of receiving 52 patients. There is an alms-house for a poor widow, supported by private subscription. In Swellan lake, about a quarter of a mile from the town, have been found, at different times, some of the largest horns of the elk that have been discovered in Ireland. The celebrated Dr. Sheridan, the friend and correspondent of Dean Swift, was for many years master of the royal school of this place, and was frequently honoured with visits from the dean; a bower in the garden, called Swift's bower, is still in existence. – See URNEY.

CLEMENTSTOWN, a village, in the parish of ASHFIELD, barony of TULLAGHGARVEY, county of CAVAN, anrd province of ULSTER, ¾ of a mile (N.N.W.) from Cootehill; containing 182 inhabitants. This place derived its name from its proprietor, Col. Clements: it is situated on the road from Cootehill to Red hills and Belturbet, and contains 44 houses. Here is a good stone bridge of four arches, crossing the Cootehill river from Bellamont forest to Lough Erne.

COOTEHILL, a market and post-town, in the parish of DRUMGOON, barony of TULLAGHGARVEY, county of Cavan, and province of Ulster, 12 miles (N.E.) from Cavan, and province of Ulster, 12 miles (N.E.) from Cavan, and 57 (N.W. by W.) from Dublin; containing 2239 inhabitants. This town is situated on the road from Kingscourt to Clones, and consists of four wide streets, containing 438 houses, nearly all of which are slated. It is on the borders of a lake, which is navigable for the greater part of the distance of seven miles between this place and Ballybay, in Monaghan; and is a considerable market for linen. The webs are principally broad sheetings of superior quality, and the

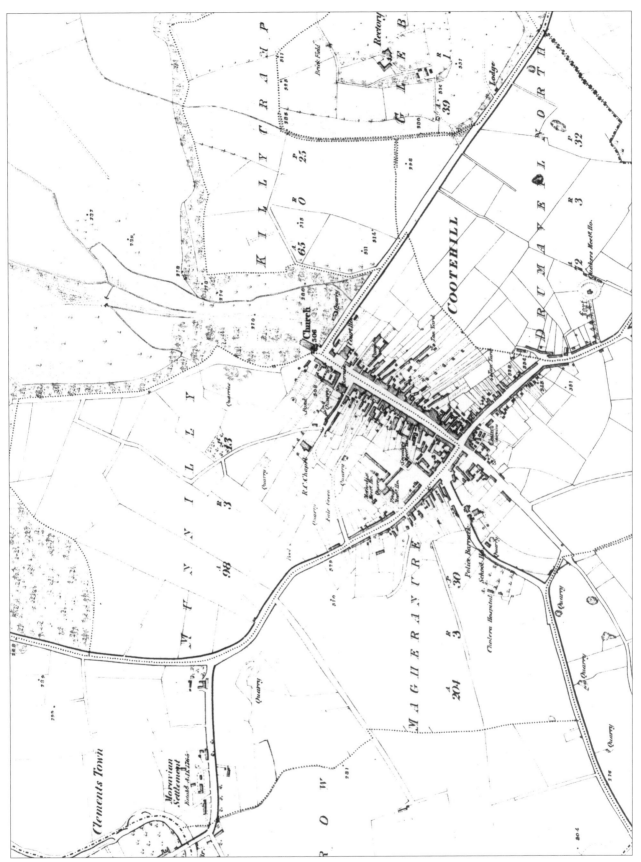

Cootehill. Part of the O.S. map of Co.Monaghan, sheet 17, published 1837 (reproduced at 140%).

number of pieces sold annually to be bleached is about 40,000. The trade, which had considerably declined, has for the last two or three years been improving. The general market is on Friday, and the corn market on Saturday, in the market-house. Fairs are held on the second Friday in each month for cattle, flax, and yarn. Here is a chief constabulary police station. Petty sessions are held every Wednesday, and quarter sessions at Easter and in October in a very neat sessions-house. The bridewell contains three cells, with separate day rooms and yards for males and females, and apartments for the keeper. The seats in the neighbourhood are very beautiful, especially Bellamont House, the residence of C. Coote, Esq., which derived its name from the title of Earl of Bellamont enjoyed, until the year 1800, by the ancient family of Coote. The house is of brick, two stories high, with a noble Doric portico of stone, and the rooms of the lower story are strikingly grand; it contains some fine paintings, among which is the death of Dido, by Guernico, also full-length portraits of the late Earl and Countess of Bellamont by Sir Joshua Reynolds, the former in the full costume of a Knight of he Bath, a fine painting in excellent preservation. The demesne comprises about 1000 plantation acres, of which nearly one- half is occupied with woods; it includes several lakes and a spa, and commands beautiful views from Dismond Hill and its several eminences. The other principal seats are Ashfield Lodge, the residence of H.J. Clements, Esq.; Annilea, of M.Murphy, Esq.; Bellgreen, of T. Brunker, Esq.; and Rakenny, of T.L. Clements, Esq. The town contains the parish church, a R.C. chapel, and two places of worship for Presbyterians, one for the Society of friends, one for Moravians, and one for Wesleyan Methodists. There are three schools, including an infants' school, also a Sunday school in the old church and at each of the Presbyterian chapels, a dispensary, and a Ladies' Society for selling blankets and clothing at half price. In an ancient fort at Rakenny a considerable quantity of god, with a large golden fibula, was found in an iron pot.

CROSSDONEY, a village and post-town, in the parish of KILMORE, barony of CLONMAHON, county of CAVAN, and province of ULSTER, 4 miles (S.W.) from Cavan, and $59^{1}/_{4}$ (N.W.) from Dublin; the population is returned with the parish. This small neat village, containing only 12 houses, is situated on the road from Killesandra to Cavan, and is surrounded by several gentlemen's seats. Fairs are held on April 5th, May 27th, Aug. 26th, and Nov. 17th. Near it is a good bleaching establishment; and at its entrance is Lismore, the seat of Col. Nesbitt, one of the oldest in the county.

DENN, a parish, partly in the barony of CASTLERAHAN, and partly in that of CLONMAHON, but chiefly in the barony of UPPER LOUGHTREE, county of Cavan, and province of Ulster, 5 miles (S. by E.) from Cavan, on the road to Ballyjamesduff; containing 5915 inhabitants. It comprises, according to the Ordnance survey, 11,600 statue acres (including 125 acres under water), of which 7774 are in Upper Loughtee, 2113 in Clonmahon, and 1712 in

Casatlerahan; 11,237 are applotted under the tithe act. Within the last few years, five townlands have been separated from it, forming, together with portions of three other parishes, the benefice and perpetual curacy of Ballyjamesduff. There are about 20 acres of woodland, and 500 of bog; the remainder is good arable and pasture land. In the northern part of the parish is the mountain of Slieve Glagh, 1050 feet above the level of the sea; and in the south western part is that of ardkilmore, 878 feet high. Fairs are held at Cross-keys, on Jan. 12th and March 17th, for general farming stock. The living is a vicarage, in the diocese of Kilmore, and in the patronage of the Bishop; the rectory is impropriate in the Marquess of Westmeath. The tithes amount to £375, of which £150 is payable to the impropriator, and the remainder to the vicar. The glebe-house was erected by aid of a loan of £618 from the late Board of First fruits, in 1817: the glebe comprises 151 acres. The church, a neat small edifice, was rebuilt by aid of a loan of £600 from the same Board, in 1812. The R.C. parish is co-extensive with that of the established Church; there are two chapels, one in the townland of Drumavaddey, and one at Cross-keys, both small buildings, and the latter old and dilapidated. In the parochial school are about 50 boys and 20 girls; and there are five pay schools, in which are about 220 boys and 70 girls.

DERRYHEEN, an ecclesiastical district, in the barony of UPPER LOUGHTEE, county of CAVAN, and province of ULSTER, 3 miles (N.W.) from Cavan, on the road to Enniskillen; containing 1771 inhabitants. This place was erected into an ecclesiastical district in 1834, by disuniting nine townlands from the parish of Urney, three from that of Kilmore, three from Castleterra, and a portion of the parish of Drumlane. It is situated on the river Derryheen, and contains some good arable and pasture land in a state of improved cultivation, though partially subject to occasional inundation from the surrounding lakes, and a moderate portion of valuable bog. The living is a perpetual curacy, in the diocese of Kilmore, and in the patronage of the incumbents of the parishes out of which it was formed:the income of the curate arises from a money payment contributed by each of the patrons. There is neither glebe-house nor glebe. The church is a neat and well-built edifice. A school at Dedris is supported by Lord Farnham, and there is one at Inishmore, together affording instruction to about 100 boys and 60 girls. Here are the ruins of some ancient buildings, called Church Urney, supposed to have been monastic: they form a picturesque object, with a burial-ground attached, used by the R.C. inhabitants.

DRUMGOON, a parish, partly in the barony of TULLAGHGARVEY, but chiefly in that of CLONKEE, county of CAVAN, and province of ULSTER, on the road from Kingscourt to Clones; containing with the post-town of Cootehill, 12,029 inhabitants. It comprises, according to the Ordnance survey, 15,475 statute acres, including 604 under water, of which 8122 are in Clonkee. Slate and lead ore abound here, but have been only partially worked; and the linen manufacture was formerly carried on to a great extent, but of late it has much declined: there is a large flour-mill and bakery. Bellamont Forest, the seat of C. Coote, Esq., stands in a forest on the banks of a beautiful lake adjoining the demesne of Lord Cremorne. The living is a rectory and vicarage, in the diocese of Kilmore, and in the patronage of the Rev. J. Hamilton; the tithes amount to £513.9.9. The glebe house was built by aid of a gift of £375 from the late Board of First Fruits, in 1820, and was rebuilt by a loan of £1384.12.0 and a gift of £92.6.0 from that board in 1831: the glebe comprises 343 acres. The church, situated in Cootehill, is a large handsome structure with a tower and spire, rebuilt by aid of a loan of £3200, in 1817, from the late Board. There is also a chapel of ease, a neat plain edifice, erected in 834, about three miles distant from the church. The R.C. parish is co-extensive with that of the Established Church, and contains three chapels, one at Cootehill, another about a mile from it and a third at Muddabawn. There are two Presbyterian meeting-houses, one in connection with the Synod of Ulster, of the third class, and the other with the Seceding Synod, of the second class; also places of worship for the Society of Friends, Moravians, and the Weslyan Methodists. There are thirteen public schools, in which are about 1080, and fourteen private schools, in which are about 640 children; also an infants' school and Sunday schools held in each meeting-house. A Society for the sale of blankets and clothing at half price is supported by ladies. The Bible Society has a repository here. Remains of an old encampment exist at Drumgoon; there are also several Danish raths, or forts. Large horns of the elk are often found, a pair of which ornament the porch of the glebe-house. The remains of the old parish church are on the townland of Drumgoon.

DRUMLANE, a parish, in the barony of LOWER LOUGHTEE, county of CAVAN, and province of ULSTER, on the road from Clones to Ballyconnell; containing, with part of the post-town of Belturbet, 8547 inhabitants. A monastery was founded here in the 6th century, by St Edan, Bishop of Ferns, which became subject to the abbey of St Mary at Kells. The cemetery was formerly the place of interment of the chieftains of Breffny, and is still a favourite place of burial. Within its limits are the remains of an ancient round tower, built of limestone and red grit. According to the Ordnance survey, the parish comprises 20,066 statute acres, of which 3074 are water, and 16,583 are applotted under the tithe act. Of these, about 400 are

Priory of Drumlane. Published by N. Hooper and engraved by J. Newton. 1794.

bog, 50 woodland, and the remainder arable or pasture. The living is a vicarage, in the diocese of Kilmore, and in the patronage of the bishop; the rectory is appropriate to the vicars choral of Christ-Church cathedral, Dublin. The tithes amount to £500, of which two-thirds are payable to the appropriators, and one third to the vicar. There is a glebe-house, which was built by a loan of £675 from the late board of First Fruits, in 1819, and a glebe of 340 statute acres. The church is a neat building with a square tower, erected in 1819 by a loan of £1500 from the late Board of First Fruits. In the R.C. divisions this parish forms the two unions or districts of Drumlane and Milltown, and has chapels at Staghell and Milltown. Here is a place of worship for Primitive Methodists. About 500 children are educated in seven public, and the same number in seven private, schools.

DRUMLOMAN, or DRUMLUMNUM, a parish, in the barony of CLONMAHON, county of Cavan, and province of ULSTER, 2 miles (E.by N.) from Granard; containing 8007 inhabitants. It comprises, according to the Ordnance survey, 17,147 statute acres, of which 1003 are water, including 541 in Lough Sheelin, 140 in Lough Gowna, and 121 in Lough Kinale. It is in the diocese of Ardagh, and is a vicarage, forming part of the union of Grnard; the rectory is impropriate in the representatives of the late Dean Blundell. The tithes amount to £526.3.1, of which £221.10.9 is payable to the impropriators, and £304 to the incumbent. The Ecclesiastical Commissioners have lately granted £161 for repairing the church. The glebe comprises 150 acres, valued at £234.8.0 per annum. There are four schools, one of which is supported by Lord Farnham, and in which about 900 children are taught; also two private schools, in which are about 70 children. Here was anciently an hospital, the endowments of which were granted by Jas. I to Sir Edw. Moore.

DRUNG, a parish, in the barony of TULLAGHGARVEY, county of CAVAN, and province of ULSTER, 5 miles (E.N.E.) from Cavan, on the road from that place to Cootehill; containing 6015 inhabitants. According to the Ordnance survey it comprises 11,475 statute acres, including 78 of water. Here are several quarries of good building stone, and it is supposed that various minerals exist, but no mines have been worked. The principal seats are Rakenny, the residence of T.S. Clements, Esq., and Fort Lodge, of J. Smith, Esq. The living is a vicarage, in the diocese of Kilmore, united from time immemorial to that of Laragh, and in the patronage of the Bishop; the rectory is impropriate in the Marquess of Westmeath. The tithes amount to £475.15.11, of which £202.4.7 is payable to the impropriator, and £273.11.4 to the vicar; the entire tithes of the benefice amount to £610.18.6. There is a glebe house, with several glebes, comprising 695 acres, and valued at £606.16.3 per annum. The church is a handsome building, lately repaired by a grant of £130 from the Ecclesiastical Commissioners. The R.C. parish is co-extensive with that of the established church, and contains two chapels, one at Dunnannah and

the other at Bannow. About 350 children are educated in three public, and 320 in seven private schools, besides those who are taught in three Sunday schools. There are several raths, one of which is called Fort William, part of King William's army having occupied it after encamping near Ballyhaise on a spot since called Camp Hill.

ENNISKEEN, a parish, partly in the baronies of LOWER KELLS and LOWER SLANE, county of MEATH, and province of LEINSTER, but chiefly in the barony of CLONKEE, county of CAVAN, and province of ULSTER, on the road from Carrickmacross to Bailieborough; containing, with the post-town of Kingscourt (which is described under its own head), 10,368 inhabitants. This place, anciently the principal seat of the Danes, was called Dunaree, and still retains that name; it is surrounded by Danish forts, and on the summits of the neighbouring hills great quantities of money and of ancient military weapons have been dug up at various times. The parish comprises 23,814 statute acres, of which about 500 are woodland, from 200 to 300 bog, and the remainder under tillage; the system of agriculture is greatly improved, and great quantities of bog and waste land have been reclaimed. Limestone abounds; there are excellent quarries of every kind of building stone, and near the rock at Carrickleck is very superior freestone, which is extensively worked for flagstones and pillars of large dimensions. On the estate of Lord Gormanstown, in the Meath district, are coal, lead and iron ore, but none is raised at present; a coal mine and an alabaster quarry were formerly worked, but have been discontinued. The principal seats are Cabra castle, the handsome residence and richly planted demesne of Col. Pratt; Corinsica, of J. Pratt, Esq.; Northlands, of the Very Rev. Dean Adams; Newcastle, of J. Smith, Esq.; Woodford, of J. Armstrong, Esq.; Lisnaboe, of – Jackson, Esq.; Plantation, of – Irwin, Esq.; Larchfield, of W. Pratt, Esq.; and Cornakill, of – Moore, Esq. An annual fair is held at Muff on the 21st of August, and there are several at Kingscourt, noticed in the account of that town, where petty sessions are also held.

The living is a perpetual curacy, in the diocese of Meath, and in the patronage of the bishop, to whom the rectory is appropriate; the tithes amount to £900. The glebe-house is a neat residence, erected by a gift of £450 and a loan of 350 from the late Board of First fruits, in 1831: the glebe comprises 28 acres. The church, at Kingscourt, is a neat plain edifice, to the repair of which the Ecclesiastical Commissioners have recectly granted 3173. The R.C. parish is co-extensive with that of the Established Church, and is called Kingscourt; the chapel in that town is a spacious and handsome edifice, in the later English style, and there is also a chapel at Muff. There is a place of worship for Presbyterians in connection with the Synod of Ulster, of the third class, and one for the Weslyan Methodists. About 130 children are taught in the public schools, and there are 16 private schools, in which are about 960 children. Between Bailieborough and Kingscourt, about two miles from the former, is a pool called Lough-on Leighaghs, or the 'healing lake', which is much resorted to by patients afflicted with scorbutic complaints; it is situated on the summit of a mountain, rising, according to the Ordnance survey, 1116 feet above the level of the sea. On a lofty eminence, about a mile from the lake, is a remarkable cairn; and about two miles from Kingscourt, on the Dublin road, is the singularly beautiful and romantic glen of Cabra. There are ruins of Muff and Cabra Castles, and some remains of an old bridge.

KEADUE, or KIDUE, a parish, in the barony of UPPER LOUGHTEE, county of Cavan, and province of ULSTER, contiguous to the town of Cavan, and on the road from Dublin to Enniskillen: the population is included in the return for Urney. The parish comprises 2893 statute acres, and is a vicarage, in the diocese of Kilmore, held by the vicar of Urney and Annageliffe; the rectory is part of the corps of the deanery of Kilmore. The tithes amount to £109.4.4, of which two-thirds are payable to the dean and one-third to the vicar. The church for the town of Cavan stands on the townland of Keadue, on a site given by the late Earl of Farnham. In the R.C. divisions it is included in the union or district of Urney and Annageliffe.

KILDALLON, a parish, in the barony of TULLOGHONOHO, county of Cavan, and province of ULSTER, 3 miles (N.) from Killeshandra, on the road from that place to Ballyconnell; containing 4246 inhabitants. It comprises, according to the Ordnance survey, 11,989 statute acres, of which 211 are water: 3233 acres are applotted under the tithe act, and there is a large tract of waste land, called Ballyheady Moor; the land is chiefly cultivated by spade husbandry. The principal seats are Greenville, the residence of Perrott Sheraten Esq.; Aughabawn, of the Rev. J. Vernon; Carn Cottage of Capt Clifford; Mackenwood, of M. Galbraith, Esq.; Belberry, of-Urwin, Esq.; and Carn of J. Benison, Esq. The living is a rectory and vicarage, in the diocese of Kilmore, and in the gift of the Bishop: the tithes amount to £203.1.6. The church is a handsome building, with a tower, erected in 1814, for which the late Board of First Fruits granted a loan of £1000. The same board, in 1821, gave £100 and lent £1200 for the erection of the glebe-house: the glebes comprise 339 acres. In the R.C. divisions this parish is the head of a union or district, comprising also the parish of Tomeegan, and containing a chapel in each. The chapel here is a large thatched building, with a neatly planted burial-ground. At Croghan is a Presbyterian meeting house, of the third class, in connection with the Synod of Ulster. About 560 children are educated in eight public, and 170 in two private, schools. On the summit of the hill of Carn is a heap of stones surrounded by a Danish rath; and at Drumboo is a holy well, at which patrons have been held.

KILDRUMFERTON, or CROSSERLOUGH, a parish, partly in the baronies of LOUGHTEE and CLONMAHON, but chiefly in that of CASTLERAHAN, county of CAVAN, and province of ULSTER, 9 miles (N.W.) from Oldcastle, on the road from Killesandra to Ballinagh; containing 9687 inhabitants. It comprises, according to the Ordnance survey,

16,436$\frac{3}{4}$ statute acres (including 207$\frac{1}{2}$ under water), of which 11,729$\frac{3}{4}$ are in Castlerahan, 4445$\frac{1}{2}$ in Clonmahon, and the remainder in Upper Loughtee, and of which 15,535 are applotted under the tithe act; about two-thirds are arable, one-third pasture, and the remainder woodland and bog. Fairs for live stock are held here on June 29th and Aug. 26th. The principal seats are Kilnacrot, the residence of Pierce Morton, Esq., and Kilmainham, of A. Bell, Esq. The living is a vicarage, in the diocese of Kilmore, and in the patronage of the Bishop; the rectory is impropriate in the representatives of Richard Earl of Westmeath, and the tithes amount to £672, of which £272 is payable to the impropriators and £400 to the vicar. In 1831, four townlands were separated from this parish to form part of the perpetual curacy of Ballyjamesduff, to the incumbent of which the vicar of Kildrumferton pays an annual stipend of £20. The church is a very neat structure, rebuilt in 1812, for which the late Board of First Fruits granted a loan of £550, and recently repaired by aid of a grant of £114 from the Ecclesiastical Commissioners. The glebe-house was built by aid of a gift of £100 from the late Board of First Fruits, in 1810: the glebe comprises 420 acres. The R.C. parish is co-extensive with that of the Established Church, but is commonly called Crosserlough; there is a large and well-built chapel at Drumkeely, and the chapel at Crosserlough has lately been rebuilt. About 400 children are educated in four public schools, one of which is supported by Lord Farnham, and about 560 in seven private schools.

KILLENCARE, or KILLENKERE, a parish, partly in the barony of UPPER LOUGHTEE, but chiefly in that of CASTLERAGHAN, county of CAVAN, and province of ULSTER, 4 miles (W.S.W.) from Bailieborough, on the road to Virginia; containing 7600 inhabitants. This parish, which is also called Killinskere, comprises, according to the Ordance survey, 15,962 statute acres, of which 131 are water, and there is some bog.The lands are principally arable, and in a tolerable state of cultivation; slate is found here, but of very inferior quality, and the quarries formerly worked have in consequence been discontinued: an ore supposed to be zinc has been discovered on the townland of Durryham, but it has not been yet worked. The living is a vicarage, in the diocese of Kilmore, and in the patronage of the Bishop: the rectory is impropriate in the representatives of Richard, Earl of Westmeath: the tithes amount to £480. The church, for the erection of which the late Board of First Fruits granted £900 as a gift, and £1200 as a loan, in 1817, is a very neat structure. The same Board, in 1816, gave £325 and lent £1050 towards the erection of the glebe-house, which is a handsome residence; the glebe comprises 380 acres. The R.C. parish is co-extensive with that of the Established Church; the chapel is a plain building, and there is also one at Clanaphillip. There is a place of worship for Presbyterians, in connexion with the synod of Ulster, of the third class; also one for those in connexion with the Seceding Synod. About 440 children are taught in four public schools, of which one is supported by Lord Farnham,

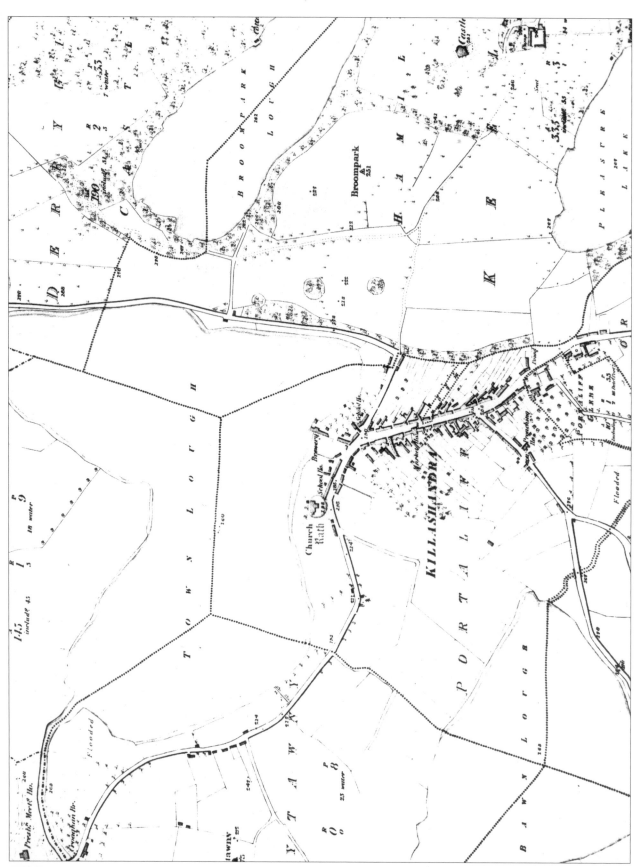

Killasandra. Part of the O.S. map of Co. Monaghan, sheet 19, published 1837 (reproduced at 140%).

and another by the Sankey family; and there are eight private schools, in which are about 480 children, and a Sunday-school. There are numerous mineral springs in the parish, some of which are used medicinally.

KILLERSHERDINY, or KILDRUMSHERDAN, a parish, in the barony of TULLAGHGARVEY, county of CAVAN, and province of ULSTER, 2½ miles (S.W.) from Cootehill, on the road to Cavan; containing 6997 inhabitants. It is also called Kilsherdany, and comprises, according to the Ordnance survey, 16,618½ statute acres, of which 15,801 are applotted under the tithe act; about 4860 are arable, 8940 are meadow and pasture, 320 woodland, 107½ water, and the remainder bog; the system of agriculture is improved. There are several quarries of common whinstone, which is raised for building and for repairing the roads. The principal seats are Annalee, the residence of M. Murphy, Esq.; Fort William, of T. Coote, Esq.; Eragle Cottage, of T. Hamilton Ennis, Esq.; Laurel Lodge, of the Rev. J. Adams; Retreat, of C. J. Adams, Esq.; Drummilton, of G. Cooney, Esq.; and Tullyvin House, of Maxwell J. Boyle, Esq. A remnant of the linen manufacture is still carried on in the parish, and there are several corn-mills, of which one belonging to Mr. Townley, of Dundalk, is very large. A lead mine, the property of T. Burrowes, Esq., of Stradone House, was formerly worked by the Irish Mining Company, but, being found unprofitable, has been discontinued. There are charters extant for four annual fairs, but one only is held in the village of Tullyvin, on the 4th of May, for cattle. The living is a vicarage, in the diocese of Kilmore, and in the patronage of the Bishop; the rectory is impropriate in the representatives of Richard, Earl of Westmeath: the tithes amount to £480, of which £230 is payable to the impropriator, and £250 to the vicar. The church, a neat plain edifice, was built in 1800, and the glebe-house in 1816: to the former the late Board of First Fruits gave £500, and to the latter £100, and a loan of £1125: the glebe comprises 285 acres. The R.C. parish is co-extensive with that of the Established Church: the chapel was built in 1825, at an expense of £700. Nearly 500 children are taught in four public schools, of which the parochial schools are supported by the vicar; and one at Tullyvin is endowed with £40 per annum late currency, and a house for the master, by the late W. Moore, Esq., of that place. There are also six private schools, in which are about 240 children. There are several forts in the parish, supposed by some to be Danish, but by others to have been raised by the native Irish as a defence against those invaders; and on the several hills on which they are situated ancient coins have been found. On the demesne of Tullyvin is an ancient vault, in which are 23 coffins, containing the remains of deceased members of the families of Moore and Boyle; and on the townland of Curravilla is a chalybeate spring, now in disuse.

KILLESANDRA, a market and post-town, and a parish, in the barony of TULLOGHONOHO, county of CAVAN, and province of ULSTER, 9 miles (W.) from Cavan, and 64 (N.W.) from Dublin, on the road to Ballinamore;

containing, with the district parishes of Arvagh and Scrabby, 14,532 inhabitants, of which number 1137 are in the town. This town, which is situated near the river Croghan and contains about 200 houses, is neatly built, and has a cheerful and thriving appearance. The linen manufacture, which is carried on extensively in the neighbourhood, has contributed greatly to its prosperity, and, upon an average, coarse linens are sold in its market to the amount of £1500 weekly. The market is on Wednesday, and is abundantly supplied with provisions; and fairs are held on Jan. 28th, March 28th, May 9th, June 22nd, July 15th, the second Wednesday in August (O. S.), Sept. 28th, and Nov. 8th. The market-house is a very neat and well-arranged building. A chief constabulary police force is stationed in the town; a manorial court is held occasionally, and petty sessions every alternate Thursday. The parish comprises, according to the Ordnance survey (including a detached portion of 323½ acres), 22,241 statute acres; 500 are woodland, and 1212 water, of which latter 74 are in Lough Oughtee. The surface is boldly undulating, and, in the southern part, rises into mountainous elevations, above which Bruce Hill is pre-eminent; and not far from the town is the steep mountain of Corhill. The lands are chiefly under tillage; the soil is tolerably fertile, but the system of agriculture is very indifferent; there is a large extent of bog. Freestone is quarried for building, and in several parts are indications of coal, but no attempt has been yet made to work it. The river Croghan, in the lower part of the parish, winds through a delightful tract of country into the magnificent lakes of Killesandra. Adjoining the town is Castle Hamilton, the seat of R. H. Southwell, Esq., a spacious mansion surrounded by an extensive and highly embellished demesne. The living is a rectory and vicarage, in the diocese of Kilmore, and in the patronage of the Provost and Fellows of Trinity College, Dublin: the tithes amount to £660. The parochial church is a very ancient structure, but in a state of dilapidation. The glebe-house has a glebe of 500 acres attached to it. There is a chapel of ease at Derrylane. The R.C. parish is co-extensive with the ancient parish of Killesandra; there are two chapels, situated in the town and at Corronee; there is also a place of worship for Wesleyan Methodists in the town. About 630 children are taught in seven public schools, of which two are supported by Lord Farnham; and there are four private schools, in which are about 230 children. Mrs. Jackson bequeathed £10 per annum to be divided by the rector among ten poor housekeepers. There are numerous raths in the parish. Dr. Hales, author of a work on chronology, and other scientific works, was rector of this parish.

KILLINAGH, a parish, in the barony of TULLAGHAGH, county of CAVAN, and province of ULSTER, 7½ miles (E. by S.) from Manor-Hamilton, on Lough Macnean; containing 5383 inhabitants. It comprises, according to the Ordnance survey, 24,783¾ statute acres, including 982¾ under water, of which 42¾ are in Lower and 806¼ in Upper Lough Macnean. The living is a vicarage, in the diocese of Kilmore, and in the patronage of the Bishop; the rectory is impropriate in Major Saunders, and the tothes amount to £290. The church was erected in 1786, by aid of a gift of £390 from the late Board of First fruits, and the Ecclesiastical Commissioners have recently granted £163 for its repair. The R.C. parish is co-extensive with that of the Established Church, and has a chapel at Killinagh, and one at Doobally. About 320 children are educated in three public, and 310 in seven private, schools, and there is a Sunday school.

KILLOUGHTER, a parish, in the barony of TULLAGHGARVEY, county of CAVAN, and province of ULSTER, 6 miles (N.N.E.) from Belturbet, on the road from that place to Cootehill; containing 6130 inhabitants. It comprises 7633 statute acres of arable and pasture land, except about 250 acres of waste and bog. The living is a perpetual curacy, in the diocese of Kilmore, formed out of the parish of Annagh in 1813, and in the gift of the Incumbent of that parish: the tithes amount to £14, and the Ecclesiastical Commissioners have granted an augmentation of £20 per annum. The church is a neat plain building, with a square tower. The glebe-house was built by aid of a gift of £450 and a loan of £50 from the late Board of First Fruits, in 1822, and has a glebe of 16a. 3r. The R.C. parish is co-extensive with that of the Established Church, and has a chapel at Red Hill. There is a meeting-house for Primitive Methodists. About 25 children are educated in the parochial school, and 460 in ten private schools.

KILMORE, a parish, and the seat of a diocese, partly in the barony of CLONMAHON, but chiefly in that of UPPER LOUGHTEE, county of CAVAN, and province of ULSTER, 3¼ miles (S.W.) from Cavan, on the road to Killesandra; containing, with part of the market-town of Ballinagh (which is separately described), 7161 inhabitants. This parish, which derives its name, signifying the "Great Church," from the abbey of Cella Magna, founded here at an early period by St. Columba, comprises, according to the Ordnance survey, 16,886 statute acres, of which 2154 are in Lough Oughter, and 14,114 are applotted under the tithe act. The soil is various, and the land in some parts under profitable cultivation; there are some quarries of good building stone, and gold and silver have been found in some parts. The principal seats are Lismore Castle, that of Major Nesbitt; the Rocks, of J. C. Tatlow, Esq.; Castle Corby, of J. Whitthorne, Esq.; Belleville, of Capt. A. Fleming; Bingfield, of H. T. Kilbee, Esq.; Drumhcel, of R. Bell, Esq.; Lisnamandra, of G. L'Estrange, Esq.; Drumcorbin, of G. T. B. Booth, Esq.; Tully, of Major R. Stafford; and Hermitage, of R. Stephens, Esq.

The DIOCESE of KILMORE does not appear to have been of very ancient foundation; the first prelate of whom any mention occurs is Florence O'Conacty, who succeeded in 1231, under the designation of Bishop of Breffny, from the territory of that name, in which the see was situated; and his successors are styled indifferently Breffnienses, and Triburnenses, or bishops of Triburna, from the small village of that name, near which they generally resided. The first who was styled Bishop of Kilmore was Andrew MacBrady,

who, in 1454, with the consent of Pope Nicholas V, erected the parish church of St. Felimy, or Fedlimid, of Kilmore, into a cathedral church, in which he placed 13 secular canons; and since that period, Kilmore has given name to the see. From the unsettled state of the district which constituted this diocese, it was not affected by the Reformation so soon as others, and it continued under the control of the bishop appointed by the Pope till 1585, when John Garvey, Dean of Christ-Church, Dublin, was appointed the first Protestant bishop, on whose translation to the see of Armagh, this diocese remained without a bishop for fourteen years, during which period it was annexed to the bishoprick of Down and Connor, till the appointment of Robert Draper, in 1603, who obtained this see, together with that of Ardagh, by letters patent of Jas. I In 1643 the see of Ardagh was united to that of Kilmore, and continued to be held with it till 1752, when it was annexed in commendam to the Archbishoprick of Tuam, with which it has ever since continued. Among the most eminent prelates were the venerable Bishop Bedell, and Bishops Sheridan and Cumberland. It is one of the ten dioceses which constitute the ecclesiastical province of Armagh; and comprehends part of the county of Meath, in the province of Leinster, part of Leitrim in the province of Connaught, part of Fermanagh and the greater part of Cavan, in the province of Ulster; extending about 74 English miles in length, and varying from 13 to 25 in breadth, and comprising an estimated superficies of 497,250 acres, of which 2200 are in Meath, 184,750 in Leitrim, 29,300 in Fermanagh, and 281,000 in Cavan. The lands belonging to the see comprise 28,531 acres; and the gross annual value of the bishoprick, on an average of three years ending Dec. 31st, 1831, amounted to £7477.17.0½. The corporation consists of a bishop, dean, and archdeacon, but there are neither prebendaries nor canons to form a chapter; even the archdeaconry has no corps, but is annexed by the bishop to any parochial living at his discretion; neither is there any economy fund. The consistorial court consists of a vicar-general, surrogate, registrar, deputy-registrar, and proctor; the registrar is keeper of the records, which are all of modern date, the earliest being a registry of wills commencing in 1693.

The total number of parishes in the diocese is 39, comprised in 38 benefices, of which 8 are unions of two or more parishes, and 30 single parishes: all are in the patronage of the Bishop, except the deanery, which is in the gift of the Crown; the living of Killesandra, in the patronage of the Provost and Fellows of Trinity College, Dublin; Armagh, in that of the Earl of Farnham; and Drumgoon, in that of the Hamilton family. The total number of churches is 45, and there are 5 other places in which divine service is performed; the number of glebe-houses is 31. By the Church Temporalities Act of the 3rd of Wm. IV, the bishoprick of Elphin, on its next avoidance, or on the demise of either of the bishops of Elphin and Kilmore, will be annexed to the diocese of Kilmore, and its temporalities vested in the Ecclesias-tical Commissioners. The cathedral, which is also the parish church, is a small ancient edifice, having at the entrance a richly sculptured Norman doorway, removed from the abbey of Trinity Island, in Lough Oughter. The Episcopal palace, an elegant mansion in the Grecian style, has been recently rebuilt on a more eligible site near the former structure, which is about to be taken down. In the R.C. divisions this diocese forms a separate bishoprick, and one of the eight which are suffragan to the archiepiscopal see of Armagh; it comprises 44 parochial benefices, or unions, containing 76 chapels, served by 80 clergymen, of whom, including the bishop, 44 are parish priests, and 36 coadjutors or curates. The parochial benefice of the bishop is Drumgoon, where he resides.

The living of Kilmore is a vicarage, united by royal authority, at an unknown date, to the vicarage of Ballintemple, and the rectory and vicarage of Keadue, together forming the union and the corps of the deanery of Kilmore, in the patronage of the Crown; the rectory is impropriate in the Marquess of Westmeath. The tithes amount to £350, of which £127.17.4 is payable to the impropriator, and the remainder to the vicar; the aggregate tithes of the benefice are £843.10.6. The glebe comprises $270\frac{1}{2}$ acres of profitable land, and $26\frac{3}{4}$ of bog; there is also, in the parish of Ballintemple, a glebe of $103\frac{1}{2}$ acres, besides which are $436\frac{1}{2}$ acres of profitable land and 47 acres of bog belonging to the deanery, though not in any of the parishes within the union. The R.C. parish is co-extensive with that of the Established Church; there are two chapels, situated respectively at Ballinagh and Drumcor, the latter built in 1809, at an expense of £150. About 350 children are taught in six public schools, of which two are parochial, and three are supported by Lord Farnham; there are seven private schools, in which are about 330 children, and three Sunday schools. In the churchyard are interred the remains of the venerable Bishop Bedell, whose death was occasioned or accelerated by the seve rities he endured while in the hands of the insurgents in 1641. In such esteem was this exemplary prelate held, even by those who had hastened his decease, that they attended his funeral obsequies with the most unbounded demonstrations of respect and sorrow. In the same vault was also interred Bishop Cumberland. On Trinity island are the remans of an abbey; and on a small island in Killekeen lake are the ruins of the castle of Cloughoughter, in which Bishop Bedell was confined.

KILSUB, or BAWNBOY, a village, in the parish of TEMPLEPORT, barony of TULLAGHAGH, county of CAVAN, and province of ULSTER, 3 miles (N.W.) from Ballyconnell, on the road to Swanlinbar; containing 24 houses and 60 inhabitants. A fair is held here on the first Monday, and petty sessions on the second Monday, in every month. Near Bawnboy is the seat of F. Hasard, Esq., in a well-planted demesne; and there is a small boulting-mill.

KILNALECK, a village, in the parish of KILDRUMFERTON, barony of CASTLERAGHAN, county of CAVAN, and province of Ulster, 8 miles (S.W.) from Cavan, on the road from Ballyjamesduff to Ballinagh; containing

64 houses and 347 inhabitants. It is a constabulary police station, and has fairs for cattle on Feb. 2nd, March 25th, May 13th, June 11th, Aug.10th, Sept. 12th, Nov. 1st and Dec. 17th.

KINAWLEY, a parish, partly in the barony of TULLAGHAGH, county of CAVAN, partly in that of GLENAWLEY, but chiefly in that of KNOCKNINNY, county of FERMANAGH, and province of ULSTER, 6 miles (N.W.) from Ballyconnell, on the road to Enniskillen; containing, with the post-town of Swanlinbar, which is separately described, 16,077 inhabitants. According to the Ordnance survey it comprises 51,004 statute acres, of which $15,346\frac{1}{2}$ are in the county of Cavan; and, including islands, $35,657\frac{1}{2}$ are in the county of Fermanagh; of the latter number, 2895 acres are in Upper Lough Erne, and $645\frac{1}{4}$ in small loughs. Agriculture is in a good state; there is a considerable quantity of bog, and limestone and freestone are abundant. Cuilcagh mountain, which, according to the Ordnance survey, is 2188 feet high, is in the Cavan part of the parish. The river Shannon rises at the base of this mountain from a deep circular gulph, 20 feet in diameter, and there is another deep gulph about three-quarters of a mile from this, in which the flowing of water may be heard. The elevation of the source of the Shannon above Lough Allen is 115 feet, and above the sea 275 feet. Petty sessions are held every fortnight at Derrilin, where fairs are held on May 27th and Oct. 27th. The principal seats are Mount Prospect, the residence of Blaney Winslow, Esq.; Dresternan, of D. T. Winslow, Esq.; Prospect Hill, of A. Maguire, Esq.; and Cloghan, of D. Winslow, Esq. The living is a rectory and vicarage, in the diocese of Kilmore, and in the patronage of the Bishop; the tithes amount to £369.4.$7\frac{1}{2}$. The glebe-house was erected in 1822, by aid of a loan of £787 from the late Board of First Fruits. There is a church at Derrilin, and one at Swanlinbar, which is in a ruinous state. In the R.C. divisions the parish forms two unions or districts, called Kinawley, in which are chapels at Kinawley and Swanlinbar; and Knockaninny, in which are chapels at Knockaninny, Glassmullen, and Drumderrig. There are eight public schools, in which about 850 children are educated, and 13 private schools, in which are about 570, also seven Sunday schools.

KINGSCOURT, a market and post-town, in the parish of ENNISKEEN, county of CAVAN, and province of ULSTER, 5 miles (W.) from Carrickmacross, and 50 from Dublin, on the road from Carrickmacross to Bailieborough; containing 1616 inhabitants. This town, which is situated on the confines of the counties of Louth, Meath, and Monaghan, was founded near the site of the old village of Cabra, by Mervyn Pratt, Esq., towards the close of the last century, and was completed by his brother, the Rev. Joseph Pratt. From the facility afforded by its situation for procuring materials for building, the advantageous conditions of the leases granted by its proprietor, the construction of good roads, and the establishment of a market, it has rapidly risen into importance, and is now a thriving and prosperous place. It

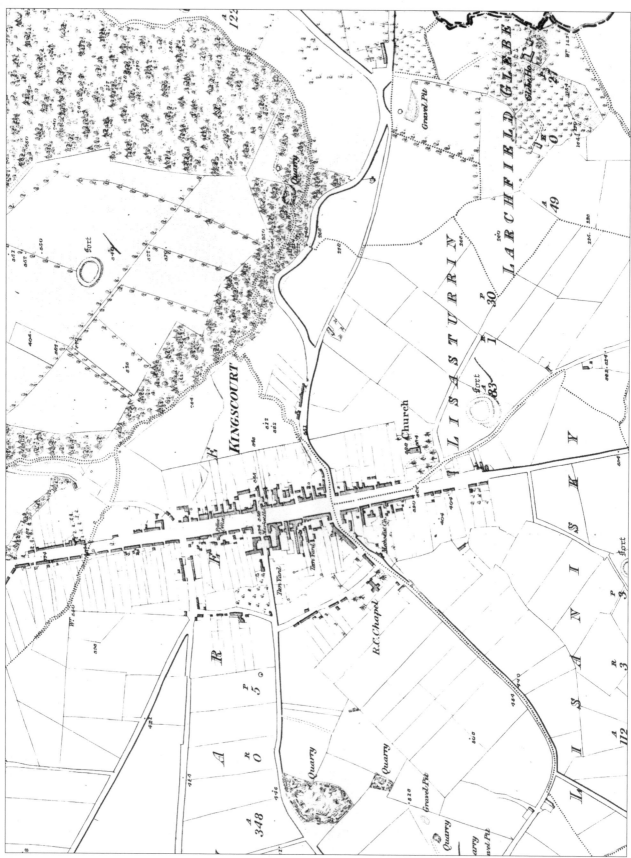

Kingscourt. Part of the O.S. map of Co. Monaghan sheet 35, Published 1837 (reproduced at 140%).

consists of one spacious street, containing 314 houses, which are well built of stone and roofed with slate; has a neat and commodious market-house, and a daily post; and is the head station for the Kingscourt district of the Irish society for promoting the education of the native Irish, through the medium of their own language.

Near the town is Cabra Castle, the seat of the proprietor, Col. Pratt, a superb baronial mansion in the Norman style of architecture, with suitable offices, situated in an extensive and beautiful demesne, comprising 1700 statute acres, and embellished with luxuriant woods and richly varied scenery. In a spacious meadow to the west of the castle, which is interspersed with stately trees of ancient growth, is an aboriginal wood covering several hundred acres, and reaching to the summit of a lofty eminence crowned with the ruins of an ancient castle and a rotundo of more modern date, commanding a rich view over several counties, terminating in the Carlingford mountains to the east, and the Bay of Dundalk, which is visible in clear weather. On a rising ground at a short distance towards the south are the tower of Kingscourt church and part of the town; and to the south-east, on a high hill, the church of Ardagh. At the western extremity of the demesne is the romantic and thickly wooded glen of Cabra, of great depth and nearly a mile in length, watered by a rapid mountain torrent, which taking a winding course over beds of rock, forms several picturesque cascades. A very romantic bridge is thrown across the glen, the abutments of which are hewn in the solid rock; the arch, raised to a very great height, is covered with ivy and ornamented with several trees of large growth, whose stems are also entwined with ivy, giving to it a splendid and imposing appearance. Near this spot, on a slight eminence, is Cabra Lodge, where the present proprietor has erected some vertical sam-mills of great power. It is traditionally recorded that one of the northern tribes, in its passage to the west of Ireland, was met in this glen by the enemy and totally routed and cut to pieces; several of the old inhabitants recollect the discovery of human bones in this place, which, it being unconsecrated ground, must have been those of bodies interred before the Christian era. This circumstance is alluded to in a note appended to Ossian's poems, a fact which would, in the opinion of antiquaries, confirm the authenticity of at least part of that work.

Contiguous to Cabra is Mullintra, the grounds of which, together with those of Cormee, the site of the present castle, now form part of the demesne, the whole having been united by the present proprietor. The market is on Tuesday; and there are fairs on April 1st, May 23rd, June 18th, Aug. 1st, Sept. 19th, Nov. 8th, and Dec. 4th and 24th. A chief constabulary force is stationed here, and petty sessions are held on alternate Tuesdays. The parish church is situated in the town, in which are also a handsome R.C. chapel and a dispensary. In the neghbourhood are several planted raths, one of which commands a very extensive and magnificent prospect.

KNOCKBRIDE, a parish, in the barony of CLONKEE,

county of CAVAN, and province of ULSTER, 5 miles (N.) from Bailieborough, on the road to Cootehill; containing 9746 inhabitants, This parish comprises, according to the Ordnance survey, 18,693 statute acres, of which 857 are under water, and 14,216 are applotted under the tithe act: there are about 1500 acres of bog and waste, the remainder being good arable and pasture land. There is a large oatmeal-mill. A court is held monthly at Corronary by the seneschal of the manor, for the recovery of debts under 40s. The living is a rectory and vicarage, in the diocese of Kilmore, and in the patronage of the Bishop; the tithes amount to £350. The glebe-house is situated near the church; the glebe comprises 188 acres. The church, a small but very neat edifice in good repair, was built by a gift of £100 and a loan of £550 from the late Board of First Fruits, in 1820. The R.C. parish is co-extensive with that of the Established Church; there are two chapels, one a good substantial edifice, erected in 1821; the other a small thatched building, about to be taken down and rebuilt. There is a place of worship for Presbyterians in connection with the Seceding Synod, of the second class, and one for Wesleyan Methodists. About 130 children are taught in two public schools, of which the parochial school is principally supported by the rector, and there are 11 private schools, in which are about 670 children.

LARAH, a parish, partly in the barony of UPPER LOUGHTEE, but chiefly in that of TULLAGHGARVEY, county of CAVAN, and province of ULSTER; containing, with the post-town of Stradone, 7808 inhabitants. According to the Ordnance survey it comprises 17,282½ statute acres, including 180½ of water; of these, are in Upper Loughtee, and 12,116 in Tullaghgarvey. The state of agriculture is rather backward, and in the upper part of the parish there is a quantity of bog. There are quarries of limestone, which is used for building and as manure. The principal seats are Stradone House, the residence of Major Burrowes, a handsome structure in a well-planted demesne; and Ravenswood, of R. Saunderson, Esq. It is a vicarage, in the diocese of Kilmore, forming part of the union of Drung; the rectory is impropriate in the Marquess of Westmeath. The tithes amount to £559.8.0, of which £221.19.9 is payable to the impropriator. and £337.8.3 to the vicar; the glebe comprises 556a. 1r. 23p. The church is a neat and commodious edifice, erected by aid of a grant from the late Board of First Fruits, in 1832. In the R.C. divisions this district is divided into Upper and Lower Larab, and has chapels at Larah and Cleffernah. There are two public schools, in which about 270 children are educated, and eleven private schools, in which are about 720 children, also two Sunday schools. On the townland of Knockatoother is a very remarkable cairn, and several Danish raths are scattered over the parish.

LAVAY, or LOWEY, a parish, in the barony of UPPER LOUGHTEE, county of CAVAN, and province of ULSTER, 4 miles (E. by S.) from Cavan, on the road to Virginia; containing 6305 inhabitants. According to the Ordnance survey it comprises 10,679 statute acres, of which 76$\frac{1}{2}$ are water. The land is highly cultivated; there are some large tracts of bog, affording an abundant supply of fuel. It is a vicarage, in the diocese of Kilmore, and in the patronage of the Bishop; the rectory is impropriate in the Marquess of Westmeath. The tithes amount to £386.5.0, of which £153.15.0 is payable to the impropriator, and £232.10.0 to the vicar. The church, a very neat edifice, was erected by aid of a gift of £900 from the late Board of First Fruits, in 1817, and has been recently repaired by a grant of £152 from the Ecclesiastical Commissioners. The R.C. parish is co-extensive with that of the Established Church, and contains the Upper chapel, built in 1820, and the Lower chapel, which has been recently built, at an expense of nearly £2000, on a site given by Major G. Burrowes. There are seven private schools, in which about 490 children are educated. Here are some Danish raths; and several heads of battle-axes and brazen spears were discovered on an artificial island while draining Lake Lavey in 1832, and are in the possession of J. Smith, Esq.

LOGHAN, or LOUGHAN, a parish, partly in the barony of CASTLE RAHAN, county of CAVAN, and province of ULSTER, but chiefly in the barony of UPPER KELLS, county of MEATH, and province of LEINSTER, 4 miles (N.W.) from Kells, on the road from Dublin by Kells to Enniskillen; containing 3795 inhabitants, of which number, 339 are in the village of Loghan. This parish, which is also called Castlekeiran and Tristelkerin, contains also the villages of Rathendrick, Derver, and Castlekeiran, and is situated on the river Blackwater, near its source in Lough Ramor. It is a rectory, in the diocese of Meath, entirely impropriate in the Marquess of Headfort: the tithes amount to £250. The impropriator allows £10 per annum to the curate of Mounter-connaught parish for performing the occasional duties of that part of Loghan which lies in the county of Cavan, and of which the Protestant inhabitants attend Virginia church: those of the Meath portion attend the church of Kells. In the R.C. divisions Loghan forms part of the union or district of Carnaross, or Dulane. At Edenburt is a national school of about 60 children, aided by the Marquess of Headfort; and at Carnaross is a private school of about the same number. On the banks of the river are the remains of a small church, dedicated to St. Kieran, with a large and richly sculptured stone cross in the cemetery; here is also a holy well, much resorted to by the peasantry on the first Sunday in August.

LURGAN, a parish, in the barony of CASTLERAHAN, county of CAVAN, and province of ULSTER, on the road from Kells to Cavan; containing, with the post-town of Virginia (which is separately described), 6387 inhabitants. It comprises, according to the Ordnance survey, 11,327$\frac{3}{4}$ statute acres, including 922$\frac{3}{4}$ acres of water, of which the greater portion is in Lough Ramor; 8423 acres are applotted under the tithe act, and there is a large portion of bog and moor. In 1831, two townlands were separated from this parish to form part of the district parish, or perpetual cure,

of Ballyjamesduff. The living is a rectory and vicarage, in the diocese of Kilmore, united by act of council to the rectory and vicarage of Munterconnaught, together constituting the union of Lurgan, in the patronage of the Bishop. The tithes amount to £233.9.0, and the gross tithes of the benefice to £381.9.0: the glebe of the union, which comprises 999$\frac{3}{4}$ acres, is valued at £694.2.6 per annum. The glebe-house, situated about two miles from the church, was erected about 1814, at an expense of £3276.18.5$\frac{1}{2}$, of which £1384.12.3$\frac{3}{4}$ was granted as a loan, and £92. 6.1$\frac{3}{4}$ as a gift from the late Board of First Fruits. The church, in the town of Virginia, was erected in 1821, at a cost of £2492.6.1$\frac{3}{4}$, of which £1846.3.1 was a loan from the same Board, and the remainder was contributed by the parishioners; having been accidentally burnt in the winter of 1830, it was repaired by subscriptions amounting to £900, contributed chiefly by the bishop and the parishioners. In the R.C. divisions the parish forms the head of a union or district, comprising also part of the parish of Loghan, in the diocese and county of Meath, and containing the chapels of Lurgan and Maghera. In the national schools at Whitegate, Caponagh, and Lattoon, and a school aided by subscriptions, about 360 children are educated; and there are four private schools, containing about 290 children.

MOUNT-NUGENT or DALYSBRIDGE, a post-town in the parish of KILBRIDE, barony of CLONMAHON, county of CAVAN, and province of ULSTER, 11 miles (S.S.E.) from Cavan, and 50 (N.W. by W.) from Dublin, on the road from Oldcastle to Granard; containing 171 inhabitants. It consists of 29 houses, the parish church, a R.C. chapel, and a school on Eramus Smith's foundation. Petty sessions are held here every third Saturday; and there is a constabulary police staion. Fairs are held on June 1st and Oct. 21st. It is near Lough Sheelin, extending to Finae, in Westmeath, where it communicates with Lough Inny, through which its waters find their way to the Shannon; in this lake are several small islands, on one of which are the ruins of a church and castle. Contiguous to its shores, at Kilrogy, near Glan, is the seat of Mrs Dallas; and on its northern side are several gentlemen's residences, among them are Arley, the beautiful cottage of Lord Farnham; and Fortland, the residence of T. Gorlin, Esq. On the opposite shore the ground is elevated and well planted; and the view of the whole, comprehending the ruins of Ross castle, is bounded by hills of considerable magnitude, among which the most remarkable is the Ben of Fore, above the village of that name, in the county of Westmeath. The lake covers 2000 Irish acres, being 8 Irish miles in length, and, in parts, 2 or 3 wide.

MULLAGH, a market town and parish, in the barony of CASTLERAHAN, county of CAVAN, and province of ULSTER, 6 miles (N.N.W.) from Kells, on the road to Bailieborough; containing 5960 inhabitants, of which number, 108 are in the town, This parish is situated on the confines of the county of Meath, and comprises, according to the Ordnance survey, 12,873 statute acres, of which 140$\frac{3}{4}$ are water, and there are large tracts of bog and mountain;

the general quality of the land is good. There is abundance of stone; some slate is found on the glebe, and coal exists, but is not worked. The town, which consists of 36 houses, is a constabulary police station, and petty sessions are held on alternate Fridays. It has a weekly market; and fairs for the sale of cattle and pigs, oats, butter, and flax, are held on Jan. 29th, March 25th, May 27th, July 29th, Sept. 30th, and Nov. 25th. Here is a dispensary. The principal seats are Lake View, the residence of – Mortimer, Esq.; Quilca House, of the Rev. Luke O'Reilly; and the glebe-house, of the Rev. Atkinson Caifrey. The living is a perpetual curacy, in the diocese of Kilmore, and in the gift of the Incumbent of Killenkere. The income of the perpetual curate is £78.2.0, of which £55 is payable by the vicar of Killenkere, and £23.2.0 from the Ecclesiastical Commissioners, out of Primate Boulter's fund: he has also the glebe, comprising 20 acres, and valued at £20 per annum; and the glebe-house, which was built by aid of a gift of £450, and a loan of £50, in 1822, from the late Board of First Fruits. The church is a neat structure in good repair, built in 1819, at an expense of £1107, being a loan from the same Board. The R.C. parish is co-extensive with that of the Established Church, and contains two chapels, one at Cornakill, and one at Chapel-Cross. There are meeting-houses for Presbyterians and Independents. There are four private schools, in which about 290 children are educated; and a Sunday school. Ruins of an ancient church and of a chapel of ease exist. The site of the castle on the western side of the lake is now occupied by the cottage of Mrs. Finlay; the castle was destroyed by Cromwell. Quilca House, in which Dean Swift wrote "Gulliver's Travels," and the "Tale of a Tub," was the residence of Mr. T. Sheridan, father of the Rt. Hon. Brinsley Sheridan.

MUNTERCONNAUGHT, a parish, in the barony of CASTLERAHAN, county of CAVAN, and province of ULSTER, 4 miles (N. by E.) from Oldcastle, on the road from Kells to Ballyjamesduff; containing 2969 inhabitants, This parish is on the confines of the county of Meath, and comprises, according to the Ordnance survey, 7432$\frac{3}{4}$ statute acres, of which 5828 are applotted under the tithe act, and 965$\frac{1}{2}$ are in Lough Ramor. It is a rectory and vicarage, in the diocese of Kilmore forming part of the union of Lurgan: the tithes aniount to £148. The church is a very neat building, erected in 1832, by a gift of £900 from the late Board of First Fruits. In the R.C. divisions it is part of the union of Castlerahan and Munterconnaught: the chapel is a good stone building. About 140 children are educated in a school aided by subscriptions; and there are three private schools, in which are about 160 children. Here was anciently an hospital, the endowment of which was granted by Jas. I to Sir Edward Moore.

REDHILLS, a village, in that part of the parish of ANNAGH which is in the barony of Tullaghgarvey, county of CAVAN, and province of ULSTER, 2 miles (N.E.) from Belturbet, on the road to Ballyhaine: the population is returned with the parish. It takes its name from the peculiarly red colour of the soil, which arise from it being strongly impregenated with iron; the roads near it are all of a deep red colour. Here is a R.C. chapel belonging to the district of Annagh East, or Killoughter.

SCRABBY, or BALLIMACKELLENNY, a post-town and parish, in the barony of TULLOGHONOHO, county of CAVAN, and province of ULSTER, 15 miles (S.W. by S.) from Cavan, and 70 (N.N.W.) from Dublin; containing 2668 inhabitants, of which number, 183 are in the town. This small town, which in 1831 contained 40 houses, consists chiefly of one street extending along the road from Arvagh to Granard; it has a sub-post-office to Crossdoney, and fairs are held on Feb. 10th, May 12th, Aug. 1st, and Dec. l2th. The parish comprises, according to the Ordnance survey, 6661 statute acres, of which 1182 are in Lough Gowna; the land is of indifferent quality. It is a vicarage, in the diocese of Ardagh, forming part of the union of Granard: the rectory is in dispute. The tithes amount to £157.16.11, of which £87.13.10 is payable to the vicar; the remainder is rectorial. The church adjoins the town.

SHERCOCK, or KILLAN, a parish, in the barony of CLONKEE, county of CAVAN, and province of ULSTER, 5 miles (N.W.) from Carrickmacross, on the road from Kingscourt to Cootehill; containing 4845 inhabitants. It comprises, according to the Ordnance survey, 8221 statute acres: the land, in general good, is chiefly under tillage, producing crops of oats, potatoes and flax. On the townland of Glasleck, about two miles south of the village and contiguous to the Bailieborough road, appears a thick stratum of coal of a very sulphureous quality, also iron ore, but neither is worked: here are several quarries of good building stone. The village, which comprises 82 houses, has a penny post to Carrickmacross, and is a constabulary police station; a manorial court is occasionally held here, for the recovery of debts under 40s, and petty sessions on alternate Thursdays. There is a market for flax, poultry, and pigs every Wednesday; and a corn market every Saturday: and fairs, where horses, cows, sheep, asses, and goats are exposed for sale, take place on the second Wednesday of every month. The weaving of coarse linen was formerly carried on here to a great extent, but of late years it has considerably diminished. Lough Sillan, or Swillan, is a fine sheet of water, some miles in circumference, and surrounded by picturesque hills formerly clothed with wood: on the north its shores are planted, and on the south the ground is elevated and covered with corn fields, the view of the whole being bounded by high hills. The gentlemen's seats are Shenan, the residence of E. Wilson, Esq.; Northlands, of Dean Adams; and the Glebe-house, of the Rev. F. Fitzpatrick.

The living is a rectory and vicarage, in the dioccse of Kilmore, and in the patronage of the Bishop; the tithes amount to £193.16.11. The glebe-house was erected by aid of a gift of £100 and a loan of £900 from the late Board of First Fruits, in 1819; the glebe comprises 292$\frac{3}{4}$ acres, valued at £406 per annum. The church adds much to the appearance of the village; it was built about 50 years since, and a tower has been recently added to it. In the R.C.

divisions the parish is united to 48 townlands of Bailieborough parish, being the ancient parish of Killan, by which name it is still called in the R.C. church: the chapel is at Kilcrossbawn. The parish school is nearly supported by the incumbent, who lately built the school-house, in which about 60 children are taught; another is supported by Mr. Singleton, at Kilcrossbawn; and there are also four private schools, in which are about 330 children, and two Sunday schools. This is the birthplace of the Rt. Hon. Richard Brinsley Sheridan, whose family resided here.

STRADONE, a market and post-town, in the parish of LARAH, barony of UPPER LOUGHTEE, county of CAVAN, and province of ULSTER, 5 miles (E. by S.) from Cavan, and 50 (N.W.) from Dublin, on the road from Virginia to Ballyhaise; containing 35 houses and 250 inhabitants. It is a station of the constabulary police, and has a dispensary. The market is on Monday; and fairs are held on Feb. 7th, March 28th, May 10th, June 24th, Aug. 16th, Oct. 10th, and Dec. 18th, for general farming stock. Stradone House, the residence of Major Burrowes, is a handsome mansion, situated in an extensive and finely wooded demesne adjoining the town.

SWANLINBAR, a post-town, in the parish of KINAWLEY, barony of TULLAGHAGH, county of CAVAN, and province of ULSTER, 8 miles (N.W.) from Ballyconnell, to which it has a penny-post; containing 398 inhabitants. This town is supposed to have derived its origin from a rich iron mine in the neighbouring mountain of Cuilcagh, which was worked at a remote period to a very considerable extent. The ore was smelted into pig iron in furnaces about half a mile distant, and manufactured into bars at some works erected upon a powerful mountain stream which flows through the village: these works were continued till all the timber of the mountains was consumed in smelting the ore, when they were necessarily abandoned. In 1786 a considerable part of the town was destroyed by an accidental fire, which consumed 22 houses. It now contains 79 houses, and is situated on the old road from Ballyconnell to Enniskillen, and surrounded by the wild mountains of the barony: it is chiefly distinguished for its mineral waters, which are strongly impregnated with sulphur, earth, sea salt and fossil alkali, and in their medicinal effect are both alterative and diaphoretick and are esteemed highly efficacious as a restorative from debility. From April to September it is the resort of numbers of the gentry of the surrounding district. The spa is situated in an enclosure tastefully laid out in pleasant walks and embellished with thriving plantations. Contiguous to the well is a handsome pump-room, in which the visiters usually take breakfast, and on reassembling an excellent dinner is provided. The surrounding mountains afford ample scope for the researches of the mineralogist, arid contain several natural and artificial caves; on the neighbouring townlands of Lurgan and Coolagh are strong indications of coal. A few linens are manufactured in the vicinity, besides other articles of clothing for the inhabitants. Fairs are held annually on

Feb. 2nd, March 30th, May 18th, June 29th, July 27th, Aug. 18th, Sept. 3rd and 29th, Oct. 26th, and Dec. 1st and 29th. A chief constabulary police station has been established; and petty sessions are held on alternate Wednesdays. On the summit of the mountain of Cuilcagh, is a fine spring of excellent water: on this mountain, which is intimately associated with much of the legendary history of the district, the Maguires anciently invested their chiefs with supreme command over the adjacent country of Fermanagh.

TEMPLEPORT, a parish, in the barony of TULLAGHAGH, county of CAVAN, and province of ULSTER, 7½ miles (N.W.) from Killeshandra, on the road from Ballyconnel to Swanlinbar; containing 10,758 inhabitants. This parish, which is situated on the confines of the county of Leitrim, comprises, according to the Ordnance survey, 42,172 statute acres, of which 1532¾ are water, and 25,767 are applotted under the tithe act. It contains not less than eight lakes: in the lake of Templeport is an island called Inch, on which are the picturesque ruins of an abbey founded by St. Macdoe, or Minodhoy, in the 6th century: attached to it is a cemetery still used as a burial-place. At Kilnavat are also the remains of an ancient monastery, of which there are no particulars on record, with an extensive burial-place still in use. The principal seats are Brackley Lodge, the residence of J. Finlay, Esq.; Corville, of G. Finlay, Esq.; and Lisnover, of J. Roycroft, Esq. Fairs are held at Ballyminegauran on May 23rd, Aug. 12th, and Nov. 23rd, which last is noted for fat cattle.

The living is a rectory and vicarage, in the diocese of Kilmore, and in the patronage of the Bishop; it was formerly united to the vicarage of Drumreilly, from which it was separated in 1835, on the decease of the late Dr. Bushe, by act of council, on the recommendation of the Pluralities' Commissioners. The tithes amount to £276.18.5½; the glebe-house was built in 1775, at an expense of £1165.4.10; there are two glebes, one of 58 acres, valued at £193 per annum; the other, formerly belonging to the parish of Drumreilly, comprising 171 acres, valued at £195. The church, a very neat edifice, beautifully situated on the margin of the lake, and for the repairs of which the Ecclesiastical Commissioners have recently granted £120, was erected in 1815, for which purpose the late Board of First Fruits granted a loan of £1500. The R.C. parish is co-extensive with that of the Established Church, and is divided into Upper and Lower Templeport; in the former are three chapels, and in the latter one. About 360 children are taught in four public schools, and there are ten private schools, in which are 520 children.

TOMREGAN, a parish, partly in the barony of KNOCKNINNY, county of FERMANAGH, and partly in that of LOWER LOUGHTEE, but chiefly in the barony of TULLAGHAGH, county of CAVAN, and province of ULSTER, on the road from Belturbet to Swanlinbar; containing, with the post-town of Ballyconnell (which is separately described), 4118 inhabitants. This parish, which is situated on the river Woodford, comprises, according to the

Ordnance survey, 10,678 statute acres, of which 3200¾ are in the county of Fermanagh, and of the remainder 2256¼ are in Lower Loughtee, and 5221 in Tullaghagh, county of Cavan; 6644 statute acres are applotted under the tithe act, and 275 are under water. The river Woodford has its source in the county of Leitrim, and after reaching Woodford, formerly the residence of the Gore family, and from which it takes its name, passes through two lakes, and becoming deep and broad might at a very trifling expense be made navigable to Lough Erne, a distance of nearly nine miles. The lands are in a very indifferent state of cultivation; a large portion that might be rendered profitable is allowed to remain waste: there is abundance of bog, affording a good supply of fuel. The mountainous parts abound with iron ore and coal, which might be easily raised, but no regular works have been established, though some of the coal has been sent to Ballyhays, Cavan, and to the great iron-works at Arigna. Slieve Russell, which borders on Fermanagh, and is the highest land in this county, is partly within the parish; it is chiefly waste and barren, the surface being in some parts very rocky, and in others a mere swamp. Lead and silverore have been brought down the stream which flows from the mountain of Ortnacullagh, in the vicinity of the parish. There are some quarries of excellent limestone and granite, and marble is also found in some of the townlands; the materials for Cavan court-house, Clancorris castle, and the episcopal palace of Kilmore, were supplied from these quarries. Ballyconnell House, the residence of John Enery, Esq., beautifully situated in a fine demesne on the Woodford river, is within the parish. There are a small bleaching-mill and flour-mill.

The living is a rectory and vicarage, in the diocese of Kilmore, and in the patronage of the Bishop: the tithes amount to £129.13.4. The glebe-house was built in 1812, at an expense of £1385 British, of which £969 was a loan and £92 a gift from the late Board of First Fruits: the glebe comprises 380 acres, valued at £381.13.3, of which 50 acres are bog, and the remainder arable and pasture land, The church was built about 80 years since at the expense of the late Col. Montgomery, and was enlarged in 1820 at an expense of £923 British, of which half was a gift and half a loan from the same Board; it has recently been further improved at an expense of £70, of which £60 was contributed by the Rev. Mr. Carson, and the remainder by the Rev. J. Storey, the incumbent; it occupies a picturesque situation on the road to Ballinamore, and with the adjacent school-house forms a pleasing object as seen from the mountains. In the R.C. divisions the parish is partly in the union or district of Knockninny, and partly in that of Drumlaine, but chiefly in that of Kildallon; the chapel, at Ballyconnell, is a plain building roofed with thatch. There is a place of worship for Wesleyan Methodists. The school-house at Ballyconnell was built at an expense of £227, of which part was defrayed by the incumbent, part by Government, and part from the Ballyconnell estate; it contains school-rooms for boys and girls, and residences for

the master and mistress, and is open to the children of all the poor. There are also schools at Cranaghan, Corramore, Mulnagorman, Gorteree, Gortenedden, and Killiwilly, aided by private subscriptions: about 600 children are educated in these schools, and about 70 in two private schools. In the mountains are some curious caves.

URNEY, a parish, partly in the barony of UPPER, but chiefly in that of LOWER, LOUGHTEE, county of CAVAN, and province of ULSTER; containing, with the town of Cavan, 6050 inhabitants. It is situated on the road from Dublin to Enniskillen, and comprises, according to the Ordnance survey, 7934 statute acres, of which 1055 are water, and of these, 530½ are in Lough Oughter: the land is of various qualities, and most of it in a profitable state of cultivation. The living is a vicarage, in the diocese of Kilmore, united by episcopal authority, apparently at an early date, to the vicarage of Annageliffe, and in the patronage of the Bishop; the rectory is partly appropriate to the Dean of Kilmore, and partly to the vicars choral of Christ Church, Dublin. The tithes amount to £156.5.8½, of which £38.15.4 is payable to the dean, £6.7.1 to the vicars choral, and £111.3.3½ to the vicar; the glebes of the union comprise 404½ acres (of which 132¼ are in this parish), valued together at £483.3.3½ per ann.; and the gross value of the benefice is £599.0.2¼. The church was rebuilt in 1816, for which purpose the late Board of First Fruits granted a loan of £4000, and the remainder of the expense was defrayed by private donations: it is a handsome structure, situated in the town of Cavan. Nine townlands of this parish have been separated from it to form with others the district parish of Derryheen. In the R.C. divisions the parish is the head of a union or district, comprising also the parish of Annageliffe, and commonly called the union of Cavan; there are two chapels, one in Cavan, a handsome edifice, erected at an expense of £2000, and one at Coolboyague, built in 1810. There is a place of worship for Presbyterians in connection with the Synod of Ulster, of the second class; and there are two for Primitive and Wesleyan Methodists. About 370 children are taught in five public schools, of which the Royal endowed school at Cavan is described in the account of that town; one in the town and another at the lodge of Farnham demesne are wholly supported by Lord Farnham, one at Coolboyague is under the New Board, and one at Drumkeen under the Society for Discountenancing Vice. There are also eight private schools, in which are about 270 children; and a Sunday school. There are some remains of a monastery.

VIRGINIA, a market and post-town, in the parish of LURGAN, county of CAVAN, and province of ULSTER, 14¾ miles (S.E.) from Cavan, and 40¼ (N.W.) from Dublin; containing 930 inhabitants. It was founded in pursuance of the plan for colonising Ulster in the reign of Jas. I, when 250 acres were allotted for the site of a town to be erected between Cavan and Kells, and called Virginia, which was to have been made a borough, but has never been incorporated. The patent was originally granted to Capt.

Hollywell Cottage, Cavan. Drawn by J.F. Neale and engraved by T. Matthews. From J.P. Neale, Views of the seats of noblemen and gentlemen in England and Wales, Scotland and Ireland *(London, 1820).*

Ridgway, but was assigned to Capt. Culme, who, in 1719, had a house and large bawn in a strong situation, and there were at that time in the town eight houses built of timber and occupied by English tenants and a minister, who kept a good school. Capt. Culme also held the lands of Lough Ramor, or the manor of Chichester, comprising 1000 acres. The town, which is pleasantly situated on Lough Ramor, consists of about 130 houses and, within the last few years, has been greatly improved by its noble proprietor, the Marquess of Headfort. The market is on Thursday, and fairs are held on Jan. 24th, March 7th, April 2nd, May 11th, July 9th, Aug. 22nd, Sept. 23rd, Nov. 21st, and Dec. 20th. Here is an extensive malting and brewing establishment, and a constabulary police station; petty sessions are held once a fortnight, and a manorial court monthly, for the recovery of debts under 40s. The parochial church, situated in the town, is a new and handsome structure in the Gothic style, with a fine spire surmounted by a gilt cross. A church was built here by a loan of £2000 from the late Board of First Fruits in 1818, but soon after its completion a storm blew down the steeple, which falling on the roof completely destroyed it; and on Christmas night, 1832, the church by which it was replaced was entirely consumed by an accidental fire. Adjoining the town, and on the north side of the lake, is Virginia Park, a cottage residence of the Marquess of Headfort. The scenery of this park is extremely diversified, and its walks and drives very beautiful: the plantations are a highly ornamental feature in the landscape. Lough Ramor contains several small islands, which have recently been planted by his lordship, who has established an annual boat race on the lough and gives as a prize a cup of the value of 30 guineas. Many curiously shaped brazen pots, supposed to be Danish, were discovered in the lake a few years since, some of which are in the possession of the Marquess at Headfort House, near Kells.

Acknowledgements

Grateful acknowledgement is due to the following for the use of illustrations in their possession: the Linen Hall Library for the three Lewis maps; the map library of the school of geography at QUB for the O.S. maps of Cos. Armagh, Monaghan and Cavan; Dr David Davin for the views from Stuart's Armagh.

For their valuable assistance thanks must be expressed to Mr John Killen, Mrs Norah Essie, Mrs Margaret McNulty, Ms Maura Pringle, Mrs Angelique Bell , Mr Patrick McWilliams, Mr Rodney Baker, the Neptune Art Gallery and Mr Jack Johnston.